WELCOME

The last British conflict of the 19th century and the first of the 20th, the Great Boer War - also known as the Second Boer War, the South Africa War, or the Anglo-Boer War - straddled a number of eras in British history. It was ostensibly a colonial conflict like many of those fought at the end of Queen Victoria's reign, but it was one fought against an enemy with modern firearms and superior artillery, and it required a level of mass mobilisation and expense that Great Britain was not prepared for.

That it was fought over vast swathes of the African interior negated Britain's traditional advantages in naval power, and that it was waged against a white foe precluded Britain outsourcing its fighting to the vast British Indian Army, local levies or regional allies. By those measures, this was Britain's first 'real' war in almost half a century and the learning curve was steep and ugly. Its bloody blunders - the

Battle of Spion Kop, for instance - and acts of neglect or inhumanity - the typhoid epidemic, the scorched earth, and the concentration camps - were all reported and debated in detail (by the likes of Arthur Conan Doyle, Rudyard Kipling and Winston Churchill no less), exposing the British Army and its decisions to a level of scrutiny it sorely needed.

The Great Boer War ended an entire swathe of storied Victorian generals and spurred on the rise of a new generation of aggressive and innovative commanders who would go on to lead the British Army through some of the darkest days of the First World War and into the cool light of victory. Names like Herbert Kitchener, Douglas Haig, John French, Edmund Allenby, Ian Hamilton, and Henry Rawlinson, all played roles both large and small in the Great Boer War.

The military legacy of the conflict can be seen in 1914. Though popular imagining

has the British Expeditionary Force as an outdated institution, led by 'cavalry generals' and expecting a quick victory, the reality is that the BEF was born in the Great Boer War. It was a small but professionalised body that looked to artillery and infantry coordination to delivery victory and used cavalry as a means for moving men rapidly into exposed flanks or gaps in the line.

Or to put it more visibly and obviously. Because of their experiences in South Africa, the British Army arrived on the Western Front in khaki serge to fight alongside the French in their red trousers and blue tunics, against the Germans in their spiked helmets.

It's true that for many nations and in many respects the First World War brought an end to 'the long 19th century' over a decade late, but for the fighting men of British Army at least, the 20th century dawned four months early in the autumn of 1899.

'First in the Trenches' by John Hassall, 1900.

Contents

A Note on Language

The racially loaded nature of white settlement in South Africa means that a lot of sources use terms now regarded as offensive. This book uses them only in the context of direct quotes and our own words aim to be as neutral as possible. We hope you understand our decision and we apologise in advance for any offence that might be caused.

RIGHT: *'Off to the front' by Maurice Henri Orange, 1899. In radiant crimson, the regimental band leads a battalion of The Prince of Wales's Own (West Yorkshire Regiment) through the grey streets under the watchful eye of Queen Victoria.*

The Boer War 1899-1902

ORIGINALLY PUBLISHED 2020

ISBN: 978 1 80282 714 9

Editor: James Hoare

Senior editor, specials: Roger Mortimer

Email: roger.mortimer@keypublishing.com

Cover design: Dan Jarman

Design: Mike Carr, Dan Jarman, and Lee Howson

Advertising Sales Manager: Brodie Baxter

Email: brodie.baxter@keypublishing.com

Tel: 01780 755131

Advertising Production: Debi McGowan

Email: debi.mcgowan@keypublishing.com

SUBSCRIPTION/MAIL ORDER

Key Publishing Ltd, PO Box 300, Stamford, Lincs, PE9 1NA

Tel: 01780 480404

Subscriptions email: subs@keypublishing.com

Mail Order email: orders@keypublishing.com

Website: www.keypublishing.com/shop

PUBLISHING

Group CEO: Adrian Cox

Publisher, Books and Bookazines: Jonathan Jackson

Published by

Key Publishing Ltd, PO Box 100, Stamford, Lincs, PE9 1XQ

Tel: 01780 755131

Website: www.keypublishing.com

PRINTING

Precision Colour Printing Ltd, Haldane, Halesfield 1, Telford, Shropshire. TF7 4QQ

DISTRIBUTION

Seymour Distribution Ltd, 2 Poultry Avenue, London, EC1A 9PU **Enquiries Line:** 02074 294000

The Cape of Storms

The Origins of the Great Boer War

For over 200 years since the Portuguese explorer Bartolomeu Dias first traversed the coastline in 1488, southern Africa had been of little interest to the seagoing European powers. It was a geographic inconvenience, serving only to frustrate and complicate ocean passage to the Far East. The Cape of Good Hope where the Atlantic and Indian Oceans met was settled in 1652 by the Dutch East India Company (Vereenigde Oostindische Compagnie or VOC). It was originally called the Cape of Storms for the unpredictable conditions around this convergence of oceans, but the process of settlement demanded a more optimistic outlook. The station that would later become Cape Town was established as a depot for company ships to take on supplies, and under the administration of Jan van Riebeeck a fort sprung up, the natural harbour of Table Bay was improved, crops were planted, and livestock purchased from South Africa's indigenous people.

The nomadic Khoisan had been resident in southern Africa for around 1,500 years in extended family groups. They were broadly divided by their means of subsistence: The San were primarily hunter-gatherers, whilst the Khoikhoi were herders. They were respectively dubbed 'Bushmen' and 'Hottentots' by the Dutch, both terms now considered offensive.

Contact and Conflict

The management of VOC had no designs on growing a colony for its own sake. Farmers, craftsmen and mercenaries (many German, Swiss and Scandinavian as well as Dutch) were hired and to tend the crops slaves were dragged in chains from the Dutch East Indies (parts of modern Indonesia and Malaysia), Madagascar, southern India, and Ceylon (modern Sri Lanka). Between 1652 and 1808, an estimated 64,000 slaves were taken to South Africa. Demand for supplies soon grew beyond the means of Riebeeck's infrastructure to provide, and Cape Town began to transform from

company town to colony, allowing settlers to farm privately and sell their produce. Many VOC employees opted to settle once their contracts were up and others were released early on Riebeeck's initiative. With land seemingly going spare, South Africa offered those who had begun life on the lowest rung of European society an opportunity to trade up. Called Burghers - meaning citizens - in contrast to the slaves and Europeans under company contract, they began to develop their own culture and world view.

With farms now springing up where the Khoikhoi previously grazed their cattle, violence followed. The Khoikhoi lost their herds, their pastures - the veldt, as the Boers called the uncultivated grassland - and their lives to these soldier-settlers who believed that firearms and faith co-signed their greed. The killer blow would come from a virus rather than violence and smallpox made landfall in 1713 with the diseased linen of a company ship. A quarter of the white population

BELOW: *Cape Colony mounted troops pursue Xhosa and cattle across the Great Fish River, 1851.*

The growing settlement at the Cape of Good Hope under VOC rule, sat beneath the Table Mountain around which clouds clung like a tablecloth. Etching by Robert Sayer, 1754

of Cape Colony died in the pandemic, but for the Khoisan - without Western medicine or the settler's understanding of what they faced - the death toll was incalculable. Perhaps only a tenth of the population survived and many of those who did fled further inland to escape.

Those few indigenous Africans who remained in the lands of their birth were little more than a beaten seasonal workforce. Their clans and culture in tatters, they were dependent on those who had destroyed them and what was left of their language and heritage disappeared with their adoption of Afrikaans - the dialect of the Boers, increasingly divergent from Dutch.

Trouble in Paradise

The spiritual life of the Boers was firmly rooted in the Calvinism of the 17th century Dutch Reformed Church (Nederduitse Gereformeerde Kerk) that saw these true believers recast as the chosen people. Patriarchal, pastoral, and devout, they had come to identify intensely with the Israelites of the Old Testament, engaged in their own search for a Promised Land.

As the Boers saw it, God had granted them a lush and fertile land and filled it with lesser races - local and imported - to toil on their farms. It was not even necessary to enslave the surviving Khoikhoi. Their dependence on their Boer masters for food and lodgings made them virtually serfs, forced to swallow contracts which in exchange for meagre pay denied them permission to leave their employer's estates. Desperation forced them to accept the cruellest of preconditions: any children born to

parents under contract would be forced to work for their master for 25 years. Even those on seasonal contracts to bring in the harvest might find their infants claimed by their master at gunpoint as they tried to leave, whilst children were also captured in raids so that they could be raised to know only a life of subservience.

The Burghers, who adopted the name Afrikaners to distinguish themselves from the Dutch-born company men, chafed under the corrupt and autocratic rule of VOC. Rather than settle in the Cape Colony hinterland, migrant farmers called Trekboers opted to drive their cattle north and east living out of

Portrait of the life-long VOC administrator and first Commander of the Cape, Jan van Riebeeck (1619-77), circa 1660.

their ox-wagons. They took their families with them, many of the mixed-race children of their Khoikhoi wives, slaves and servants.

As Trekboers moved further and further inland, they collided with the first of the Nguni people of the South African interior and eastern coast, the Xhosa. Whilst small groups of San who resisted the intrusion into their lands with poisoned arrows were easily dispatched by mounted posses of fighting-age Boers called commandos, across the Great Fish River the Xhosa - from the Khoisan word for 'fierce' - were another matter. Their warrior culture, honour code and iron-worked weapons made them more dogged opponents and the Xhosa defended their territory with throwing spears and hardwood war clubs. Nguni cultivated land as well as herded livestock, which supported significantly larger clan groupings which in turn could confederate with other clans to form formidable nations.

The first of the nine Cape Frontier Wars - also known as the Xhosa Wars - began in 1779 and would roll on for two decades. Instigated by Boer intransigence, each conflict increasingly pulled the boundaries of Cape Colony further east as the administration - VOC and then British - struggled to keep up, keep the peace, and keep the belligerent settlers firmly in check.

Under New Management

In 1795 Great Britain occupied the Cape. It was briefly returned to the Dutch in 1803 by treaty and then in 1806, Britain took Cape Colony outright. Two unbending moral missions were now set on a collision course. ➤➤

ABOVE: *An 1804 depiction of nomadic Khoikhoi, called 'Hottentots' by the Dutch settlers, packing up their camp.*

In a 1772 court case, slavery was deemed to have no basis in English law, in 1778 Scotland followed, and the long-term implications for the British sugar plantations of the Caribbean were obvious. In 1807 the slave trade itself was banned as cruel and inhuman, although ending the existing system of slave labour was more challenging. Narrow victories in the House of Commons were jealously denied by the plantation shareholders who occupied the House of Lords, but for all its cynicism and hypocrisy, Great Britain was defining itself as a moral superpower.

From 1808 the Royal Navy's West African Squadron - initially based out of Cape Colony - acted as a maritime police force to run down slave ships and release their captives. The Atlantic slave trade was rapidly becoming unprofitable and although the Indian Ocean trade from Portuguese-run Mozambique endured, it had driven the price of human stock beyond the means of many Boers.

While the Dutch administration seemed to regard the Boers with varying levels of disinterest or irritation, the British appeared to be directly threatening the very fabric of their society. In 1812, missionaries began to agitate against the abuse - and murder - of Khoisan contract labourers in the remote Eastern Cape. As they were not their employer's 'property' like slaves, the farmer had no incentive not to treat them harshly as he did not risk his investment by beating them to death. British circuit judges - derisively called the 'Black Circuit' - brought 17 Burghers to trial in open courts. All were ultimately dismissed, but the spectacle of black witnesses and victims giving their testimony against white accused turned Boer stomachs as surely as it swelled British hearts with the transparency of their legal system. That it had failed to secure justice of any sort was beside the point.

In 1828 the contract labour system was significantly weakened to restore the freedom of movement to Khoikhoi trapped in oppressive servitude, and then finally in 1833, slavery was ended throughout the British Empire.

Freedom for Persecution

The equality of all races under the law was an enormous affront to beliefs of the Boers, and many opted to join the Trekboers in a massed migration to outrun the writ for their own law of the whip. Between 1835 and 1837 around 5,000 Voortrekkers (literally 'fore-trekkers', or pioneers) and 5,000 of their servants made the migration, pushing well

An ox-drawn wagon makes slow progress through the interior, taken from the book Journal of a Visit to South Africa *(1818).*

beyond the Orange and Vaal Rivers into the lands of the Zulu, Sotho, Ndebele and other Nguni people, triggering a fresh round of violence over the veldt.

Three Boer republics sprung up through right of conquest, the Nguni unable to overcome the ring of ox-wagons bristling with guns that the Afrikaners called a 'laager'. The Zulu were humiliated and slaughtered by fewer than 500 Voortrekkers at the Battle of Blood River (December 16, 1838) to found the Natalia Republic. Later, the Ndebele were defeated in a series of bloody exchanges which pushed their frontiers further and further back so that the Voortrekkers could settle what became the Orange Free State (Oranje-Vrystaat), and beyond that the South African Republic (Zuid-Afrikaansche Republiek), known to the British as Transvaal. Everywhere the Voortrekkers went, crops were unrooted, water sources

ABOVE: *A depiction of the Weenen Massacre by the artist Thomas Baines. An early encounter with the Zulu during the 'Great Trek' that left 530 Voortrekkers dead.*

were seized, herds were stolen, and indigenous people forced into servitude or driven off.

The least of the three, the Natalia Republic was wedged between the Eastern Cape and Zululand, and it was gripped by political infighting. It was easy pickings and in 1843 it became the Colony of Natal, but Orange and Transvaal remained too remote and their peoples too rugged to rule. Negotiations to bring them into the protective embrace of Britain failed and the idea of waging war for the possession of endless acreage of tall grass and hostile Nguni did not appeal. However, possession of Natal on the eastern coast of South Africa gave Britain paramountcy over Boer affairs. With the two remaining republics landlocked, Natal was Transvaal's closest source of trade whilst Orange exported enormous quantities of wool via Cape Colony.

This suited Britain fine. Cape Colony was a costly endeavour, but its value as a supply post en route to British India, Australia and the Far East made it a necessary expense. Beyond the quays and storehouses, South Africa was little more than a source of irritation and the constant border wars were a drain on the Treasury. With the most disagreeable of the Trekboer having ridden off into the sunset, perhaps things would start looking up.

Caught unawares by a Zulu sneak attack, the British tried foolishly to hold them off in an extended line. 'The Battle of Isandlwana' by Charles Edwin Fripp, 1885.

Diamonds Are Forever

In 1886 what once was the British Empire's unstable backwater, was suddenly filled with promise. Teenager Erasmus Jacobs was playing on his family farm by the Orange River in 1867 when his head was turned by a glittering pebble. His father sold it. In a few short years, the land to the west of the river became the diamond mining capital of the world. Claimed by the Orange Free State which overlaid part of the diamond field, Cape Colony encouraged a mutiny amongst the miners who drove the Boers from the diamond field. By the end of 1870, 10,000 British settlers had moved into the area and West Griqualand formally became a colony on October 27, 1871 and was later annexed by Cape Colony.

Seasonal workers - mostly black - left their pastures in the Boer republics and flooded the diamond fields. With their earnings they improved their lot considerably. Their wages were far below that of whites, but it was considerably more than was offered to agricultural workers and the effects on the Burghers were considerable: it decimated their access to low-cost labour and once their work was up, many black miners returned to their families able to afford dignity and guns, neither of which was welcomed by their white neighbours. No longer a burden on the Treasury, Cape Colony was awarded self-government in 1872 (and Natal followed in 1893) with an elected parliament and prime minister to manage its internal

affairs. This - 'responsible government' - replaced the system of 'representative government' where despite an elected assembly, power still resided with a governor appointed by the British Crown. Even as early as 1852, the vote was offered equally to all men regardless of race so long as they owned property and in this traditional land ownership was judged the equal of the white homestead. The constitution of the new government was stridently colour blind, pledging to treat all men as equal. This noble endeavour was not to last, but if the Boers were trying to build a Promised Land, what they were witnessing from the south was Sodom and Gomorrah.

Aspirations in both London and Cape Town turned towards ➡➡

RIGHT: *An early depiction of Xhosa warriors fighting with cowhide shields and hardwood war clubs, 1810.*

ABOVE: *Members of the Natal Native Police in 1890. Differing attitudes to the treatment of South Africa's black population was a significant cause of tension between Boer Republics and the British colonies.*

Fortunately, Transvaal was an economic and political liability. A failed attempt to build a railway to Delagoa Bay in Mozambique (therefore circumventing Natal) had not accounted for the Pedi whose land it crossed. The Pedi resisted, and the investment was lost. Dispute with King Cetshwayo kaMpande over their shared border with Zululand was also threatening to escalate. Despite Boer victories against the Zulu, Cetshwayo could raise an army 30,000 strong and they had a reputation for disembowelling and mutilating their victims.

In 1877, the persuasive colonial fixer Sir Theophilus Shepstone set out from Natal with an escort of mounted police and a warrant to raise the Union flag. The Transvaal Boers were not happy but did not protest too loudly. Though wary of Britain's creeping reach, their government was discredited, the economy had ground to a halt, and they were being hemmed in by the Zulu and the Pedi. The Volksraad (people's assembly) acquiesced - incentivised by British wages - with opposition coalescing around the stern Vice-President, Paul Kruger.

Two years later in 1879, the scarlet-clad circus came to town as Cape Colony manufactured casus belli for an invasion of Zululand. The formidable warrior state had proven the bitterest check to Boer expansion, but the Afrikaners showed precious little enthusiasm for the cause of white 'civilisation' against black 'barbarism'. The benefits of British administration in Pretoria seemed entirely chimerical: the economy was still in tatters, the concerns of the Burghers were completely ignored, and the only investment seemed to go straight into the pockets of the Volksraad.

Britain's calamitous first engagement - the Battle of Isandlwana (January 22, 1879) - carried another vital lesson for the Boers. The army of the British Empire had faced its greatest and most humiliating defeat in almost half a century, and its greatest defeat ever against an indigenous foe. For the Boer who had made a craft of frontier warfare, conditions seemed favourable to restore Transvaal's independence.

federation: creating a single nation from the quilt of separate colonies as they had successfully done in Canada a few years earlier. Partly this was vanity on behalf of the colonial functionaries, but also a single legal system with fair treatment for black as well as white South Africans, would bring peace and order to what was an unpredictable and unstable land. Yet, South Africa was not Canada, where the English-speaking population dwarfed the French speakers, and the indigenous peoples were fewer and not in open war. Taken as one, the two British colonies (Cape and Natal) and two Boer republics (Orange and Transvaal) would become a nation where the Afrikaner outnumbered the English speakers three to one, and the black population outnumbered them both by a factor of ten in some of the more remote regions.

Two Tribes go to War

As good neighbours, if Britain saw their fellow man chaffing under a corrupt and incompetent administration, it was their duty to intervene.

ABOVE: *A Boer on horseback, sketched from life by Lieutenant Charles Manners, 15th King's Hussars, during the First Boer War.*

RIGHT: *Church Street, Pretoria at the time of the First Boer War. The capital of the South African Republic, or Transvaal Republic, was still little more than an underdeveloped country town.*

ABOVE: *Miners on the Witwatersrand gold fields - known as the Rand - in 1891.*

"The British were unprepared for a highly mobile foe with firearms."

First Blood to the Boers

On December 16, 1880 - with the Anglo-Zulu War (1879) over and the bulk of its troops having been shipped home - Paul Kruger led Transvaal in rebellion. Cape Colony massively underestimated the scale of the rising and the fighting abilities of the Boers, and by the time reinforcements were requested it was too late. The British battalions garrisoning South Africa had found a war-winning formula for overcoming the Zulu, but they were unprepared for a highly mobile foe with firearms and familiarity with the harsh terrain of Transvaal.

The garrisons of Pretoria and the other towns were besieged in their barracks and a column of the 94th Regiment was ambushed on the road, with 156 of its strength killed or wounded at the Battle of Bronkhorstspruit (December 20, 1880). As the war escalated, volunteers from Orange rushed to join their brothers and Cape Colony began to fear that its own sizable Afrikaner population would also rise up. The British government - distracted by large-scale unrest in Ireland and the need to untangle its troops from Afghanistan - agreed to an armistice.

Major General Sir George Pomeroy Colley dutifully made peace overtures but was resolved to throw the Boers from their positions on Laing's Nek, a vital ridge on the road from Durban to Pretoria, whilst they thought about it. In the early hours of the morning, a scratch force of 92nd (Gordon Highlanders), 58th (or the Rutlandshire) Regiment of Foot and armed sailors moved onto a mountain overlooking Laing's Nek. Colley failed to give orders to dig in and took himself off for a doze, whilst the Boers crept up the slope on their stomachs. The disastrous Battle of Majuba Hill (February 27, 1881) ended with the terrified British fleeing as bullets whistled at their backs. Colley, knowing he faced disgrace and most-likely court martial, chose to die fighting.

The humbled British government restored internal self-rule to the Transvaal Republic and withdrew the besieged garrisons on August 3, 1881. Just shy of full independence, the Pretoria Convention that concluded the First Boer War (December 16, 1880 - March 23, 1881) gave Britain full control of Transvaal's foreign relations. Just as the diamond fields first put federation on the agenda, the discovery of the Witwatersrand gold fields in 1884 brought it back. Gold attracted prospectors, prostitutes, missionaries, and all manner of seasonal labourers, both black and white, and as with Kimberley, a rough frontier town quickly grew that still cherishes the nickname 'the City of Gold': Johannesburg.

ABOVE: *The disastrous Battle of Majuba, recast as a valiant last stand with Major General Sir George Pomeroy Colley at its head by Melton Prior for the Illustrated London News.*

The Schemes of Cecil Rhodes

The larger than life Cecil Rhodes was as impressive as he was immoral. As managing director and major shareholder of DeBeers Consolidated Mines Ltd, he dominated Kimberley, the de facto capital of the diamond fields, and to these immense commercial interests he added political ones. In 1889 he was issued with a charter for his British South Africa Company to settle what would become - with all due modesty - Rhodesia (modern Zimbabwe), and a year later became Prime Minister of Cape Colony. ➤➤

An Afrikaans Primer

Afrikaans: Language spoken by the Afrikaners, derived from Dutch but incorporating other influences.
Afrikaner: Literally 'African', but specifically a white South African of predominantly Dutch origin.
Biltong: Literally 'tongue-strip', strips of dried and cured meat often used as stores when on the move.
Boer: Literally 'farmer', used to refer to rural Afrikaners but also inhabitants of the Orange Free State and South African Republic.
Burgher: A citizen of the Boer republics.
Donga: From the isiZulu 'udonga', a narrow ravine that fills with water in the rainy season.
Eerste/Tweede Vryheidsoorlog: First/Second Freedom War, the Afrikaans name for the two Boer Wars.
Handsupper: A collaborator, a Boer fighting with the British.
Highveldt/Highveld: The inland plateau 1,500 feet above sea-level which covers much of the interior of Transvaal.
Kaffir: From the Arabic for 'non-believer', used by Boers and British to mean black South Africans. Now considered highly offensive.
Kakebeenwa: Jaw-bone wagon, a rugged and hard-wearing Boer ox-wagon.
Kleurling/Coloured: A person of either mixed European/African heritage, or of Indian or Asian descent. Considered by white South Africans to be 'semi-civilised', but inferior. Now offensive.
Kommando/Commando: Literally 'an order' but referring to the irregular mounted units formed by the Boers in times of war.
Kopje/Koppie/Kop: Literally 'little head', a small hill or outcrop.
Kraal: From Portuguese, an indigenous African village within a wooden stockade.
Laager: Literally 'camp', referring to the circling of the ox-wagons axle to axle with the ox in the centre to make a fort.
Nek: A narrow neck of land, such as a ridge, connecting two hills.
Rooinek: Literally 'redneck', the British whose pith helmets rarely offered protection from the sun.
Uitlander: Outlander or foreigner, a non-Afrikaner resident in the Boer Republics.
Veldt/Veld: Grassland or pasture.
Volk: People or ethnic/national community.
Volksraad: People's assembly, the governing bodies of Orange and Transvaal.

Rhodes believed in federation, but unlike the officials imposed by London, he had no intention of paying lip-service to racial equality. The banks and businesses of Cape Colony needed free access to the gold mines of Transvaal for both to benefit. Federation meant investment, which meant railways, roads, telegraph lines, hospitals, universities, and economic growth. Britons and Afrikaners could both prosper and manage their own affairs, but only with access to an enormous cheap and obedient - and black - labour force. In 1892 the Rhodes government raised the property threshold to restrict the number of black voters and in 1894 it passed an act to drive the Xhosa from their traditional lands and into the labour market. Speaking in the Cape Parliament in 1887, Rhodes asserted: "The native is to be treated as a child and denied the franchise. We must adopt a system of despotism, such as works in India, in our relations with the barbarism of South Africa."

and the growth of Johannesburg had been due to investment by what the Burghers called 'Uitlanders', predominantly English-speaking 'outlanders' from the Cape and beyond. They were taxed heavily, denied representation in the Volksraad (ironically, the Burghers feared the effects of a British voting block as much as Rhodes had feared a black one), and refused to sell them dynamite for blasting.

The plot involved an uprising by the Johannesburg Uitlanders and a simultaneous invasion from the British Bechuanaland Protectorate (modern Botswana) by Dr Leander Starr Jameson - a fascinating character with the distinction of inspiring Rudyard Kipling's poem 'If' - with 500 men from the British South Africa Company's private police force.

The Uitlanders got cold feet and Rhodes tried to call the coup off, but by that point Jameson was already on the move. The Jameson Raid (December 29, 1895 – January 2, 1896) was a failure, causing embarrassment

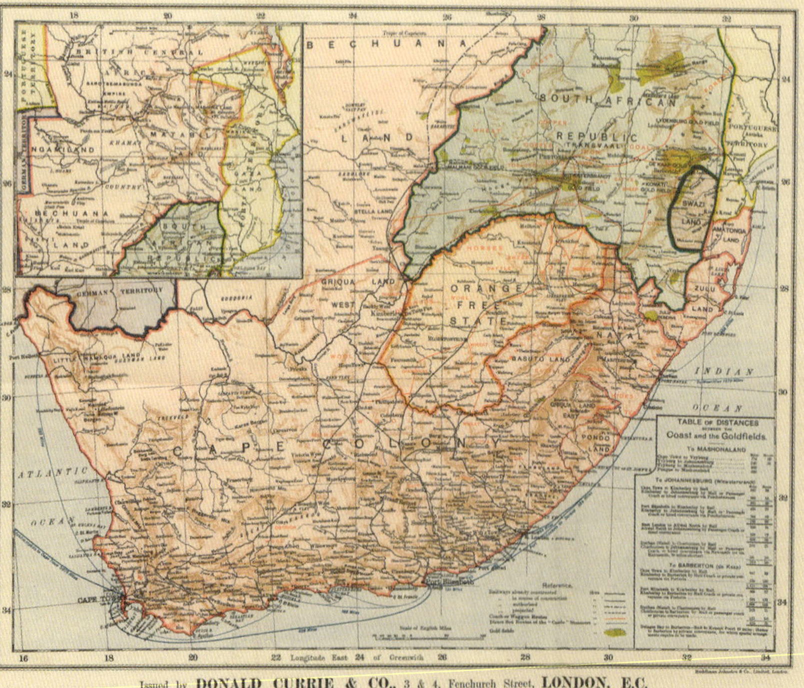

ABOVE: *South Africa in 1891 between the Boer Wars, showing Boer republics ringed by British colonies and protectorates, as well as the locations of its gold fields.* **BELOW RIGHT:** *An ox-wagon crossing a South African drift or ford, circa 1890.*

The Right Honourable Joseph Chamberlain MP, painted following his appointment as secretary of state for the colonies. Oil on canvas by John Singer Sargent, 1896.

for both Great Britain and Cape Colony, and renewing the wariness of Transvaal and the Orange towards their neighbours. Rhodes was forced to stand down as PM and Jameson was tried back in Britain, although his actions were celebrated in the press and the injustices endured by the Uitlanders continued to excite popular imagination. Gold, meanwhile, continued to excite the fears of the British government who saw a wealthy Transvaal as a challenge to their dominance and an obstruction to the eventual federation of South Africa. In fact, by 1899, Transvaal was arguably the wealthiest state in the entire continent with annual gold exports of £24 million and Johannesburg was rivalling Cape Town as the centre of gravity in the region.

The charismatic Joseph Chamberlain, Britain's Secretary of State for the Colonies, had been supportive of the Jameson Raid but somehow dodged the fallout despite telegrams implicating him in the coup. He continued to champion the Uitlander cause as a vehicle for federation and dispatched the unassuming but cold-blooded British High Commissioner for Southern Africa, Sir Alfred Milner, to negotiate voting rights for the Uitlanders, who now outnumbered the Afrikaner population of Transvaal.

Milner was polite but firm in his demand that the 14-year residence to qualify for the vote

Ironic then that the first Cape Colony representative to be cut from the same cloth as the Burghers (and indeed he became PM thanks to the support of Cape Afrikaners) would seek to overthrow them. More than anything else, Rhodes was an ultra-capitalist buccaneer and Pretoria's attitude to the mining companies which had flooded into Transvaal with the gold rush was an impediment to prosperity.

An Invasion of Uitlanders

With relations brittle, Rhodes decided to sponsor the so-called Jameson Raid. As he saw it, the development of the mining industry

be reduced to five. Pretoria was unwilling to compromise so to rev up the British press, Chamberlain released Milner's private dispatches which made the case for armed intervention in frank and emotive terms. The Transvaal President, Paul Kruger - a stubborn man but not one willing to lead his people to war without good reason - accepted the five year limit but on the condition that Britain refrain from intervening further in the affairs of Pretoria. Chamberlain responded by pushing for even more concessions. If his intention were to antagonise the old Boer, he was successful: Kruger withdrew the five-year limit and instead offered a seven-year one.

Assured by Milner, Rhodes, and the Johannesburg gold barons that Kruger would fold if threatened with war, Chamberlain piled on the pressure. A force of 10,000 troops were dispatched to Natal, largely from India and Malta, whilst an army corps of 47,000 in Britain was mobilised under the Anglo-Zulu War hero Sir Redvers Buller. A final offer, an ultimatum was tabled.

Stephanus Johannes Paulus 'Paul' Kruger, four-times elected President of the South African Republic (Transvaal), photographed in 1900 at the age of 75.

BELOW: *One of the many top hats owned by Paul Kruger that came to define his austere image, more like a lay preacher than a President.*

"If Kruger chose war, than Britain would be forced to fight one."

Chamberlain demanded that voting rights be given to all Uitlanders who had been resident for at least a year - which would give the British control of the Volksraad - lower costs for the miners and labour, a limit on armament purchases by Transvaal, and a new convention that would guarantee British supremacy.

Gambling the Peace

Privately, the British Prime Minister - the infirm Robert Gascoyne-Cecil, 3rd Marquess of Salisbury - feared that it was Britain, not Transvaal, that had the most to lose by 'blinking'. If Kruger chose war, then Britain would be forced to fight one or bring the whole imperial house of cards tumbling down and "all for people whom we despise and for territory which will bring no power."

Despite his reports to the contrary, Milner also had doubts that Kruger would accept so humiliating a demand, but whilst

Chamberlain was trying to bully Pretoria to a compromise without bloodshed, Milner wanted their federation to be born out of war. He fully expected the Boers to strike at Natal and Kimberley before the 10,000 reinforcements arrived - and he hoped they would, as demonstration of their belligerence would be all the license needed to refashion South Africa not as a shotgun wedding between Briton and Boer, but born of victory and flooded with British settlers.

Pretoria also expected war. The select committee might have absolved Chamberlain of the Jameson Raid, but in Kruger's eyes he was guilty. Kruger viewed the entire negotiation as a pretext for hostilities and when news arrived on September 9, 1899 that 10,000 British soldiers were sailing for Natal, his suspicions were seemingly confirmed. His protege, the lawyer and journalist Jan Smuts, proposed an invasion of Natal as Milner had

foreseen believing that if they moved fast they would be able overrun the British garrison at Durban and the Cape Afrikaners would rise in support. By the time the 10,000 troops landed, all South Africa would be a Boer republic. The Orange Free State President, Martinus Steyn, stayed their hand. He had yet to come to accept the Transvaal President's fatalistic view of the negotiations and despite Smuts' urging, the pre-emptive strike was dropped. On September 22, British newspapers reported that the 47,000-strong invasion force had set sail and the Boers set their jaws.

It was now the turn of Pretoria and Bloemfontein to issue an ultimatum to Cape Town and London. Kruger and Steyn demanded that Britain accept that it had violated its earlier treaties, accept international arbitration of their differences, withdraw the troops in South Africa, and recall the armies in transit. Failure to do so within 48 hours would be a declaration of war.

Soldiers of the Queen

The British Army in South Africa

The calculating colonial hawk Sir Henry Milner and the charismatic jingo Joseph Chamberlain, MP were to have their war, but once conflict was on the table, they lost influence over how it was to be pursued.

The closest thing they had in South Africa to a professional fighting force was the Cape Mounted Police and the Natal Mounted Police, both of which were old hands at frontier warfare, but they were widely dispersed and few in number. Some towns, especially those with a clique of wealthy farmers prepared to spend their weekends playing soldier, had volunteer units to draw upon, but the war would now be won and lost by whatever forces were cobbled together by the British Parliament, the War Office, and by the opaque and idiosyncratic leadership of the British Army.

Although Britain - and particularly the British public who had been whipped to a frenzy by Chamberlain's gung-ho PR campaign - were prepared for war, they were not necessarily expecting one. The claim by Cecil Rhodes that Kruger would "bluff up to the cannon's mouth" was largely accepted as fact, creating a heady brew of confirmation bias that translated the Transvaal's willingness to fight as hot air.

Two battalions of regulars had been in Natal since August 1899 and they were to be reinforced immediately by a further 10,000 men at a cost to the taxpayer of £350,000 (over £27 million in today's money), diverted piecemeal from their deployments across the empire. Henry Petty-Fitzmaurice, 5th Marquess of Lansdowne, the Secretary of State for War, had been hoping that British India would provide the majority. They dutifully freed up 5,500 men, which began embarking from Calcutta and Bombay (now Kolkata and Mumbai) within days to join the forces already in Natal.

Field Marshal Garnet Wolseley, 1st Viscount Wolseley, the British Army's reformist commander-in-chief, set about making up the difference. He managed to wangle the 1st The Royal Irish Regiment from Egypt, the 1st The Border Regiment from

ABOVE: A wash prepared for a January 1900 issue of The Graphic showing the crew of the passing HMS Amphion cheering a troop transport on its way to war.

MAIN PICTURE (FAR LEFT): Sons of Empire' by Harry Payne, a patriotic image showing an array of uniforms worn by British Empire fighting men in 1899. Several figures can be seen in khaki, reflecting the uniforms worn in South Africa.

BELOW: A jingoistic stereograph showing men in khaki field uniforms fighting for the 'Restoration and defence of British liberty in South Africa' circa 1899.

Malta, and the 2nd The Rifle Brigade from Crete. Including the troops already in South Africa, this would give them 15,000 men in total and as far as Wolseley was concerned this was ample for mopping up gangs of disgruntled backwoodsmen.

The General

At an eye-watering cost of £5 million (£390 million) - so much for making the South African colonies pay for themselves - the cream of the British Army was being mustered at Aldershot as the newly formed 1st Army Corps. Some 50,000-strong, this was the largest force assembled by Great Britain since the Crimean War (1853-1856) and it was placed under the command of Major General Sir Redvers Buller, VC. A squat and surly-looking chap, Buller was actually fairly anxious and shy in that way which made him appear brusque and tactless. He had the distinction of being one of the few heroes of the Anglo-Zulu War, where he was awarded the Victoria Cross for courage in the field. ➤➤

Buller was a man who got things done, but his greatness had come under the command of others, and he had never directed a campaign, and certainly not one against a foe with firearms. But he was Wolseley's pick and the old warhorse was determined to have his way as a point of principle. The irony was that he was not even that fond of Buller. He had appointed him to command an infantry brigade in Sudan in 1882 and found him wanting, but if Buller was unimpressive, he was at least Wolseley's man. Buller himself was the first to accept his limitations, admitting in 1895: "I have never really been tried as a head man - personally, I am always inclined to think myself a better second fiddle than a leader of thought."

The Infantry

The British Army of 1899 was an extremely professional and versatile force, but its half-century as an imperial gendarmerie, putting down uprisings throughout the colonies and cowing princelings, had allowed its war-fighting - as opposed to battle-winning - abilities to atrophy.

The Cardwell and Childers Reforms of 1870-81 had transformed the culture most profoundly at the battalion level. Terms of service were cut from (an often short and brutish) life to 12 years, with six served in reserve, which widened the pool of potential recruits beyond its traditional base of the most desperate dregs of Victorian society. Recruitment was done locally, significantly strengthening the esprit de corps well beyond their esoteric regimental traditions, archaic names, and ornate heraldry.

ABOVE: *A squadron of Lancers in the Boer War with their carbines holstered on their saddles. Painted by Frank Feller, 1900.*

BELOW: *Staff officers in a mixture of slouch hats and foreign service helmets, with one wide-brimmed Worsley helmet and one side cap, or forage cap, which was typically worn around barracks. Sir Redvers Buller is front row, second left.*

"Buller was a man who got things done, but his greatness had come under the command of others."

Pre-existing regiments were merged as the 1st and 2nd battalion of what was usually a county regiment, or at least one with a strong local affiliation. One battalion would always be on home service at the barracks, while one was posted overseas, usually garrisoning Britain's far-flung empire. County militia and other volunteer formations were then attached as the 3rd and 4th battalions and so on, although the numbers might vary. Very rarely would both the 1st and 2nd battalion be in the field at the same time, and instead, the higher numbered militia and volunteer battalions were used as a pool of reinforcements for 1st or 2nd. Each battalion consisted of eight companies of 100 men.

The exceptions to the system were the prestigious Guards Brigade (the Coldstream, Grenadier, and Scots Guards, with the Irish established in 1900) and the swashbuckling green-clad rifles regiments - the Rifle Brigade and the King's Royal Rifle Corps - who were permitted to form their own additional battalions and had their pick of recruits.

ABOVE: *A British soldier in khaki with his regimental flash on the side of his foreign service helmet, by George Montbard, 1900.*

The purchase system which allowed officers to buy their postings and positions was replaced with promotion by merit, which professionalised the officer corps although there was still a class divide between commissioned officers and other ranks. As officers were expected to purchase their own uniforms, kit, and cover their food and lodgings - as well as maintain the exclusive social life of the late Victorian gentleman - it easily priced out those from humble backgrounds. The purchase system had been abolished in 1871, but a number of the more senior staff had begun their careers with one hand in their purse.

ABOVE: *A caricature from Vanity Fair showing the senior commanders in South Africa in 1899. Lord Roberts is seated in the centre, whilst Buller wears a tropical helmet.*

For all the progress of the previous half-century, the very top of the military establishment was the most moribund, one so bloated with opinionated and out-of-touch old generals of Crimean War vintage that it was virtually indistinguishable from the Royal Hospital at Chelsea. Prior to Sir Garnet Wolseley's appointment as commander-in-chief in 1885, the post had been held for 39 years by Field Marshal Prince George, Duke of Cambridge, a grandson of King George III and first cousin of Queen Victoria. True to form, he had last muddied his boots in the Crimea and had doggedly resisted anything approaching meritocracy.

In the decades of stagnation, Wolseley had gathered around him promising young officers, helping their careers along and handpicking them for assignments. The core members of the 'Wolseley ring' had served with him in the Ashanti Wars to capture the Gold Coast, but now he had finally secured the top job most of his more capable collaborators were too long in the tooth for active service, whilst the Secretary of State for War was closer to his rival, Field Marshal Frederick Roberts, 1st Baron Roberts. Just as Wolseley had used Africa for his patronage system, Roberts used India where he had served since the bad old days of the East India Company. The 'Africans' and the 'Indians' were locked in a bitter battle for influence, more a product of having languished for so long in the whiskery shadow of the Duke of Cambridge waiting for their moment than any real ideological difference between the men sardonically nicknamed 'Britain's only general' and 'Britain's only other general'.

Maj Gen Sir George Pomeroy Colley, who fell at the Battle of Majuba Hill in 1881, was one of the 'Africans', as was Maj Gen Sir Redvers Buller, but the 'Indians' were gaining ground. While Wolseley had successfully pushed for Buller to lead the 1st Army Corps, Lord Lansdowne had managed to appoint the 'Indian' Lt Gen Sir George White as the commander in chief in the Colony of Natal, and he brought with him a staff of fellow 'Indians', Colonels Henry Rawlinson and Ian Hamilton.

Wolseley, who rose thanks to his mastery of small wars in Africa was about to be felled by a big one, all because he judged his clique more important than competence. The rivalry, once taken root at the very top of the general staff and the War Office, was so toxic as to endanger lives. While Buller assembled the 1st Army Corps at Aldershot, he found himself completely out of the loop, not even being appraised of White's actions let alone having any direct contact with him. From Landsdowne came only silence.

"They say the smell of curry all over the War Office is very overpowering," griped Wolseley later.

The Uniforms

From 1897 khaki had been adopted as the foreign service dress of the British Army, although it had been used in campaigns much earlier. From the Urdu for 'dusty', the first khaki uniforms had been worn by mounted regiments of the British Indian Army for service on the frontier during the mid-19th century and it had been adopted ad hoc since, although to their detriment campaigns in South Africa had clung to the eye-catching crimson for both the Anglo-Zulu War (1879-80) and the First Boer War (1881). Nonetheless, it was common for soldiers to blacken their buttons, cap badges, and other tell-tale bits of metalwork which might glint in the sun and the more ostentatious bits of frippery such as silver braid was soon discontinued once they began to draw bullets. It was considerably harder to pick out officers than it had been in the First Boer War (1880-81), but the keen-eyed knew to look for men with revolvers, swords and leather Sam Browne belts in contrast to the light-coloured Slade-Wallace webbing of the infantryman. Eventually, these too were discarded and towards the end of the conflict the infantry officer fought and

ABOVE: *A New South Wales mounted regiment - most likely one of the very earliest judging by their foreign service helmets - receive a rapturous send-off.* Courtesy of the State Library of New South Wales.

BELOW: *A standard-issue British khaki service tunic worn by Trooper John Purcell Campbell Simpson, 9th New Zealand Contingent. Note the ferns on the collar.* © Auckland Museum CC BY

dressed much like his men. Uniforms were originally made from light drill cloth which was worn in India and North Africa but offered little warmth in South Africa where the nights could dip below freezing and was replaced with a darker khaki serge.

The standard headgear for service in the warmer climates was the cork foreign service helmet, sometimes called a pith helmet (as it was manufactured from sholapith, or 'Indian cork') with a regimental flash on the left side. It provided limited shade for the neck and nose, but its primary benefit was the shape which allowed heat to rise and escape from a vent in the crown. The wider-brimmed Wolseley pattern helmet provided greater protection from the sun and was preferred by officers and some Canadian regiments.

The slouch hat or bush hat, which became more common during the second year of the war came to the Boer War from Australia and New Zealand. A derivative of the typical hat worn by agricultural labourers in the Antipodes, it was first adopted by

ABOVE: *Corporal Jack McBean of the 4th Imperial Bushmen's Contingent, wearing a typical Australian mounted uniform of slouch hat, khaki tunic, and bandolier, 1900.*

the volunteer Victorian Mounted Rifles in 1885, who pinned up the brim on the right for performing the 'Eyes right' in a review. Later, the left side was pinned up instead so that the hat would not be knocked askance when the trooper took his rifle from his shoulder. Offering greater protection from the sun, the slouch hat was issued in huge numbers to many newly arrived reinforcements due to shortages in the foreign service helmet.

The Cavalry

The cavalry had managed to escape the cultural vandalism of the Cardwell and Childers Reforms to retain the exceptionalism of its regimental identities. Here the esoteric, archaic, and ornate still held superficial sway. Each regiment remained a single battalion of 650 men divided amongst four squadrons. Unlike infantry, recruitment recognised few territorial restrictions.

Despite their colourful names, dragoons, hussars, and dragoon guards regiments were generally equipped and deployed in a similar fashion with swords and carbines, short-barrelled rifles which could be fired from the saddle. Only lancers, with their nine-foot bamboo lances, were an exception although they still carried a holstered carbine on their saddles.

To reflect the way cavalry were now expected to fight - as a reconnaissance or scouting force, or for flanking and running down infantry - from 1890, the sword was transferred to a scabbard on the saddle so that it didn't obstruct the trooper as he fought on foot. Ammunition was worn on the body, slung from shoulder to hip on a 50-round bandolier first introduced for Sudan in 1898. Red and blue tunics, which had clung on as service dress in mounted regiments who had not seen any large-scale warfighting for the best part of a century were finally replaced with the khaki before being dispatched to South Africa.

Despite the modernisation of British cavalry doctrine and kit, their popular image lost none of the dash and glamour it had traditionally revelled in. Dress uniforms remained a fiesta of ruffles, fur and polished plate, and membership of a cavalry regiment was to

Maxim Gun Mark I

Fed by a 250-round .303 calibre belt and effective up to 2,000 yards, the water-cooled Maxim was the first modern machine gun. Unlike its hand-cranked predecessors, the recoil of the round being ejected pulled a new one into the barrel to give it a theoretical rate of fire of 600-rounds a minute. Although some commanders struggled to know what to do with them, at an institutional level they were recognised as an effective support weapon and each infantry battalion and cavalry regiment had a machine gun section. A larger 1.46-inch calibre Maxim, known as a 'Pom-Pom' for the sound of its rounds being fired, was also used although mounted on a gun carriage rather than a tripod.

One of the four Maxim guns purchased by New Zealand in 1901 for use in the Second Boer War. © Auckland Museum CC BY

Lee-Metford Mark II

The first of a new type of firearm utilising James Lee's box-loading mechanism that would stay with the British Army through two World Wars, the Lee-Metford used a spring-loaded 10-bullet magazine which pushed a new round into the chamber when the bolt was pulled back to eject the spent one. The gun's .303 calibre lacked the stopping power of the .450 Martini-Henry it replaced, but its rate of fire was much improved.

A 1895 British-made Lee Metford Mark II from the collection of the Swedish Army Museum. © Armémuseum CC BY

Lee-Enfield Mark I

Essentially a modification to the Lee-Metford, the Lee-Enfield was designed to handle .303 cordite cartridge rather than gunpowder bullets but until a formula could be issued that was stable in the tropics, the Metford was issued as a stopgap. Obsolete from the second it was in service, at the start of the Second Boer War the British Army was part-way through replacing it with the Lee-Enfield Mark I and its cavalry carbine counterpart.

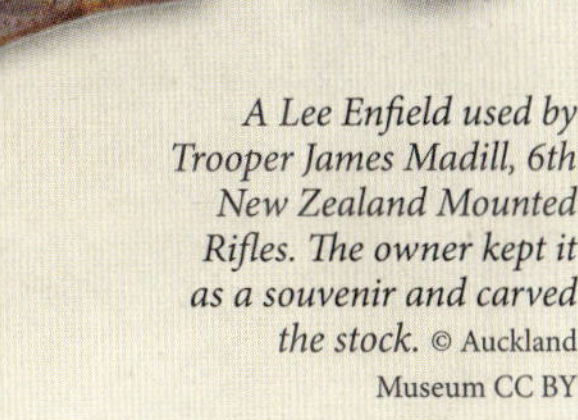

A Lee Enfield used by Trooper James Madill, 6th New Zealand Mounted Rifles. The owner kept it as a souvenir and carved the stock. © Auckland Museum CC BY

belong to the social elite. It was a self-selecting club that still expected every trooper to be a gentleman.

The fact that mounted regiments attracted the sons of the middle class and minor nobility (mess bills often eclipsed wages) produced an egalitarianism of sorts. Cavalry officers were far more likely to have been promoted from the ranks than infantry officers (although far fewer cavalry troopers began their careers in the gutter) and there were far more instances of 'gentleman rankers' - men from high-status backgrounds who served as private soldiers but often dined in the officers' mess.

In addition to the usual drain on a Victorian officer's wages, cavalry officers were also expected to provide two horses for their use (which might include hunting and polo, given the social obsessions of the cavalry) - including one charger of the appropriate breed. These latter steeds were usually purchased from the Army Remount Department, part of the Army Service Corps responsible for training and supplying horses and mules.

The cavalry equivalent of the militia - although few cavalry regiments would accept shared billing - was the yeomanry. Most of these glorified social clubs traced their origins to the French invasion scares of a century earlier and despite their fantastic uniforms, the feeling was by 1899 that they had outlived their usefulness. Though statute forbade their use outside of the country, they would later become a vast source of manpower.

The Colonial Contingents

The colonial militia - which was more likely to be mounted like the yeomanry - was far more relevant to the needs of the Second Boer War. South Africa, Australia, New Zealand, and Canada all produced hardy frontier folk with skill at hunting, riding, and tracking - and more still urban dwellers who fancied themselves the aforementioned. Regiments were often formed to confront a particular crisis, but some - such as South Africa's Cape Mounted Rifles or the New South Wales Lancers - had a lineage as storied (or pompous) as that of the Great British yeomanry regiment. Most of these formations functioned as mounted infantry rather than traditional cavalry, in that they used horses for manoeuvre and not for combat. Instead, they would dismount to shoot and only occasionally fire from the saddle, most often to cover a retreat as a horse seldom made for a stable firing platform.

With the outbreak of the Second Boer War, the six colonies of Australia (it federated on New Year's Day 1901) - Tasmania, Western Australia, New South Wales, South Australia, Queensland and Victoria - raised contingents of mounted troops from their militia and these arrived between November 1889 and March 1900. Later contingents were drafts of older militia veterans or young single men, leading to a disintegration of morale both at home and in the field. In total, an estimated 16,000 Australians served in South Africa between 1899 and 1902, with one in every 50 fighting-age men in khaki.

War was greeted equally enthusiastically in New Zealand and there was even talk of a 500-strong Māori contingent being formed, which was refused by the British government who baulked at the principle of using non-white troops against white foes. A few Māori enlisting under British names or men of mixed heritage did successfully join, however. One of their number, Walter Calloway, composed a haka which became the official war chant of the estimated 6,500 New Zealanders who went on to serve in the campaign:

"*Kia kaha nu Tereni/Wha whai maea mo to Kuini to Kianga/Ake.*" ("*Be strong New Zealand/ Fight bravely for your Queen, for your country/*

Ever! Ever! Ever!")

Despite any real or imagined affinity for the terrain of South Africa, the colonial contingents of Australia and New Zealand were often poorly trained and equipped, and lacked experienced officers. All of which made the Canadian contribution to their nation's first overseas engagement more valuable.

Unlike Australia and New Zealand which relied on Britain (and the vastness of the Pacific Ocean) for defence, Canada had a standing army called the Permanent Active Militia or Permanent Force, which gave it the core of professional soldiers from which to build battalions for the first contingent. Whilst most of the 7,000 Canadians to serve in South Africa did so in mounted units, first into the fray was the newly raised 2nd Royal Canadian Regiment of Infantry. The Canadians were equipped like their British counterparts in cork foreign service helmets, but the second contingent brought with them a more distinctly Canadian identity. Arriving in early 1900, it included men recruited from the ranks of North-West Mounted Police who wore wide-brimmed Stetsons.

The Irish-born journalist James Grattan Grey wrote in *The New York Times* of the view from New Zealand: "To outside nations, it will appear not a little odd that self-governing

"*The 15-pdr and 6-pdr were only issued with shrapnel shells.*"

ABOVE: *The Ordnance BL 15-pdrs of the Royal Artillery lie still as the horses forage in their camp outside of Pretoria, 1900.*

BELOW: *The 37th Field Battery of the Royal Artillery haul their Ordnance BL 5-inch howitzer up Maddox Hill, 1900.*

colonies 7,000 miles away from the scene of strife should send off bodies of men to do battle against people they have had no quarrel with, or that they should think it necessary to assist in the subjugation of a people who claim the right of self-government the same as they do; but the jingoistic spirit at the Antipodes is too inflamed just now to care anything about the rights or wrongs of the question."

The Artillery

Infantry support came from Royal Field Artillery batteries of six Ordnance BL 15-pounder guns or Ordnance BL 5-inch howitzer, whilst the cavalry was accompanied by the Royal Horse Artillery which used lighter Ordnance BL 12-pounders. RFA guns were pulled by six horses, with the crew mounted on two of the horses, the limber (the 'cab') or the gun carriage itself. For mobility, an RHA crew rode only on their own mounts with extra horses assigned for outriders.

Large calibre naval guns from HMS Monarch and HMS Doris mounted on crude 'Percy Scott Carriages', 1900.

Despite the professionalism of the Royal Artillery, in matters of firepower, they were considerably outmatched by the Boers. The Royal Garrison Artillery's siege batteries of heavier calibre 5-inch and 6-inch guns did eventually arrive in South Africa, but for the first months of the war, a solution was to detach larger pieces from coastal batteries and bring them inland with their gun crews. That this was possible was down to Captain Percy Scott of HMS *Terrible*. An innovator in naval gunnery and communications, Scott quickly engineered stable carriages that allowed QF (quick-firing) 4.7-inch guns to be used in the field.

LEFT: *View from the high ground overlooking a British Army camp in the veldt, 1901.*

BELOW: *An officer and his escort in the field, 1901.*

The 15-pdr and 6-pdr were only issued with shrapnel shells, which had been used to decimate charges of sword-wielding enemy infantry in Afghanistan and Sudan. The shell was packed with steel balls which sat on a percussion cap and would detonate in the air at 3,700 yards (a later cap was slower-burning and detonated at 5,800 yards) scattering steel balls over the unprotected foe.

With most field guns now specialised for infantry, this left the mean-looking 5-inch howitzer for hammering open earthworks. It threw a 50lb shell upwards in a high arc, which reduced the effective range to just under 5,000 yards. The shells were packed with lyddite which replaced gunpowder in 1898 and despite enthusiastic reports from Sudan, its promised devastation was often found wanting when it failed to detonate.

"It Is My Country You Want"

The Boer Army in South Africa

Much of the Boer character could be found in the person of Paul Kruger himself. Known to his constituents as Oum (Uncle) Paul, the president of the Transvaal Republic since 1883 lived a spartan existence, devoted to his Bible, his large family, and his community. He spoke in a great stentorian rumble - tones suited to religious sermons delivered in guttural Afrikaans - and spent much of the day puffing on his pipe and sitting on his front porch, where he was presented with as many questions on animal husbandry as he was pressing affairs of state.

Kruger had done all he possibly could to further the cause of peace in South Africa. As talks collapsed in face of escalating British demands, he was said to have cut the British negotiator, Sir Alfred Milner, down with a statement of truth softly delivered: "It is my country you want."

He returned to Pretoria with tears streaming down his face, but love for peace did not preclude a willingness to wage war. His family had never owned slaves, but they emigrated on the Great Trek where the 11-year-old Kruger was counted amongst the 35 Voortrekkers who fought off 400 Matabele warriors at the Battle of Vegkop (October 16, 1836). Like most Boers who settled on the high veldt, Kruger learned to shoot from a young age, reputedly killing his first lion at the age of 14. After his gun blew up in his hand whilst hunting rhino, the 20-year old amputated his own thumb with a pocketknife rather than let a doctor take his entire hand. These were not people who would give up easily.

BELOW: 'The Last Man of the Family' *by Edward J. Austen, showing a commando heeding the call during the First Boer War.*

otherwise what exactly were they fighting for? Even then, individual Burghers were well within their rights to disobey an order if they believed it flawed or signal their displeasure by leaving the commando altogether and heading home. Discipline was impossible to enforce, manpower fluctuated wildly, and democracy was not always meritocratic, with 'elder statesmen' parachuted into combat roles that they were not necessarily the best candidates for.

Armies were led by generals, who were elected in Orange Free State but appointed in Transvaal. Uniquely amongst that select brotherhood, the Transvaal General Petrus 'Piet' Joubert held his role in peacetime and seemingly for life. Like Kruger he had refused to return to the Volksraad after the annexation of Transvaal in 1879 and went on to lead the victorious Boers at the Battle of Majuba (February 27, 1881), which afforded him a certain mythic reputation.

The Commando

As with the First Boer War and the myriad conflicts with the Swazi, Zulu, Xhosa and others, the commando remained the heart of the Boer military machine. Despite deeply-ingrained hostility towards what would now be called 'big government', Boers recognised that individual survival rested on everyone pulling together to protect the community and every male Burgher between the ages of 16 and 60 were required to present themselves with a mount if mustered for war.

Despite the increased urbanisation of both Transvaal and Orange Free State, the values of self-reliance, horsemanship and marksmanship remained so integral that even the most urbane of Afrikaners could be made ready for frontier warfare at the first cry of "Vertroue in God en die Mauser" – 'Trust in God and the Mauser'.
Each Burgher belonged to a wyk, a ward or district, summoned and led by an elected veldkornet (field cornet) who in peacetime functioned as a magistrate, resolving local disputes and collecting taxes. The veldkornet distributed rifles and other equipment, although some Boers preferred to fight with their own firearms.

As many six neighbouring wyks were then gathered to form a commando, which meant the actual number of Burghers per commando could range anywhere from a few hundred to a thousand depending on how populous any given region was. The commando was led by a commandant, who like the veldkornet was elected by his men and despite his seniority, most strategic decisions were made by the whole commando during a war council called a krygsraad. This form of consensual decision making was vital to the Boer way of war,

The Artillery

Despite the rough-and-ready individualism of the Boer commando, both Transvaal and Orange had been unwilling to approach artillery with the same hobbyist attitude. As early as 1875 the Transvaal Republic had invested in a dedicated artillery corps, recruiting Captain Otto Riedel from Germany to raise Batterij Dingaan, which consisted mainly of foreign artillerymen who, like Riedel, sought gold and glory in the 'dark continent.'

After annexation, the men of Batterij Dingaan were perfectly content to draw British wages and went on to fight for new masters against their old ones in the First Boer War. Consequently, Pretoria had to build a new artillery corps from scratch and like its predecessor, the 650-strong Staatsartillerie van de Zuid-Afrikaansche Republiek (State Artillery of the South African Republic) ➤➤

ABOVE LEFT: General Petrus 'Piet' Joubert and his men pose by a wagon. Joubert was considered a 'progressive' in the Transvaal Volksraad and ran against Kruger for the presidency. ABOVE RIGHT: The Transvaal Staatsartillerie in their Austrian-style uniforms of dark blue tunics and shakoes. Zuid-Afrika Huis

enticed foreign veterans with the necessary expertise and experience. This time an Austrian subject of Czech origin, Captain Adolph Zbořil, was entrusted with breathing life into the corps and he saw that they were clad in finery worthy of the Austro-Hungarian Empire. Regular artillerymen wore a dark blue tunic with three rows of buttons, black collar and shoulder cords, and fussy hussar-style braid. All ranks also wore fur busbies, or shakoes (round caps with a peak), and carried swords, with officers denoted by their gold braid. Fortunately, a khaki service dress and slouch hat were introduced in 1890, with only dark blue piping and the letters 'SA' or 'A' on the cap to denote their membership of the corps d'elite.

Orange had a far smaller artillery corps of around 450 men, which had been reformed in the 1880s by Major F.W.R. Albrecht. Prussian by birth, he introduced a dress uniform that would have put the curl in the Kaiser's moustache: dark blue tunic with orange piping and a Pickelhaube, the daunting spiked helmet of the Prussian and then Imperial German Army. Likewise, common sense prevailed over showmanship and the Oranje-Vrystaat (OVS) Staatsartillerie fought in khaki.

The Uitlanders

Whilst the majority of Uitlanders on the Witwatersrand were of British origin and fled for Cape Colony on the outbreak of war, the gold rush had lured men and women of all nations to seek their fortune, many of whom had no affection for the British Empire.

Perhaps as many as 2,500 foreigners fought with the Boers, the largest contingents being Dutch and German (an estimated 600 and 750 volunteers respectively), who felt a cultural affinity for the Afrikaners. The attitude of the Transvaal government was one of non-committal acceptance, they were happy to arm and feed these Uitlanders but not to pay them, and they made it clear that whilst foreign help was accepted, it was by no means needed.

Irish and Irish Americans made up the third-largest group of pro-Boer Uitlanders with around 500 volunteers who saw something of their own relationship with the British Empire in the fight. Colonel John Blake, a US Cavalry

"Perhaps as many as 2,500 foreigners fought with the Boers."

BELOW: *Orange Free State's Winburg Commando makes an awesome show of force.* Zuid-Afrika Huis

veteran of Irish descent, was elected commander of the 100-strong First Irish Brigade which was recruited from the Irish miners of the goldfields and reinforced by the volunteer Irish American Ambulance Corps who travelled from Chicago to South Africa, shedding their Red Cross armbands and taking up arms. Blake's brigade published a manifesto on September 13, 1889, which refought old battles:

"England has been a vampire, and has drained Ireland's lifeblood for centuries, and now her difficulty is Ireland's opportunity. The time is at hand to avenge your dead Irish. England's hands are red with blood, and her coffers filled with the spoil of Irish people, and we call upon you to rise as one man and seize upon the present glorious opportunity of retaliating upon your ancient foe."

Roland Schikkerling wrote in his memoir, *Commando Courageous* (1964): "[The Irish] were lively boys, and the finest of company [...] Where the German and Hollander, nearer to us in blood perhaps, felt and looked out of place, you could not pick Patrick out of a herd of the wildest Boers."

ABOVE: *Major F.W.R. Albrecht and the Prussian-inspired pomp he brought to the Orange Staatsartillerie.* Zuid-Afrika Huis

Other companies formed from the expatriate population of Johannesburg, included 113 Scandinavians under a Swedish commander, Captain Axel Christer Helmfrid Uggla, and an Italian Volunteer Legion led by Colonel Camillo Ricchiardi. Something of a full-time friend to liberation movements in the grand tradition of Giuseppe Garibaldi, Ricchiardi honed his skills as a guerrilla in the Philippine Revolution (1896-1898) against Spanish rule and went on to marry one of Kruger's granddaughters. ➤➤

ABOVE: *An immense 155mm Creusot BL 'Long Tom' in the Boer lines around Mafeking, 1899.*

The Boers had no shortage of older and obsolete artillery, but in the wake of the Jameson Raid and growing suspicion towards Great Britain, both republics sought out some of the most sophisticated guns commercially available.

Unlike the British and German guns, the 75mm Creusot QF was a genuine 'quick fire' piece in that it used a hydraulic recoil buffer that absorbed just over 11-inches of movement. If you consider that the average artillery piece was likely to 'jump' backwards with the immense force of the firing and had to be moved back into position before it was fired again, recoil buffers speeded up the process considerably.

Though this would become commonplace in the decades which followed, the technology was still in its infancy and even the buffer of the 75mm Creusot needed support from an axle spade which was dug into the ground to anchor the gun in place and drag shoes wedged under the wheels. Another innovation was that the barrel could be traversed from left to right, which reduced the need to haul the gun into a position to find its target. Though imperfect, the later generation of 75mm Creusot would gain a reputation as the best artillery piece of World War One.

It was, however, the larger calibre Boer artillery that gave the British cause to worry. Both the 120mm Krupp howitzer BL and 155mm Creusot BL, nicknamed 'Long Tom', outranged anything the Royal Artillery could bring to bear by at least 1,000 yards and 3,000 yards, respectively.

The Long Tom was not designed as a field gun but for fixed defence mounted on a timber base. However, the Boers immediately entered the war with four of them adapted for transport. The trunnion - the thick cylindrical pin which the barrel pivoted up and down on - was levered out of its cradle and the immense barrel was slid down the carriage to move the centre of gravity and keep the gun from toppling over as it was manoeuvred uphill. A second set of detachable wheels were added to the 'tail' of the gun for stability on the road.

The Boers also fielded a larger-calibre Maxim machine gun than the British Army, at least for the first phase of the war until the purchasing power of the War Office overtook the governments of Pretoria and Bloemfontein. The 37mm Maxim-Nordenfelt - which also has the distinction of being the only artillery-scale weapon in South Africa with a shield for its crew - fired explosive shells rapid-fire from a 25-round belt with devastating effect. Ironically at least some of these had been purchased directly from the Maxim Nordenfelt Guns and Ammunition Company in London, although the ammunition was of German origin.

LEFT: *A 'Long Tom' packed for transport with the barrel detached and moved down the carriage to distribute the weight more evenly.*

RIGHT: *A 37mm Maxim-Nordenfelt 'Pom-Pom' gun parked next to two 75mm Creusots, 1900. The two wheeled wagons at the rear of each gun is the limber, which carries ammunition and the driver.* Zuid-Afrika Huis

ABOVE RIGHT: *The khaki field dress and slouch hats of the Transvaal Staatsartillerie during the Siege of Ladysmith, 1899.* Zuid-Afrika Huis
ABOVE LEFT: *Dutch volunteers - the second-largest foreign contingent to fight with the Boers - moving out to the front, October 1899.* Zuid-Afrika Huis

The most celebrated of the foreign adventurers was Major General Georges de Villebois-Mareuil. Whilst the French government urged its citizens in South Africa towards neutrality, Villebois-Mareuil was a founding member of the ultra-nationalist and antisemitic Action Française political party and saw the conflict as an opportunity to avenge French humiliation. He wrote: "[England] gave us a Hundred Years' War, and for a hundred years, she has robbed the [Boer] farmers from the Cape. Since then she has violated every peace treaty. Her hatred being even fiercer against the Boer, for there is French blood flowing through their veins."

Whilst foreigners had to win rank by popular vote like their Afrikaner counterparts, Villebois-Mareuil was an exception. Having led troops in the Franco-Prussian War (1870-1871) and then in Algeria and Tunisia, he was enthusiastically embraced as a military advisor and in March 1900 was given overall command of the foreign volunteers.

The Agterryers

Though both sides tried to preserve the illusion that this was a 'white man's war' - as if such a thing were possible in a land where the black population outnumbered the white many times over - the farmstead needed black labour and so too did the commando.

An agterryer - literally 'after-rider' - were domestic servants who joined their master in the saddle in what was supposed to be a strictly non-combatant role, agterryers tended to the Burghers' horses, guarded their supplies and ammunition, collected firewood, cooked and washed, and undertook all manner of menial tasks, but they also fought as and when needed.

ABOVE: *The highly decorated Major General George de Villebois-Mareuil, he attained the rank of colonel at the age of 45, making him the youngest in the French Army.*

An estimated 15,000 agterryers accompanied the commandos during the Second Boer War, but these are difficult numbers to track. For many Boers, agterryers barely merited a second thought and their contributions went unnoticed because they were expected. Their sacrifice was seen as the natural order of things. For others, there was an erosion of the old certainties that saw the black servant regarded, if not anywhere near an equal, then at least having some worth as a human being.

Speaking in the 1960s, Klasie Grobler recalled the service of a 'coloured' servant called Willem Gorrel who stayed by his father's side throughout the war and alludes to an understanding of sorts: "After the peace, my father gave him £2 and he went off to Johannesburg to find his family. We never saw him again."

It is impossible to say for certain how the Boers' black auxiliaries felt about the war they were fighting. It is certainly true that many were genuinely loyal to a profoundly unequal society which endured only because of their exploitation. But who can blame them? For many, this life was all they knew. According to Hans du Plessis, an African servant called Windvoël joined his father Commandant Casper du Plessis's commando - not as an agterryer, but as a combatant bringing with him a rifle and horse. He refused to be turned away and replied: "I am going to help defend my country, the land of my master's children."

7mm Mauser M1896

ABOVE:
An M1896 Mauser taken as a trophy in the Second Boer War.
© Auckland Museum CC BY

As with the push to acquire the latest artillery, the Jameson Raid also convinced Orange and Transvaal of the need to replace their single-shot .405 Martini-Henry (also brought from Britain). Firing from a clip rather than a magazine (which had to be reloaded round-by-round), the 7mm Mauser M1896 was significantly quicker to reload than the British Army's Lee-Metford and Lee-Enfield, and over 50,000 of them were purchased by the two republics. Rounds with a soft lead nose which expanded on impact to cause horrific wounds, called dumdums, were used by both sides to much moral outrage from the other.

The Hand of God

The Invasion of Natal, October 11, 1899 - October 30, 1899

The ecstatic Sir Henry Milner, who was already imagining himself the father of united South Africa, had correctly anticipated the Boer response to British bullying, and he was likely correct about their strategy too. It was clear that the Boers would strike pre-emptively at Natal to their east and across their western frontiers where tempting targets lay within their grasp. The great diamond mines of Kimberley were on land previously claimed by the Orange Free State and Mafeking - the capital of the Bechuanaland Protectorate and vital hub on the route to Rhodesia - was disputed territory on Transvaal's frontier.

Although his dual roles as British high commissioner for South Africa and governor of Cape Colony made Milner the paramount imperial official on that side of the Sahara, his actual powers were nebulously defined. Both Natal and Cape Colony had elected governments (and in Natal's case, its own governor), but whilst Natal already had British reinforcements in place, the Cape prime minister was reluctant to take any action that might be deemed provocative.

A peacemaker with a more conciliatory attitude towards both the Boers and the blacks than Cecil Rhodes, William Schreiner was the human embodiment of backlash against the Jameson Raid. German-born and married to an Afrikaner, he had undermined the pro-war party by publicly applauding Kruger's proposals and even now he refused Milner's urging to dispatch colonial troops to defend Kimberley. Rhodes, meanwhile, had stubbornly refused to exit stage-left. As tensions mounted, he rushed to Kimberley, the source of his immense wealth, to organise

BELOW: *The Boers fire into the advancing Gordon Highlanders at the Battle of Elandslaagte by German artist Fritz Neumann, 1900*

the town's defence - a move so guaranteed to irritate the Boers that Kimberley's mayor tried to stop him.

The Place of Stones

Neither were the town's appointed defenders overjoyed, suspecting that Rhodes's presence would make attempts to utilise the formidable resources of the De Beers mining company more difficult. Despite Schreiner's prevarications, he had allowed Major Scott-Turner to raise the town guard and the Diamond Fields Volunteer Artillery. These colonial troops were subordinate to Lieutenant Colonel Robert Kekewich, whose four companies of the Loyal North Lancashire Regiment were garrisoning the town. Rhodes for his part threw his money at the raising of the Kimberley Light Horse, guaranteeing a great diffusion of leadership.

Maxim guns were ensconced in redoubts raised atop the great heaps of tailing - discarded material from the mines which formed sheer manmade plateaus on the outskirts of Kimberley - and rather than

ABOVE: *Colonel Robert Baden-Powell in 1900. Sent to South Africa for 'special service', Baden-Powell's experiences at the Siege of Mafeking made him a national hero and led to his formation of the Scout Movement.*

General Pieter Arnoldus 'Slim Piet' Cronjé outside of Mafeking, 1899. He is the smaller figure in the top hat, holding a whip.

leaving the cattle outside the town for the Boers to plunder, De Beers' chief engineer, an American called George Labram, hit upon the idea of building an underground refrigeration plant in the silent mines themselves.

Milner had better luck with Mafeking. Colonel Robert Baden-Powell had been sent north to recruit volunteers to hold Rhodesia and Bechuanaland, and after talking the gallant special service officer out of a raid on Transvaal, Milner persuaded him to take Lt Col C. O. Hore's Protectorate Regiment to Mafeking instead. Contrary to Milner's directive that indigenous Africans should not be used as combat troops, Baden-

Powell took the highly controversial step of arming the black townsfolk with obsolete firearms. Around his 500-strong core of white Australian and South African mounted infantry, was a company of 500 armed Tshidi-Baralong. The Tshidi-Baralong were the traditional inhabitants of Mafeking (which they called Mahikeng, the Place of Stones) and their own settlement was Buda to the white man's Pest. They had been fighting the Boers for two years, and as tensions with Transvaal mounted they made clear their intentions to defend their homes and cattle.

With the flight of the British gold magnates from the Witwatersrand, the black population of Mafeking grew with returning migrant workers and refugees, these miners and labourers were quickly put to use in work gangs digging a formidable ring of trenches and earthworks.

"From the outside, the town looks as if a series of gigantic mounds had been suddenly created," wrote *The Times* correspondent J. Angus Hamilton. "At different points tiers of sandbags, several feet high, protect the more exposed places, and to these again has been added, as an exterior facing, banks of earth. Within such a position as I am now describing there is a deep trench, which is of that depth which enables a man standing upright to fire through loopholes between sacks of sand. Behind the trench is a low shelter of deals with an upper covering of sandbags, intending to serve the garrison of the fort as protection against shell fire."

Cutting the Cord

With Paul Kruger's declaration of war on October 11, the Boers immediately took the initiative. As Milner had predicted it was a war over two frontiers. In the west, General Piet Cronjé would strike for the towns of Mafeking and Kimberley, while in the east, a larger force would bear down on Ladysmith. This was the gateway to Natal, with a long and porous border to both Transvaal and Orange on three sides. ➤➤

The Boers preparing to fire on Mafeking, 1900.

crossed the Modder River south of Kimberley while the Boshof Commando simultaneously uprooted the rails ten miles to the north and diverted the water supply to the town. On October 14, the telephone line from Kimberley was silenced and the Siege of Kimberley had begun.

The way cleared by Rey's sortie, Gen Cronjé's main force of 5,000 crossed the border for Mafeking and on October 16 - after Baden-Powell politely refused the invitation to lay down his arms - Boer artillery opened up.

The defence of Natal was initially co-ordinated by Major General Sir William Penn Symons KCB who resolved to fight at the border. When Lieutenant General Sir George White VC arrived with a view to making a stand further south behind the natural barrier of Tugela River, he deferred to his experienced predecessor and the urging of the Natal Governor, Sir Walter Hely-Hutchinson, who feared an indigenous uprising if the British were to show any hint of hesitance.

The result was White at Ladysmith with 8,000 men, and Penn Symons some 40-odd miles further north at Dundee with a garrison of 4,000. Too late, White found his voice and ordered Penn Symons back just as two

By cover of darkness, Gen Koos de la Rey led the Potchefstroom and Lichtenburg Commandos over the Transvaal frontier 37 miles south of Mafeking where the railway hugged the border. In the small hours of the following morning, they happened across the armoured train 'Mosquito' carrying ammunition and artillery north and derailed it, seizing the railway siding and its token defenders at the Battle of Kraaipan (October 12-13, 1899). The first engagement of the Great Boer War was almost a game, at no cost to Rey's command they inflicted nine wounded and took 30 prisoners, severing both the telegraph and railway south. Without these strands which trailed like a dull thread through hundreds of miles of the veldt, Mafeking was alone. The same morning as 'Mosquito' was swatted, the Jacobsdal Commando cut the railway line where it

ABOVE: *A map of Northern Natal reproduced from Arthur Conan Doyle's* The Great Boer War, *1900. It shows not just the locations of Dundee, Elandslaagte and Ladysmith, but just how vulnerable the land north of the Tugela was.*

On November 14, Commandant Cornelius Wessels demanded that Kimberley surrender and Lt Col Kekewich likewise deferred. Three days later, the Krupp chorus sounded over the diamond fields as the Boers began to shell the town.

The Battle of Talana Hill

It was in the east that the real war began. Commandant-General Piet Joubert had at his disposal 14,000 Transvaalers and an additional 6,000 Free Staters and they advanced in four great columns of rattling wagons and rising dust clouds. The teenage Deneys Reitz recalled later in life: "As far as the eye could see, the plain was alive with horsemen, guns and cattle."

columns under Gens Lukas Meyer and D. J. E. 'Maroela' Erasmus began to move in on Dundee. Penn Symons ignored the order completely, just as he went on to ignore the first desperate request for support from a patrol which encountered Erasmus's Boers in the afternoon of October 18. Critically, Penn Symons also ignored the dire warning that this first exchange of fire contained and failed to occupy the high ground around Dundee, so confident was he that the Boers would shy away from engaging directly.

On the dull and misty morning of October 20, the camp was going about the usual business of an army in the field, when a soldier glanced up to see the nearby kopje of Talana

ABOVE: *Major General John French, photographed just prior to the Second Boer War. French was a dashing cavalry commander with a chequered personal life.*

Hill bristling with Boer artillery. During the night, Maj J. F. Wolmarans had hauled the Staatsartillerie to the top of Talana and Gen Meyer had taken Lennox Hill which faced it across the road. Gen Erasmus had led his force onto the commanding Impati Hill further to the north. As shells fell, the British sprang into action. Despite having unhitched their guns, the 16th and 69th Field Batteries galloped across the town to return fire with canisters of shrapnel which burst high above the Boer positions, scattering Wolmarans and his gun crews with jagged metal thorns.

For all the Boers' skill in frontier wars, few had seen field pieces fired, let alone come under the disciplined sights of the Royal Artillery. Some bolted, most took cover, and Wolmarans was forced to pull back his guns. The initiative had passed to Penn Symons and he ordered the 2nd Royal Dublin Fusiliers forward in extended order, followed by the 1st The Royal Irish Regiment and the 1st The King's Royal Rifle Corps. No sooner had the tide turned, when it turned again with the Dubliners tumbling helplessly into a concealed ravine. As their officers tried to restore order, Boer rifles cracked wickedly above them. The wood beyond the donga offered some respite and when the infantry hesitated to move out of its shade and into the open, Penn Symons galloped forward to urge them on. Dismounting to peer around a low stone wall, the general turned back and timidly admitted that he had been shot in the stomach.

Whilst Penn Symons carried himself down the hill to die of his wounds, Brigadier General James Yule carried on the charge into the devastating fire of the Boers. As they closed on the enemy, they found their shrapnel had begun falling amongst Boer and Brit alike. Finally, they signalled to the guns to cease fire and the Dubliners were able to occupy Talana. The Boers - including Meyer's commandos which had been giving supporting fire from Lennox Hill - began to withdraw to the east.

Meanwhile, the inexperienced 18th Hussars and some colonial mounted infantry had been skirting Impati Hill through the drizzle when

they saw the Boers in flight. With a fleeting echo of the Light Brigade at Balaclava, Lt Col Bernhard Drysdale Möller charged barely more than 100 men right into the path of the Boer retreat. As the scale of their folly dawned, the hussars attempted to make their escape but found Erasmus's commandos descending Impati and bearing down on them through the mist. The cavalry was herded to a cluster of farm buildings eight miles from Dundee, where they made a desultory stand until the Staatsartillerie was brought to bear.

Deneys Reitz arrived just in time to see their surrender, writing: "The soldiers had thrown down their arms and were falling in under their officers. Their leader, Colonel Möller, stood on the stoep [veranda] looking pretty crestfallen."

The Battle of Elandslaagte

Whilst Meyer and Erasmus advanced on Dundee, Gen Johannes Kock led his column into the village of Elandslaagte on the rail line between Dundee and Ladysmith and took it without resistance, seizing a supply train at the station and cutting off communications.

On October 20, news of the costly victory at the Battle of Talana Hill reached White, and he dispatched Maj Gen John French to drive the Boers out of Elandslaagte and secure the line retreat from Dundee. French had taken command of White's cavalry only two days earlier but by the morning of October 21, he was in a position. Kock's force - 1,000 men in all - was considerably larger than French had anticipated, and the heavy Krupp guns pummelled the diminutive Natal Volunteer Field Battery into silence. The Boers took up positions on the higher northern arm of a horseshoe-shaped ridge east of the village whilst French pulled out of range.

Reinforced by the innovative Col Ian Hamilton with three battalions of regulars, the 1st The Devonshire Regiment launched a frontal attack on the high ground, whilst the 1st Manchester Regiment and the 2nd Gordon Highlanders ascended the southern arm of the ridge and attacked the Boer flank. They were followed by the locally raised Imperial Light Horse, who dismounted to fight as ➤➤

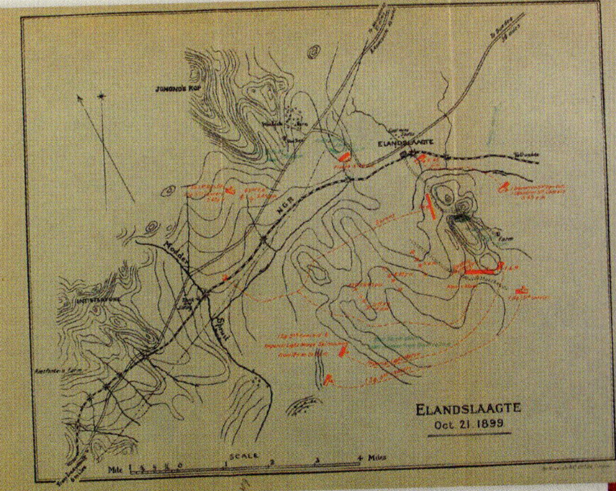

LEFT: *A contemporary sketch by W. F. Mondriaan showing the charge of the 2nd Gordon Highlanders at Elandslaagte, 1899.*

infantry on the Highlanders' right. On each side of the British line, a squadron each of the 5th (Royal Irish) Lancers and 5th (or Princess Charlotte of Wales's) Dragoon Guards made ready beneath cover for the foot-sloggers to drive their prey into the veldt.

As storm clouds swirled and opened a deluge, the bagpipes wailed and the men bellowed "Remember Majuba!" By the time the Gordons reached the top of the ridge, half of their officers had fallen under the murderous fire of the Boers and Hamilton dashed forward with his staff to stiffen their resolve. The momentum regained, the Gordons charged, and the others followed, bayonets turning the khaki dark with blood.

Whether through duplicity or the notorious individualism of the Afrikaner, a Boer raised the white flag and the British obligingly faltered. Surrender was not on Kock's agenda, however, and he led his commando forward to open fire. The Imperial Light Horse, their colonel's leg, chest, and skull shattered in turn by a sharpshooter, began to retreat. A lieutenant of the Gordons dashed forward to rally the colonials, but he too was riddled with bullets and sent crashing to the sodden earth. Desperately, Hamilton and other officers turned the rout with curses and exhortations. With Kock mortally wounded, the Boers broke and fled, some on foot and some on horseback. They soon discovered that a cavalry charge knows no mercy.

To the Boer, the lance was simply a spear - the weapon of a savage - and those who threw up their hands in surrender discovered the

ABOVE: *5th (Royal Irish) Lancers run down the defeated Boers in the veldt around Elandslaagte. Photogravure etching from original artwork by Richard Caton Woodville, 1900.*

"Both forces had become lost in the darkness and strung out across the battlefield."

moment for civilisation had passed. Private W. Tuxford, 5th (Royal Irish) Lancers wrote home: "We charged them, and they went on their knees, begging us to shoot them rather than stab them with our lances, but in vain. The time had come for us to do our work and we did it."

The Battle of Ladysmith

Two battles were won, but at a cost which the British had not expected to pay - and so far from home, could they afford to? Talana Hill left them weaker by 41 killed, 185 wounded and as many as 200 captured, whilst the butcher's bill at Elandslaagte was 55 dead and 205 injured.

By October 25, the bulk of the British Army in Natal had withdrawn to Ladysmith in such haste that both French and Yule left provisions and prisoners scattered behind them. This was scarcely an overreaction; the Boers had come within an inch of cutting the force in half: they were more numerous and moving more swiftly than White had anticipated.

The Boer freedom of movement had been curbed somewhat, however, by the orgy of looting that followed the occupation of Dundee, behaviour that sent Joubert into a fury. The hero of Majuba was essentially a decent man. He attributed his victories to God and bore the British no grudges - once he had finished browbeating his subordinates over their criminality and indiscipline, he wrote a letter of condolence to Penn Symons's widow, Jane.

The Boer columns which had entered Natal were now staggered by events and White resolved to strike before they were able to concentrate their forces against the town. Whilst Ladysmith made an ideal supply hub, it was a miserable citadel which gifted its

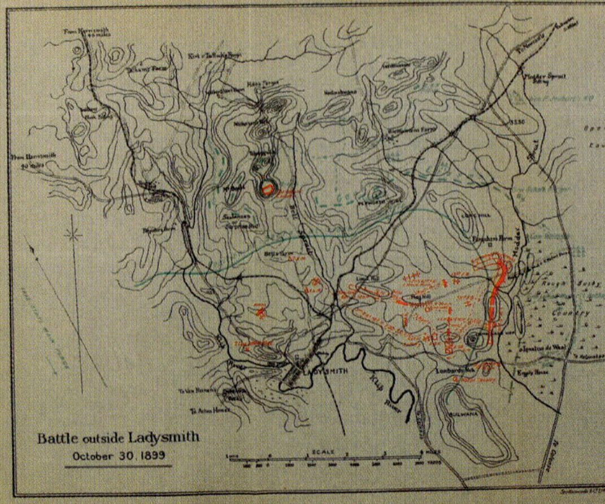

LEFT: *A Boer commando advances across a river somewhere in the vicinity of Ladysmith, 1899.*

ABOVE: *Two Boers and their shelter during the Siege of Ladysmith, either late 1899 or early 1900.*

enemies a ring of hills from which they could lob explosives with impunity.

Called the Battle of Ladysmith (October 30, 1899), what unfolded were two engagements conjoined by their disastrous outcomes: The Battle of Nicholson's Nek and the Battle of Lombard's Kop. Col Hamilton was to lead the main assault on Pepworth Hill where the Boers had been seen manoeuvring their artillery, with a companion action by Col Geoffrey Grimworth against Long Hill to the right of their line. Maj Gen French's cavalry brigade would secure the Grimworth's flank and six batteries of Royal Artillery would support the attack. Further north, Lt Col Frank Carleton was to hold Nicholson's Nek in case one of the other Boer columns began to advance.

The British moved into position by the cover of darkness and when the sun rose Grimworth discovered only half his brigade was where he expected them to be. Nor were French's cavalry

ABOVE: *Lieutenant General Sir George Stuart White, VC. He was awarded his Victoria Cross for twice leading an attack on an enemy position during the Second Anglo-Afghan War (1878-1880).*

in position. Both forces had become lost in the darkness and strung out across the battlefield. Grimworth pressed on regardless and assaulted Long Hill, which he promptly discovered was completely deserted. The Boers had placed their artillery on Lombard's Kop instead and once the British realised their mistake, Gen Louis Botha opened fire into Grimworth's unprotected right flank. Simultaneously, the guns on Pepworth Hill hammered their left flank catching the British in a devastating crossfire.

Hamilton was forced to divert troops to try and cover Grimworth's retreat. Piece by piece, the attack collapsed, and only divine intervention saved Ladysmith. As his staff clamoured to give chase and make good their victory, the cautious Joubert quoted an old Afrikaans proverb: 'When God offers you a finger, it's not right to take the whole hand'.

Mournful Monday

Incredibly, Lt Col Frank Carleton managed to have an even more humiliating morning. He was supposed to be in place on Nicholson's Nek by dawn on October 30 but going was slow and he decided to spend the night on the side of Tchrengula Hill instead. As they climbed the rugged slopes, the mules hauling their ammunition, water, artillery, and heliograph stampeded.

Raising rocky 'sangers' as best they could on the hillside without tools, as dawn broke the silence was broken too. The Boers - who had been alerted to Carleton's movements by a hundred panicked pack animals - opened fire, killing 38 and wounding 105 before Carleton surrendered the rest. Almost 1,000 British soldiers were taken prisoner at the Battle of Nicholson's Nek, more than had been lost in a century.

Both battles lost, the boom of the 'Long Tom' on Pepworth Hill offered no right of reply as it rattled the windows and door frames of the panicked town. Their spirits were lifted only by the fortuitous arrival of a train of heavy guns and naval gunners from HMS *Terrible* that had the calibre to at least worry the Boers in the hills and keep them from levelling Ladysmith and riding into the empty ruins.

As night fell on 'Mournful Monday', Ladysmith, like Mafeking and Kimberley before it, was under siege.

ABOVE: *Medics search the battlefield for the wounded by darkness. Watercolour sketch by Frank Craig, 1899.*
Wellcome Collection. Attribution 4.0 International (CC BY 4.0)

Drawing-Room Generals

Buller's First Campaign, October 31, 1899 - December 15, 1899

General Sir Redvers Buller, VC, arrived in South Africa on October 31, 1899, for his first battle in 15 years with the carefully qualified triumphs Elandslaagte and Talana Hill followed at a gallop by the large-scale humiliation of Ladysmith. It was clear that Ladysmith needed to be urgently relieved so that its defenders could be put to use, but the obnoxious Cecil Rhodes was also demanding the relief of Kimberley. Commandos were pushing across the Orange River and into the north of Cape Colony where Cape Afrikaners, also called 'Cape rebels', were rising to join them. Mafeking at least could wait, as Colonel Baden-Powell seemed to be managing well enough to frustrate the enemy.

Buller was forced to discard his original plan of a push north into Orange and from there into the soft underbelly of the highveldt, and he prepared the 1st Army Corps for a war across multiple fronts.

A division of 8,000 men under Lieutenant General Paul Standford, Lord Methuen was to make haste for Kimberley to relieve the diamond capital and stop Rhodes from making a nuisance of himself. A token force under Lt Gen Sir William Gatacre - dubbed "back-acher"

A highly stylised depiction of an attempt to recover the guns at the Battle of Colenso. In the actual event, the Boer fire was far more distant but it captures the desperation and carnage.

ABOVE: *Paul Sanford Methuen, Lord Methuen pictured in 1910 by which time he had been promoted to full general and appointed governor of the Colony of Natal.*

for the way in which he relentlessly drove his men - was to resist further incursion into Cape Colony and deter Afrikaner insurrection. Buller, meanwhile, sailed to the relief of Natal.

The Battle of Belmont

A Wolseley Ring stalwart, Methuen began to march on the Orange River Station with some of the most prestigious regiments in the British Army. The British division followed the Western Railway from Cape Town, sheltering in the cover of an armoured train and crossed the Orange River on November 21. Not only was Methuen not keeping his movements quiet, but he seemed determined to make as much noise as possible, announcing to a subordinate: "My good man, I intend to put the fear of God into these people."

Their destination and route had appeared in the British press days before their departure and the Free Staters had ample time to pick their battlefield.

Methuen, of course, could have ignored them. The veldt was wide enough to skirt any foe, but then he would have relieved Kimberley only to find a few thousand Boers sniping at his exposed flank, rather than his front. He was also tasked with rescuing the civilians in the

besieged town and escorting them back to safety by train. He could hardly do that if larger numbers of hostile Burghers were still prowling the veldt, ambushing his columns and tearing up the rails.

The Boers dug in around the railway station at Belmont under the untested Commandant Jacobus Prinsloo and 1,500 Free Staters. Lord Methuen - who had only a small cavalry contingent - lacked the men for thorough reconnaissance (another good reason to follow the railway, on balance). As they neared Belmont, he knew enough to know that the Boers were occupying two chains of hills which faced Belmont from the east running parallel to the railway, although their exact disposition was a mystery. The first line was divided between Table Mountain on the left and Gun Hill on the right.

The Battle of Belmont (November 23, 1899) began with the coffee-fueled 9th Brigade advancing under the cover of night, the darkness shielding them from the fire of the defenders. The 2nd Northamptonshire Regiment and 1st Northumberland Fusiliers seized Table Mountain by first light and pressed on to the key kopje in the second line, the commanding Mont Blanc. The Guards Brigade meanwhile had

stumbled catastrophically. Half an hour late to their starting position, they became lost in the darkness and 3rd Grenadier Guards began their approach just as the sun began to rise, leaving the guardsmen silhouetted by the glow to their backs. In the face of devastating losses, the Grenadiers eventually drove the enemy from Gun Hill at bayonet point.

Despite the blunder, Methuen's pre-dawn

ABOVE: *A stereoscopic photograph of British infantry firing on the withdrawing Boers from the hills to the east of Belmont, 1899.*

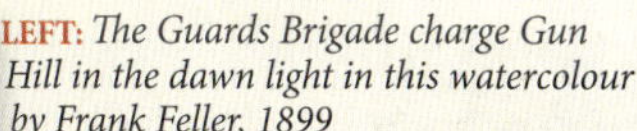

LEFT: *The Guards Brigade charge Gun Hill in the dawn light in this watercolour by Frank Feller, 1899*

offensive had spared both brigades heavy losses, and he ordered them onwards in three extended lines. Whilst he remained committed to the British Army doctrine of a decisive charge, his extended order ("Men getting quickly from rock to rock," marvelled one officer) was beyond anything encouraged by a drill sergeant and reflected a response to the challenges of the terrain and their foe. The 9th Brigade was supposed to bear the brunt of the assault, whilst the Guards supported their advance but the bumbling Grenadiers had thrown the line further to the right. As the unsupported Northamptons and Northumberlands began to take heavy casualties, Methuen pivoted the attack to the Grenadiers and poured in his reinforcements until the Boers finally broke.

Left on the field were 150 Boer dead and wounded, and 300 British. It was another costly hurrah and the press were unforgiving of what they saw as murderous folly. With only 850 mounted troops for a force of

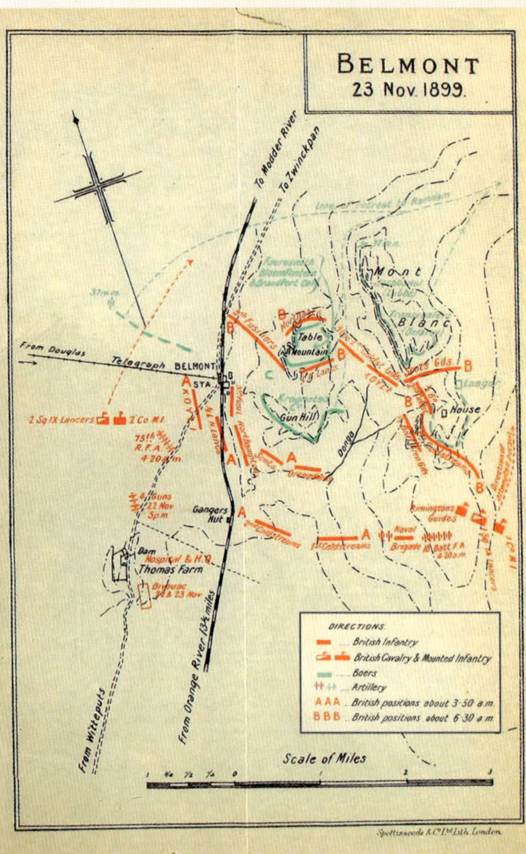

Spottiswoode & C? Lth London.

LEFT: *That the conflict was ongoing didn't stop The Times newspaper from publishing The Times History of the War in South Africa (1900), from where this detailed map of the Battle of Belmont is taken.*

BELOW: *A wounded soldier helps a dying bugler down Graspan Kopje in the aftermath of the bloody battle.*

BELOW RIGHT: *A detailed map of the Battle of Graspan, from The Times History of the War in South Africa (1900).*

force drove the Boers back from the hill. Of the 20 killed and 165 wounded, 16 dead and 101 injured came from the ranks of the Royal Navy - a toll so considerable that Queen Victoria sent her condolences.

The Battle of Modder River

The Boers withdrew again to form a new fighting line further north where the Modder and Riet Rivers met 25 miles outside of Kimberley. Gen Piet Cronjé was ostensibly in command, with Rey as his advisor, but the old 'Lion of Potchefstroom' found him so difficult to work with that he left his subordinate to it. Using the high banks of the Modder itself as a trench, Rey set about ordering concealed artillery positions erected and rifle pits dug. The number of Boers, though still outnumbered, was by now as high as 3,500 with six artillery pieces and at least three Maxim guns of the OVS Staatsartillerie.

Knowing that the railway bridge had been destroyed, Methuen had originally planned to avoid the Modder altogether. He hoped to leave

8,000, Methuen was unable to make anything other than a frontal attack without thorough reconnaissance. After all, you cannot outflank an enemy if you're not sure where their flanks begin.

The Battle of Graspan

Methuen's inability to run down the mounted Boers once they bolted left him keenly aware that he would be facing the same Burghers again before they reached Kimberley. Leaving two companies of 1st Royal Munster Fusiliers and 2nd Scots Guards to hold Belmont and dispatching the rest of the Guards Brigade to escort the baggage, Methuen led the 9th Brigade, the Naval Brigade (a mixed force of armed sailors and Royal Marine Light Infantry) and the Royal Field Artillery towards the Graspan railway siding at Enslin station. There he believed some 400 retreating Boers had dug in to fight a rearguard action.

The Battle of Graspan (November 25, 1899) marked the only time in the Boer War that the Naval Brigade - really a half battalion of 365 men - were used as infantry. It was another night march and then a bold frontal attack on Graspan Kopje, but whilst the 9th Brigade attacked in extended order, the seamen leading the charge bunched up to rush the Boer positions.

Their officers, standing tall with their swords drawn and belt-buckles gleaming as if they were on the foredeck of a frigate, were easy prey for the enemy guns and the attackers discovered that the number of the defenders

was far closer to 3,000. The Free Staters were bolstered by 500 Cape Afrikaners and 800 hard-bitten Transvaalers under the formidable Gen Koos de la Rey, a veteran of the First Boer War who quickly sidelined the timid Prinsloo. Once he realised how steeply the odds were stacked, Methuen signaled for the Guards Brigade to move up from the rear.

Finally, cold steel and brute

General Jacobus Hercules 'Koos' de la Rey, by the Dutch correspondent Thérèse Schwartz. Rijksbureau voor Kunsthistorische Documentatie

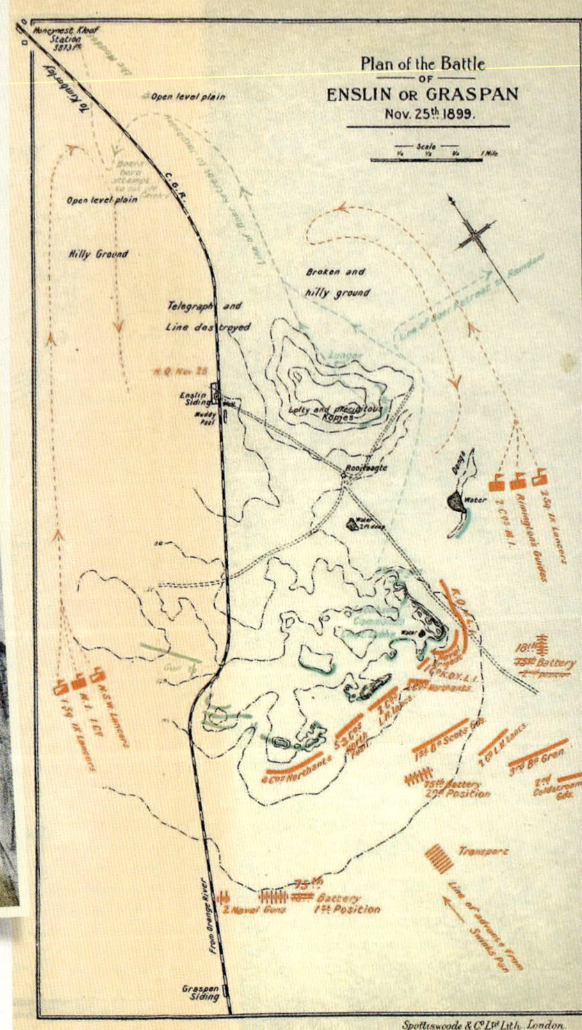

Spottiswoode & C? Lth. London.

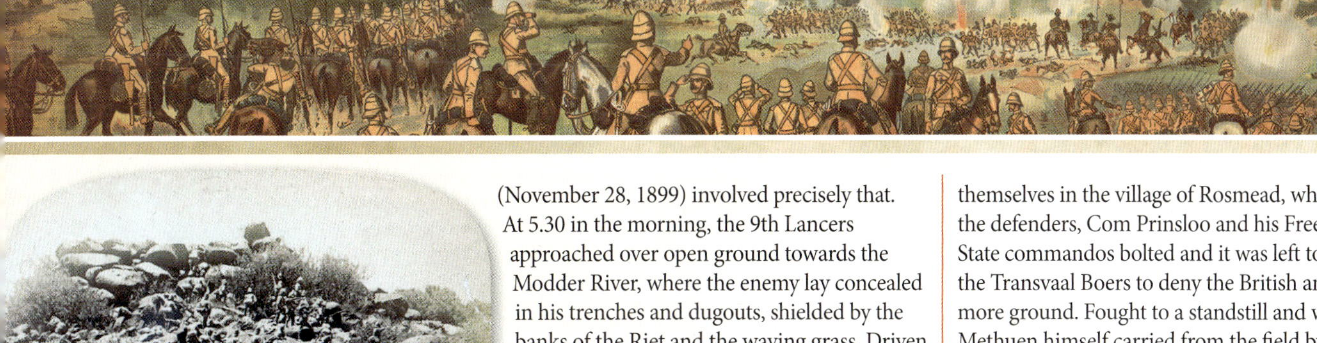

(November 28, 1899) involved precisely that. At 5.30 in the morning, the 9th Lancers approached over open ground towards the Modder River, where the enemy lay concealed in his trenches and dugouts, shielded by the banks of the Riet and the waving grass. Driven back by the crack of rifles from the Boer left, the Lancers raced back to the British camp and Methuen eagerly ordered the infantry up and out.

Thinking that the Boers were only holding the riverbank to the east of the ruined bridge, the Guards advanced towards on the right and the 9th Brigade on the left, reinforced by the 1st (Princess Louise's) Argyll and Sutherland Highlanders. Only by becoming a tempting line of targets did they reveal the extent of the Boer deployment and over the rest of the day. Eventually, the 9th Brigade were able to push across the river. They waded through the chest-deep water and entrenched

themselves in the village of Rosmead, where the defenders, Com Prinsloo and his Free State commandos bolted and it was left to the Transvaal Boers to deny the British any more ground. Fought to a standstill and with Methuen himself carried from the field by a shrapnel wound to the leg, the British dug in for the night at a cost of approximately 60 British killed and 300 wounded. When they awoke, the Boers had withdrawn completely, unable to hold the two rivers without the Orange contingent.

The Battle of Stormberg

Finally battered to a standstill after their rapid advance, Methuen's division spent two weeks recuperating at the two rivers, bringing up reinforcements from Major General Andrew Wauchope's 3rd (Highland) Brigade, the 12th Lancers, some artillery - including a 4.7-inch naval gun patriotically nicknamed 'Joe Chamberlain' - and an observation balloon. ➡

the safety blanket of the railway and cross into Orange to raid the town of Jacobsdal before sweeping west again towards Kimberley. He would have most likely caught Cronjé and Rey completely by surprise, but after scanning the horizon with his binoculars, Lord Methuen decided that another frontal attack would be the order of the day.

The war correspondent Alfred Kinnear claimed to have observed a conveniently wry exchange in his book, *To Modder River with Methuen* (1900). Speaking to a fellow officer, a colonel of the Guards Brigade was quoted as saying: "It seems to me that our leaders find the strongest position of the enemy, and then attack him on the front."

His colleague replied: "It appears to me that they attack him first and find out his position afterwards."

The conversation may have been a piece of invention, but the Battle of Modder River

ABOVE: *Another stereoscopic photograph showing the British infantry moving up during the Battle of Graspan.*

BELOW: *A 1899 lithograph showing a panorama of the Modder River engagement from behind Methuen's position.*

The Grenadier Guards creep over the open ground towards the Boer positions on the Riet in this wash by Frank Dadd, 1899.

As the Highlanders advanced to the front, the lines of communication and supply back to Orange River Station were held by newly arrived contingents of Australians and Canadians.

There was no great rush on Kimberley from either Methuen or Cronjé. Despite the constant hectoring of Cecil Rhodes, Lt Col Robert Kekewich was keeping Methuen abreast by the flashing of a great searchlight portentously called 'Rhodes's Eye', and he knew the situation wasn't critical. The periodic bark of the Krupp guns aside, the Boers had chosen to maintain the siege rather than to try and take the diamond town.

The first battle of what became known as 'Black Week', a hat trick of catastrophe, didn't begin with Lord Methuen, or even Gen Buller, but with the hard-driving Lt Gen Gatacre. A man whose career had been defined so far by his invention of the mess tin, Gatacre had decided to head for the railway junction at Stormberg and drive out the Boers from their boltholes in the hills.

Gatacre gathered his force at the dusty town of Molteno for a night march on the Kissieberg, the hill at the centre of the Boer line. Only two full battalions of British regulars were present - 2nd The Northumberland Fusiliers and 2nd The Royal Irish Rifles - the order for reinforcements was written but never sent. Already weary by the time they arrived at Molteno, they gnawed on rations and whatever they could barter with

Lieutenant General Sir William Forbes Gatacre, KCB, DSO pictured just before 1899.

the locals before marching at nightfall. At the last minute, Gatacre decided to amend his plan and attack the flank, rather than the front of Kissieberg, taking the road to the west rather than following the railway.

Relying on the Cape Mounted Police to guide them, it turned out that they had oversold their local knowledge and Gatacre took a wide arc

that further added two miles to the exhaustion. Meanwhile, Col John Edge, RAMC, was leading some Maxim guns, the field hospital and other support units along the railway, not having been told of the change of plan. Unable to find Gatacre ahead, Edge turned back and was met by a couple of staff officers and reserve ammunition wagons also literally and figuratively in the dark. Edge decided to stay put.

As dawn broke on the Battle of Stormberg (December 10, 1899), Gatacre's nervy company came within sight of a single 75mm gun of the OVS Staatsartillerie and 60 startled Boers who immediately opened fire. Gatacre ordered the Irish to take a small kopje to his left, detached from the Kissieberg. A toxic mixture of exhaustion, excitement and miscommunication saw only some of the Irish move to the correct location, the rest - and without orders, the entirety of Northumberlands - flung themselves at the Kissieberg. With no infantry left to hear him, Gatacre called for his two batteries of RFA who, facing into the glare of the rising sun, poured shrapnel over their own men.

Even losing was badly executed. As mounted Boers began to arrive and harry them from all sides Gatacre ordered a retreat, leaving 633 of his men behind where they were encircled and captured. Staggering back to Molteno, Gatacre burst into tears in the drab little railway station when he realised the immense scale of the disaster he had curated.

The Battle of Magersfontein

Methuen spent two weeks rebuilding his force and laying a pontoon bridge across the Modder, then decided to simply continue his monomaniacal advance along the railway line. This was what the Boers were counting on and they had used the breathing space to install themselves along the Magersfontein ridge, only another six miles along the line. If Methuen had taken to correcting his earlier mistakes and using his bolstered mounted contingent to more thoroughly recce the landscape, it was a task made impossible by the barbed wire fences which divided plots of farmland.

Gen Rey's realisation after Graspan was that taking up position on the high ground actually gave the British some advantages, primarily it made them obvious targets for the more numerous enemy artillery and the awkward trajectory of firing downhill meant as soon as the British began their ascent they were effectively shielded from the Boers. Instead, at Modder firing over level ground from entrenched positions had proved far more effective and to Cronjé's horror, Rey resolved to dig in at the base of the hills instead of on their crests.

By now the army had swollen to an estimated 8,500 men and the Free State President Martinus Theunis Steyn toured the lines giving impassioned speeches. Steyn's intervention settled the disagreement between Cronjé and Rey over strategy in the latter's favour, winning over the krijgsraad to his scheme, and raised morale by dismissing the craven Prinsloo.

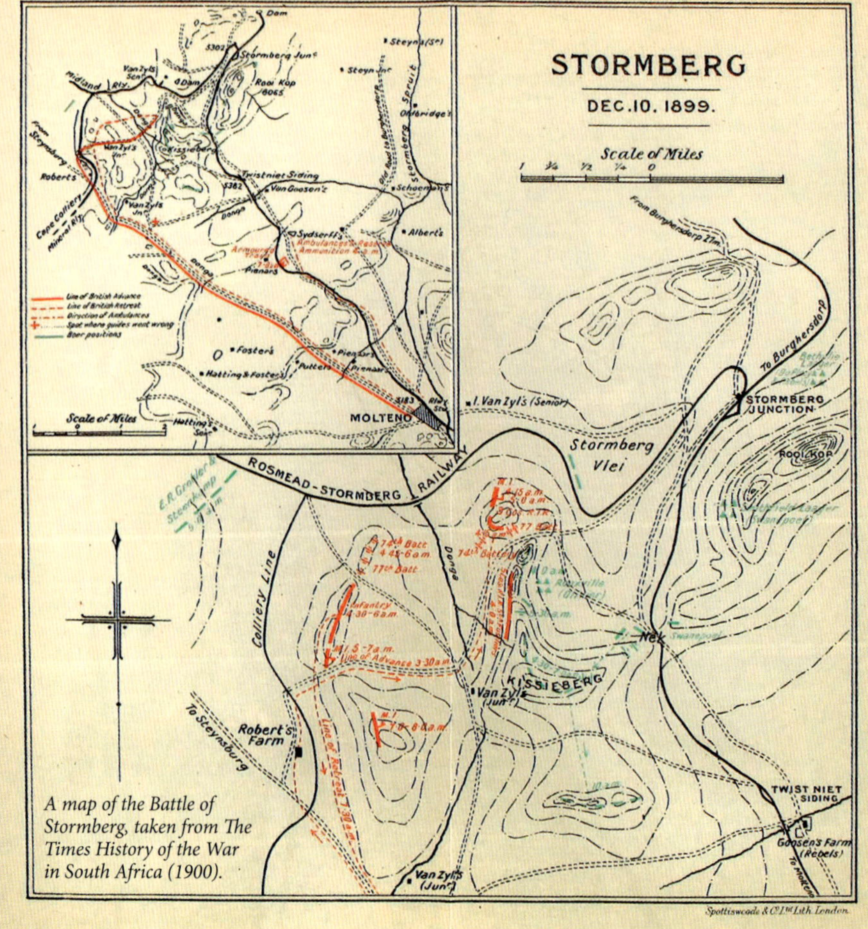

A map of the Battle of Stormberg, taken from The Times History of the War in South Africa (1900).

ABOVE: *An inaccurate depiction of the 3rd (Highland) Brigade at the Battle of Magersfontein, realistic only in its depiction of the utter chaos.*

RIGHT: *A detailed map of the Battle of Magersfontein from The Times History of the War in South Africa (1900).*

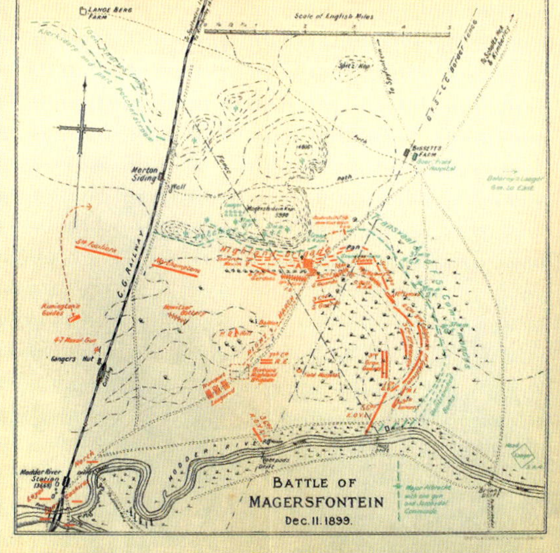

The Battle of Magersfontein (December 11, 1899) began as Lord Methuen had begun all his battles. The 3rd (Highland) Brigade advanced towards the hills through the pouring rain and darkness of early morning counting on the previous day's ferocious artillery to have softened up the Boers on the ridge. To prevent the columns losing position or twisting their ankles on the uneven ground, they crept forward in close order with knotted guide ropes when at 400 yards the Boers opened fire. Colour Sergeant McInnes, 1st (Princess Louise's) Argyll and Sutherland Highlanders, wrote: "The front of the hill was lit up by the flashes of rifles as if someone had turned on a million electric lights."

Maj Gen Wauchope was killed along with Lieutenant Colonels John Coode of the 2nd The Black Watch (Royal Highlanders) and Gerald Goff of the 1st Argylls, but the doughty 3rd (Highland) Brigade fought on as best they could. With dawn breaking, they found themselves pinned down, forced to seek shelter in whatever scrub they could find as Boer snipers strained their eyes for the telltale flash of dark plaid amongst the dampened dirt. In the desperate fight for survival before the Boer lines, an officer of the Royal Army Medical Corps (RAMC) earned the Victoria Cross as he crawled on his belly to treat the wounded.

Methuen was so convinced that the Highlanders would carry the day that he had no more cards to play. The Guards Brigade in reserve were three miles back and only G

Battery, Royal Horse Artillery offered a rebuke to the Boers, expending 1,250 rounds over the course of the day. They were joined by the 12th Lancers, who advanced on foot with their Maxim gun section. Fighting so fearlessly as infantry to draw the Boers away from the guns that he earned a mention in despatches, the aristocratic Lt Col David Ogilvy, 11th Earl of Airlie approached his artillery counterpart, leant on his sword nonchalantly and drawled: "Dear fellow, this really isn't my game."

There was no chance of turning the tide and Methuen's only order was to hang on until dusk when the Highlanders could be safely withdrawn and hope that by morning the Boers had melted away. As the light faded, the men limped back to Modder River having taken 971 casualties, with the Black Watch paying more than their fair share - 17 out of their 22 officers, and 338 out of 948 other ranks had been killed or wounded. The total Boer losses were fewer than that one regiment alone at 250. One Black Watch private damned his commander in doggerel:
"Such was the day for our regiment,
   Dread the revenge we will take.
   Dearly we paid for the blunder
   A drawing-room General's mistake."

Buller Loses Faith

The Tugela River which wound its way through northern Natal was a far more formidable barrier than the Modder. The approaches were flat and exposed, whilst beyond the northern banks the landscape grew progressively more rugged and uninviting until it reached the foothills of the Drakensberg Mountains which divided Natal from the highveldt.

The road and railway to Ladysmith crossed the Tugela at Colenso, which nestled in a crook of the winding river, ➤➤

A view down the concealed Boer trench line in front of the Magersfontein hills. Zuid-Afrika Huis

before climbing through a steep nek between Red Hill and Grobelaar Hill. It was being held by 5,000 Boers under the command of Gen Louis Botha, who had replaced Piet Joubert after the old warrior had been thrown from his horse. Botha covered the hillsides in trenches, many of which were left empty to deceive the British of their strength and disposition.

Gen Buller had long judged a direct attack on Colenso to be a fool's errand, telling the Secretary of State for War, Henry Petty-Fitzmaurice, 5th Marquess of Lansdowne: "There is a deep defile commanded on both sides by high rocky hills to be ascended, and at the top is a very favourable position for the enemy."

With the bulk of the 1st Army Corps at his elbow, Buller had the numbers to worry the entire Boer line and he planned a noisy diversionary attack on Colenso whilst he crossed 25 miles upriver and turned the Boer flank. On December 12, he ordered up the guns to begin bombardment of the hills around Colenso and then telegraphed both Lord Lansdowne in London and Lieutenant General Sir George White in Ladysmith that he would be striking on December 17.

News of Gatacre's shambolic expedition at Stormberg hit him like a punch to the gut, but Magersfontein sent him reeling. Two costly defeats - and the failure to relieve Kimberley - following so sharply on one another's heels destroyed Buller's confidence in his grand manoeuvre entirely. In fact, it drove him to repeat Gatacre and Methuen's mistakes, whilst finding all-new ways to outdo them. Without updating London or Ladysmith of his thinking (or lack of), Buller fixed a new attack for December 15 and ordered his three brigades to effect a crossing at three points.

In all three cases, their orders were imprecise and based on a threadbare understanding of the terrain. On the left of the British line, Maj Gen Arthur Fitzroy Hart was to cross a drift to the west of a spruit (a small tributary) with the 5th (Irish) Brigade and push north, but there were two tributaries with drifts to their west and only one was passable on foot. In the centre, Maj Gen Henry Hildyard's 2nd Brigade was to cross the iron bridge in Colenso, but the village had two iron bridges - road and rail - which crossed at different points and only the road bridge was still intact. On the right, Col Douglas Cochrane, 12th Earl of Dundonald, commanding the 1,000-man Mounted Brigade, was instructed to take the only piece of high ground on this side of the Tugela, Hlangwane Hill, almost as an afterthought. Over 3,000 feet high, it was the crack in Botha's fastness and he had been forced to leave it in the hands of a token force of defenders. For Buller though, it seems he regarded it only ever as a diversion.

In reserve, covering the 5th (Irish) and 2nd Brigades was Maj Gen Neville Lyttleton's 4 Brigade, whilst Maj Gen Geoffrey Barton's

ABOVE: *Major-General Andrew Gilbert Wauchope CB CMG in his Black Watch tartan, 1899. According to one account, his dying words were: "Don't blame me for this, lads."*

TOP: *Douglas Cochrane, 12th Earl of Dundonald, in the uniform of a junior officer in the Life Guards, circa 1870.*

RIGHT: *A map of the Battle of Colenso showing troop movements, from The Times History of the War in South Africa (1900).*

6th (Fusiliers) Brigade was instructed to cover Hildyard's right and support Lord Dundonald if necessary.

The Battle of Colenso

Unlike the first two battles of 'Black Week', the Battle of Colenso (December 15, 1899) began by daylight with Buller's force advancing on their targets at the first light of what would become a suffocatingly hot summer's day. The Boers waited nervously in their trenches as the broad veldt beyond the Tugela swarmed with men, horses and guns. The young Willie Pohl looked to the Burgher next to him for guidance and he received it: "Trust in God, lie low, and don't waste ammunition."

First into battle was the newly arrived Col Charles Long who rushed ahead with 14th and 66th Batteries, Royal Field Artillery and a detachment of naval guns to - as he so eloquently put it - "smash the buggers." He was supposed to be moving in support of Hildyard's brigade, but his carriages clattered on by the startled infantry to within 700 yards of the riverbank and around a mile ahead of the 2nd Brigade. Parking his guns smartly as if readying them for inspection, the entire Boer line opened up. Unbelievably, Long's guns kept firing until they had expended all of their ammunition, then with 12 killed and 29 wounded - including Long who took a piece of shrapnel in his liver - they withdrew.

Long wasn't the only officer to comport himself with a level of pig-headedness that went well beyond parody. Maj Gen Hart, known as 'General No Bobs' as he never flinched or ducked when under fire, followed a well-trodden road to where one would reasonably expect to find a drift. Instead, Hart took the advice of his guides that the drift was elsewhere and veered off the to the right where the 5th (Irish) Brigade found themselves trapped in a bend of the river with Boer trenches on three sides. As murderous

Boer artillery overlooking the Tugela River at Colenso.
Zuid-Afrika Huis

Boer pickets on the slopes of the hills around the Tugela. Zuid-Afrika Huis

fire tore into the Irish from all sides, one officer tried to detach his men and search for the drift further upstream but Hart pulled him back and urged them onward. A bugle sounded the charge and some men fixed bayonets and poured into the Tugela where they downed. Eventually, Buller sent Lyttleton in to cover the Irish retreat and the bloodied brigade limped back for shelter having taken 532 casualties.

The dashing Lord Dundonald meanwhile had done as instructed and managed to get his dismounted Mountain Brigade to the base of Hlangwane Hill where the defenders were holding them off. His request for reinforcements from Barton was refused as Buller had by now decided to give up on his left and right flanks and concentrate entirely on the centre column at Colenso.

Despite Hildyard's dearth of battlefield experience, he led the 2nd Brigade well. They advanced in extended order and once amongst the buildings, Hildyard began to cover the Boer trenches on the river with such punishing fire that the defenders were forced to pull back to positions higher on the hillsides. Buller by now had lost all view of the wider battle unfolding along the Tugela and was down at the front where he was fixated on getting Long's artillery out of the donga where they were sheltered from the Boer bombardment.

Captain Harry Schofield, Royal Horse Artillery, asked for volunteers and two staff officers stepped forward to join the limber teams of the 66th Battery. Lieutenant the Honourable Freddy Roberts - the only son of the Worsley Ring's arch-rival Field Marshal Frederick Roberts, 1st Baron Roberts - was shot from his saddle after 30 yards, and Cap Walter Congreave had his horse shot out from under him, but miraculously survived and crawled to the mortally wounded Roberts. Two guns were recovered and another attempt was made at equally heavy cost. Gen Botha who watched the entire saga through his binoculars said later: "I was sick with horror that such bravery should have been so useless."

Seven Victoria Crosses were earned in

'The Last Shot at Colenso', a fanciful scene which appears to combine Colonel Charles Long's battery firing its last shot, with the desperate attempt to withdraw the guns later in the battle.

sheer bloody folly to reclaim the guns, and confronted only with a panorama of the dead and wounded Buller judged that all was lost. Arguably it wasn't, other guns were available to reinforce Hilyard, Lyttleton and Barton's brigades had seen barely any fighting, and Dundonald could still have occupied Hlangwane with some aid from other quarters. Buller had lost all perspective, in every sense.

Across the battlefield, many fought on with the order taking an hour to reach Hilyard alone. Eventually, the guns smoked in silence and the field was left to the dead and dying, circling vultures, sombre samaritans, and the sounds of Long's lost guns being pulled up into the hills.

The British counted 143 dead, 755 wounded, and 240 unaccounted for. An American newsman who visited the scene, W. K.-L. Dickson wrote: "It was the most harrowing thing I have ever seen. Khaki uniformed men lying about everywhere, deluged in blood, faces horribly distorted and swollen and black. A piece of shell had caught one in the head and opened up his brain."

A copy of Sidney Paget's 1906 watercolour of the guns being limbered under intense fire from the Boer positions across the Tugela.

A Dangerous Experiment?

The Imperial Yeomanry and Volunteers

News of 'Black Week' blew like a chill wind through a particularly dreary British winter, but jaws were set. Too much had now been sacrificed to contemplate anything other than victory and like Britain in the wake of Dunkirk, Britons began to volunteer for service in huge numbers. When Arthur Balfour MP attempted to engage Queen Victoria on events in South Africa, the monarch who had come to personify grief rebuked him with the full force of stage one, denial: "Please understand that there is no one depressed in this house. We are not interested in the possibilities of defeat; they do not exist."

In *Yeoman's Letters* (1901), Corporal P. T. Ross of the 69th Sussex Company, Imperial Yeomanry frothed: "Who does not remember with pride the great outburst of patriotism, which, like a volcanic eruption, swept every obstacle before it, banishing party rancour and class prejudice, thus welding the British race in one gigantic whole, ready to do and die for the honour of the Old Flag, and in defence of the Empire which has been built up by the blood and brains of its noblest sons[?]"

The War Office, desperate to funnel the immense public feeling into something constructive, broke with its traditional distaste for citizen-soldiers and on December 13, 1899, announced that 20,000 mounted volunteers would serve in South Africa. They were recruited on a county basis in part from existing yeomanry regiments to form the

BELOW: *The City of London Imperial Volunteers scramble across the rocks on the outskirts of Jacobsdal, Orange Free State. Reproduction of the drawing by Henry Charles Seppings Wright, 1900.*

Imperial Yeomanry, which received the Royal Warrant on December 24. The government would supply their arms, ammunition and kit, and pay for their transport, but they were left to supply their own horses and saddles, the War Office's ability to do so for its own cavalry having been pushed to breaking point. The cost of equipping a mounted trooper for war was £170 (approximately £13,000 in modern terms). In theory, this attracted a 'better class' of soldier - educated, moral and patriotic men. These gentleman recruits would be stiffened by a good number of who had already received training in the county yeomanry.

The commander-in-chief, Field Marshal Garnet Wolseley, 1st Viscount Wolseley, was deeply unimpressed by the whole affair. On December 28, 1899, he barracked the Secretary of State for War, Lord Lansdowne: "To go into the highways and byways and pick up any civilians who will volunteer to go to South Africa quite regardless of whether they have ever learnt even the rudiments of discipline and to form them into companies or battalions in the proportion of three of such men to one of the very imperfectly drilled and disciplined yeomanry man also volunteering is, according to my knowledge of war, a dangerous experiment."

Disaster in the field, however, had resolved the conflict between the army and the War Office in the latter's favour and Wolseley's days at the top were numbered.

Although the vast majority of 'Black Week's eager new recruits saw service with the Imperial Yeomanry, Volunteer Service Companies were also raised from the volunteer battalions affiliated to the regular infantry in the reforms of 1881. The militia (3rd) had already been tapped and now the War Office looked to the 4th, 5th and beyond. Unlike the IY which formed its own battalions and served under its own staff, Volunteer Service Companies reinforced depleted infantry battalions in the field, coming under the command of experienced officers. Recruited through the existing regimental system, the quality was generally higher - or at least more consistent - and their experiences were not dissimilar from those of the regulars they accompanied.

In total, some 34,733 men served in South Africa with the Imperial Yeomanry and another 15,305 with the Volunteer Service Companies.

ABOVE: *The City of London Imperial Volunteers (CIV), the earliest and arguably most prestigious of the volunteer troops march across Westminster Bridge prior to their departure for the Cape, 1900.*

ABOVE: *A cigarette card showing the uniform of the City of London Imperial Volunteers (CIV) as they appeared in Britain. The dark greatcoat was issued as it was winter in the northern hemisphere when they sailed.*

The Eager East Kents

Some effort had been made months earlier by the more zealous of the jingoes to persuade the government to ship out volunteers from the county yeomanry. Chief amongst the amateur soldiers was George Harris, 4th Baron Harris, the cricket obsessive and disastrous former governor of Bombay (now Mumbai), who was lieutenant colonel of the East Kent Yeomanry, styled the Royal East Kent Mounted Rifles. Harris felt so strongly about the prospect that when he was turned down by the War Office, he encouraged willing volunteers from the East Kents to travel to South Africa at his expense, taking all their own equipment and uniforms, and on their arrival enlist in the Imperial Light Horse in Cape Town. Of the 50-odd part-time troopers he claimed were keen, only 11 followed through and Harris treated them to a star-studded send-off in London. Their adventures were followed in detail by the local press, with the coverage helped along by the fact that Sergeant Charles Mudford was the proprietor of *The Kentish Observer*, which dutifully ran his missives from the backside of the front.

'Black Week' and the intense reaction it caused transformed the jingoistic drumbeats of the Harrises and their acolytes into a national cacophony, shared by eager young men from all levels of society. The educated and urbane middle classes who had boomed over the 19th century were galvanised in a way that would only be matched - and overshadowed - by 1914, but it was 1900 when the suburbs first marched out to join the slums.

The surely negligible contribution of this band of Kentish men to the Imperial Light Horse was now a useful propaganda tool and Buller singled out the Royal East Kent Mounted Rifles in the national press as "among the best." ➤

LEFT & ABOVE: *Captain the Honourable Schomberg Kerr McDonnell took a hiatus from his role as principal private secretary to the prime minister to fight in South Africa. His 1894 caricature in Vanity Fair shows him in his civilian guise, testament to the calibre of volunteers in CIV.*

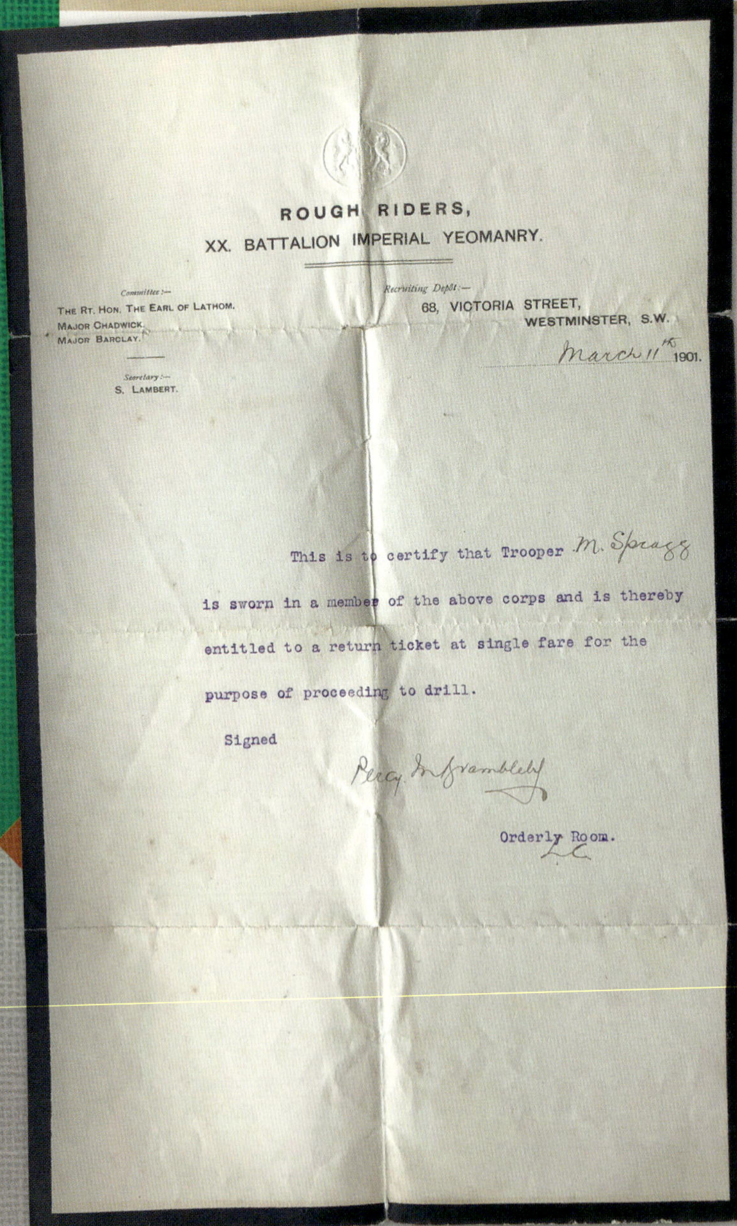

LEFT: *A 1901 travel warrant Issued to Trooper Montagu Spragg and signed by Quartermaster Sergeant Percy Mead Brambleby, 20th (Rough Riders) Battalion, a Special Corps inspired by the US cavalry of the same name. Both men eventually went to South Africa with the 22nd (Rough Riders).*

BELOW: *Edward, Prince of Wales, reviews the Imperial Yeomanry before they leave for South Africa. Wash for* The Graphic *by Henry Marriott Paget, 1900.*

hand, will have to be particularly watched and nursed on the march, in the camps or on the battlefield."

Spirits nonetheless remained high enough away from the bunting and cheering of the capital for one man to compose the following:

"Sons of the Empire marching on to war, With our brave Colonials going on before, CIV will conquer and break old Kruger's jaw."

The Piccadilly Heroes

It was the glamour of the Imperial Yeomanry, however, that captured the public imagination. Incredibly, the smartly turned out City of London Imperial Volunteers were not even the most well-to-do of the square mile. If the clerks marched with the CIV, their

The City Leads the Way

One of the most prestigious bodies founded in this outburst of martial fervour was the City of London Imperial Volunteers (CIV), raised by the Lord Mayor of London, Sir Alfred Newton, from the best of the volunteer forces within the square mile, the capital's traditional home of finance, law, and business. They were equipped by public subscription of £100,000 (almost £8 million in today's money), which paid for everything from slouch hats to a Maxim gun and six 12.5-pounders. By merit of public largess, CIV consisted of an artillery battery (its men supplied by the Honourable Artillery Company), an infantry battalion and two companies of mounted infantry, and by merit of its white-collar constituency, saw a calibre of recruit long missing from the British Army. Amongst this intake were nine barristers, seven architects, four schoolmasters, two bankers and 30 civil servants, all placed under the command of Colonel Henry Mackinnon, a lifelong servant of empire who began his career in the Grenadier Guards.

Following a ceremony at St Paul's Cathedral on New Year's Day, the first detachment of 500 CIV sailed for the Cape of Good Hope aboard the mail steamer *Ariosto*, provided free of charge by the public-spirited Thomas Wilson Sons & Co of Hull. Aside from their ages, attestations of their performance in the Volunteer Forces, and a medical examination, little effort had been made to bond them together as a single fighting force, or even to weed out those ill-suited to the adventure they had embarked upon. Instead, all their training and drilling took place at sea. Lance Corporal J. Barclay Lloyd wrote in his memoir, *One Thousand Miles with the C.I.V.* (1901): "Officers and NCOs are beginning to find out of what their men are made, to know on whom they can best depend, and who, on the other

chairmen, landlords and MPs rode with the 47th Company (Duke of Cambridge's Own). One of the many Special Corps formed outside of the county yeomanry system by merit of influential patrons or deep pockets, the 47th funded their own passage, mounts and kit, and donated their wages to the Imperial War Fund for Widows and Orphans of Soldiers. So prestigious was this brotherhood that one anonymous old Africa hand offered a £2,000 donation and a brand new Maxim gun if he could serve, but was refused when he failed his medical, whilst another unfit would-be yeoman demanded a second opinion.

Other gentlemen volunteers were 51st, 52nd, 68th and 73rd Companies, IY which made up the 19th (Paget's Horse) Battalion, although the PH on their sun helmets was said by some wags to mean 'Piccadilly's Heroes' or 'Perfectly Harmless'). Raised by the imperial adventurer George Thomas Cavendish Paget who placed adverts in gentlemen's clubs, the barrister-turned-ranker Private Cosmo Rose-Innes discovered to his horror that his uniform bridged the class divide. He wrote in his memoir, *With Paget's Horse to the Front* (1901): "The friendly offers of navvies to 'ave half a pint' in the street [...] was the most embarrassing. We were clad as troopers, but flattered ourselves we bore the impress of officers and hence a conflict of emotions, the desire to be rollicking good fellows qualified by surprise that our would-be host should not detect the gentleman under the plain khaki."

More Yeomanry, More Problems

Expectations on all sides rarely survived their collision with reality. Although many volunteers had already served in the county yeomanry, their abilities to do anything other than escort visiting dignitaries to and from the town hall were untested. That was the best-case scenario, at worst recruits had received no training beyond a few lectures and drills at sea, and their health, marksmanship and horsemanship left much to be desired. Corporal P. T. Ross noted: "It is curious to note that in many cases men

ABOVE: *Two watercolours by Christopher Clark showing the uniforms of the Imperial Yeomanry, 1902.*

who claim to have roughed it in various parts of the world have been amongst the worst to stand the roughing here."

The first contingent of 550 officers and 10,731 men - 20 battalions of three to four companies each - arrived between February and April 1900, and the majority were simply dumped in a hastily assembled camp just outside of Cape Town. There they at least had time to acclimatise and, in some cases, embarrass themselves. After witnessing his company's first parade, Lieutenant W. S. Power, 8th (Derbyshire) Company, IY, wrote to his cousin: "Oh! What a time, these men are the greenest, most useless devils on earth; why did they come out? You have to do everything for them, and they won't remember, but what can you expect when they have never put a saddle on before." ➡

"These men are the greenest, most useless devils on earth."

BELOW: *The Maxim Section of one of the Imperial Yeomanry companies supplied by the Northumberland Hussars in South Africa.*

ABOVE: *Senior officers of the 14th (Northumberland and Durham), 15th (Northumberland) and 55th (Northumberland) Companies in a mixture of uniform types pose with Honorary Colonel J. B. Cookson, Northumberland Hussars.*

"'Company - right turn!' bred the most dreadful confusion."

"I believe there is in the Chinese army, a body of Tiger Braves, whose function it is to inspire terror by their antics," recalled Tpr Rose Innes, Paget's Horse. "I do not think they can be more grotesque than we sometimes were. So simply a command as 'Company - right turn!' bred the most dreadful confusion."

With their terms of service fixed at a year, by the time experience had made competent combatants of the Imperial Yeomanry, they were returned to Britain. There was no means by which the trial and error of the earliest contingent were shared with their latter arrivals, a flaw highlighted in the post-war Elgin Commission.

In particular, the leadership of the second contingent of Imperial Yeomanry was much diminished. With the most capable officers and NCOs having been signed up in the first wave, there was no choice but to accept geriatric, inexperienced or physically infirm half-pay heroes. The disastrous consequences of waiting until the men were actually in South Africa before finding out whether they were any use to the war effort was finally reversed in January 1902, with the third contingent facing examinations and being drilled for two or three months at Aldershot and elsewhere, however by the time the new model yeomanry were ready for action, the war had ended.

LEFT: *Captain C. L. Bates and Lieutenants M. R. Blackhouse and G. S. Clayton of 14th (Northumberland and Durham) Company, Imperial Yeomanry. All former members of the Northumberland Hussars, Bates was later awarded the Distinguished Service Order.*

FAR LEFT: *A member of the Imperial Yeomanry by the Victorian military artist Richard Simkin showing his usual attention to detail in matters of equipment and uniform.*

Deployed and Despised

It was not just their commanders who were unimpressed by the capabilities of the Imperial Yeomanry, the men themselves found the adventure and glory they had been promised was not as advertised. Despite Buller's fulsome praise for the East Kent Mounted Rifles and his enthusiastic use of battle-hardened colonial volunteers such as the Imperial Light Horse, New South Wales Lancers, and the Royal Canadian Corps of Infantry, the Imperial Yeomanry were generally viewed as mostly inexperienced, often unreliable, and sometimes dangerously incompetent. Fortunately, there are no useless men in wartime, and the Imperial Yeomanry was often used for patrolling, piquet duties, escorting prisoners, supplies and remounts, and other tedious but vital tasks so that the regular cavalry and veteran irregulars could be put to better use elsewhere.

ABOVE: *A heroic depiction of the CIV taking the top of a kopje by Richard Caton Woodville, 1900. The illustration does not appear to be inspired by any particular incident as even the gallant city boys found themselves reduced to less glamorous duties.*

For the City of London Imperial Volunteers who had left with much fanfare and at such expense, it was a rude awakening. Colonel Henry Mackinnon wrote in August 1900: "Our principle duties were to put out of their misery the many dying animals left behind by the column, and to awaken all the exhausted men who had dropped asleep on the veldt."

Then, of course, was the changing nature of the war itself which bore no resemblance to the triumphant and chivalrous action promised by Henry Newbolt's 'Vitae Lampada', which had successfully convinced a generation of grammar school boys that the British Empire's many foes could be put to flight with notions learnt on the cricket team. Men grew bored and mutinous, desertions, theft and disobedience increased, and darker deeds still in what would now be termed the 'counter-insurgency' of 1901. "I am sure if [the recruits] knew what was in store for them," Private John Paterson, 17th (Ayr and Lanark) Company, IY wrote to his father, "they would infinitely prefer staying at home."

Despite similar levels of enthusiasm from members of the county artillery volunteers as their infantry and cavalry counterparts to serve in South Africa, the War Office baulked at sending contingents of Volunteer Service Companies to join the Royal Field Artillery and Royal Horse Artillery. The main barrier was the expense in arming newly-raised batteries, as the guns used by the volunteers were typically obsolete mid-century pieces (although one would also hope that the highly professional nature of British Army artillery no doubt played a role in quashing a flood of have-a-go gunners).

Noting the example of CIV and the Honourable Artillery Company, Lt Col C. Allen offered to purchase a battery of the latest quick-firing guns for the Sheffield Volunteer Artillery to take to South Africa. For the steel city of Sheffield - home of Vickers, Son and Maxim Ltd - the opportunity to take to the field with guns they had built themselves was a point of pride, but it would fall to another northern industrial powerhouse to make this dream a reality.

It was not that the 1st Army Corps had lacked artillery generally, but specifically, it found itself outranged by the heavier guns of the Boers, and naval guns were pressed into service on an ad hoc basis. The wealthy widow, banjo player and socialite Lady Valerie Meux had previously sprayed her fortune on a pair of zebras to pull her carriage and over 1,700 Ancient Egyptian artefacts, but the headlines from the Boer War affected her tremendously.

Lady Meux commissioned a battery of six QF 12-pounder naval guns with a range of 10,000 yards from Armstrong Mitchell & Company of Newcastle-upon-Tyne. Armstrong rushed them into the field, using guns which were being set aside for a Japanese battleship, and mounted them on carriages at the Elswick Ordnance Works. When the War Office refused her generous offer, she presented them to Field Marshal Frederick Roberts, 1st Baron Roberts as a gift to him personally and he was more than happy to put them to use. As with Sheffield's Artillery Volunteers, local industrialists maintained close links with the local volunteers and one of Armstrong's directors asked that his men be allowed to crew them. Roberts agreed and so 244 men of the Elswick Ordnance Works were formed into the 1st Northumberland Volunteer Artillery (Elswick Battery) and sailed out to South Africa under Major Harvey Scott.

Amazingly, every man of the Elswick Battery made it back to Newcastle alive. They were praised for their accuracy and pragmatism, but as engineers would appreciate, metal speaks louder than words: two Elswick gunners were awarded the Distinguished Conduct Medal and two officers - Scott was one - were awarded the Distinguished Service Order.

ABOVE: *The flamboyant and fantastically wealthy Lady Valerie Meux, an unlikely investor in heavy artillery. Portrait by James Abbott McNeill Whistler, 1881.*

The Elswick Battery pictured at the front, 1901.

Bloody Heights

Buller's Second Campaign, January 10, 1900 - February 28, 1900

ABOVE *The bitter and bloody close quarter fighting to take the crest of Spion Kop by the German artist Fritz Neumann, 1900.*

The reputation of General Sir Redvers Buller had been a lifetime in the making and 24 hours in the undoing. After withdrawing from the field at Colenso, Buller messaged the Secretary of State for War to report that he had been turned back by 85,000 Boers from Transvaal alone (which Lord Lansdowne knew only had a total population of 90,000) and then messaged Ladysmith's defender, Lieutenant General Sir George White, advising him to surrender. Fortunately, Lansdowne attached no credibility to the report and the horrified White refused the suggestion.

It was clear that Buller could no longer continue in his position and Lansdowne - always a friend to the 'Indians' - appointed Field Marshal Frederick Roberts, 1st Baron Roberts his replacement as overall commander in South Africa, but allowed Buller to remain in command of the Natal Field Force. Known as 'Bobs', or 'Little Bobs' for his diminutive stature, Roberts had been Lansdowne's first choice as General Officer Commanding (GOC) the 1st Army Corps, but concerns about his advanced years - he was 67 - and a turf war with the 'Africans' had forced him to compromise. Joining Roberts as his chief-of-staff was the seemingly unbending figure of Major General Herbert Kitchener, 1st Earl Kitchener, who despite having built his reputation in North Africa was a fully paid-up member of the 'Indians'. Wolseley was entirely left out of the decision-making, his role as the British Army's commander-in-chief was increasingly empty and now being measured by weeks rather than years.

The day after Roberts was appointed, he learned of the death of his only son, Freddy, at the Battle of Colenso. One can only imagine the grief he must have felt and who could have blamed him if he held Wolseley or Buller responsible, or for feeling that had he been

ABOVE *Lieutenant General Sir Charles Warren, photographed prior to the Second Boer War. A former Royal Engineer, Warren had not seen active service for decades and was called out of retirement to serve in South Africa.*

appointed GOC of the 1st Army Corps from the very start that his son would be amongst the living?

Before he departed for South Africa, Roberts met with Queen Victoria. She wrote in her journal on December 22, 1899: "He knelt down and kissed my hand. I said how much I felt for him. He could only answer, 'I cannot speak of *that*, but I can of anything else.'"

Buller's Bane

Buller was relieved to be relieved. He had been open from the very beginning that overall command was not his calling and replied to Lansdowne that "[He] is kind enough to suggest that the decision may be distasteful for me, but I trust that any decision intended for the interests of the Empire is acceptable to me."

After a Christmas of ugly stalemate, Buller marched into 1900 numerically better off than he had been in the closing months of 1899. Reinforcements had brought his numbers up to 30,000 whilst the Boers had dwindled through sickness and disinterest to around 14,000, half of whom were focused on maintaining the Siege of Ladysmith. Whilst Buller had been busy losing battles, the Boers had spent the quiet months losing the war and no attempts had been made to resolve Kimberley, Mafeking and Ladysmith in their favour, or chase down the beaten Lieutenant Generals Sir William Gatacre or Paul Stanford, Lord Methuen. Leaving Maj Gen Geoffrey Barton's 6th (Fusiliers)

ABOVE *Major General Neville Lyttelton was commander of the 4th Brigade at the Battle of Spion Kop. One of the few officers to come out of the battle with reputation intact.*

LEFT *A group of Boers standing in front of the northeast side of Spion Kop.* Zuid-Afrika Huis

Brigade to hold the camp, on January 10, 1900, some 19,000 infantry, 3,000 cavalry and 60 guns advanced towards the Tugela River through the sweltering heat of the southern hemisphere's high summer. The plan was the same as it had been before the doubts of 'Black Week': to effect a crossing of the Tugela and flank the Boers. This time the offensive would consist of two simultaneous crossings from where they would be able to sweep down on trench-lined ridges of ➡

thus far, he was not put on this earth to be number one.

Wasting Time on the Tugela

Taking three complete infantry brigades, 36 artillery pieces, and the Mounted Brigade, Warren was tasked to cross the Tugela at Trichardt's Drift to the west of Spion Kop. On the opposite bank, he was to hold fast and then extend his lines along the three-mile Tabanyama Range, which ended at Bastion Hill. This would give them command of the road to Ladysmith, allow them to bathe Spion Kop with artillery and force the Boers to pull back.

East of Spion Kop, on the British right, Maj Gen Neville Lyttelton was to take the 4th Brigade over Potgieter's Drift as a diversion. Warren demanded the long-range naval guns

ABOVE *General Louis Botha, at the Battles of Spion Kop, Vaal Krantz and Tugela Heights, the worst of British leadership met the best the Burghers could offer.* Zuid-Afrika Huis

RIGHT *A stereoscopic photograph of the view from the fortified Boer positions on Spion Kop, looking down towards the Tugela River.*

the 1,400-foot high Spion Kop or Look-Out Hill. The name was soon to become infamous as the costliest British battle of the conflict and arguably its greatest blunder in a war riddled with them.

Unfortunately, Buller decided to place this strategy in the hands of his newly arrived second-in-command, Lt Gen Sir Charles Warren, a man clearly sent to Natal as a 'corrective', although how Buller's performance could have been improved by the pompous and needling Warren is a mystery. The former chief commissioner of the Metropolitan Police disgraced by his inability to catch Jack the Ripper, Warren immediately put Buller on the defensive by asking pointed questions about Colenso and the decision not to press on Hlangwane Hill. What is more, he came equipped with a 'dormant commission', which would be activated in the event of Buller's death or incapacity and would immediately enthrone Warren as commander of the Natal Field Force.

Why Buller responded by making him almost solely responsible for the battle, can only be explained by his deflation after Colenso. Perhaps he believed that the appointment of Warren as his second and successor was an implicit suggestion that he should let the newcomer lead, or perhaps he was genuinely taken in by Warren's abrasive self-confidence as much as he disliked the man. As Buller continued to remind people, despite all the valour and victory of his career

"The success of Buller's plan relied on speed and decisiveness."

be part of his contingent, arguing that without them he would be forced to immediately occupy Spion Kop for his own protection. Buller strongly disagreed but held off from explicitly ordering him not to, the first of a series of vague non-commands issued that day.

It was effectively a plan for men like Buller to execute - at least the Buller of the 1860s and 1870s. In the first hour of January 17, Warren's force reached Trichardt's Drift where they could have easily crossed on foot and taken up positions on the far bank as only 500 Boers stood watch. Instead, Warren - who had the tidy mind of a Royal Engineer - waited for first light and set about constructing a pontoon bridge for his ox-laden wagon train and began dribbling men across the river. By January 19, he was still at it, and the 500 Boers had been significantly reinforced with Gen Louis Botha rushing up to supervise new earthworks.

Colonel Douglas Cochrane, 12th Earl of Dundonald was apparently the instinctive tactician that Warren was not. Left with only

700 of his Mounted Brigade (the rest had been peeled off to guard the oxen), he was tasked with holding Warren's left flank but had impatiently begun to feel out the right of the Boer lines, sweeping right around Tabanyama ridge and ambushing a commando moving up along the road to reinforce Botha. Seeing the Boer flanks wide open - as per Buller's original plan - the swashbuckling Dundonald sent a rider back to Warren for reinforcements, expecting infantry and guns. What should have been the Battle of Spion Kop… was not. Warren ordered the Mounted Brigade back to the river and gave Dundonald a condescending dressing down, telling him that the correct role of cavalry was to ride ahead of an infantry column, not to dash about willy-nilly.

On January 20, Warren decided he had herded enough cattle and attacked Three Tree Hill, the rightmost corner of Tabanyama. A daring uphill assault later, Three Tree Hill turned out to be completely empty. Later that afternoon Maj Gen Arthur Fitzroy Hart's 5th

ABOVE *The officers of 3rd The King's Royal Rifle Corps pictured prior to their departure for the Cape. Lieutenant Colonel Robert Buchanan-Riddell is in the centre of the front row.*

ABOVE RIGHT *Surviving NCOs of the 2nd Duke of Cambridge's Own (Middlesex Regiment) about to be transferred to the 3rd Battalion following Spion Kop.*

BELOW *'Trying for one stone" - the British dead on Spion Kop. The bodies have clearly been searched and stripped of weapons and valuables.* Zuid-Afrika Huis

(Irish) Brigade stormed Tabnyama itself only to discover that Botha had pulled back the defenders to the highest part of a sloping glacis which offered its now-heavily entrenched defenders a field of fire over the hills below. Despite his disastrous turn at Colenso, the notoriously hot-headed Hart was perfectly happy to draw his sword and lead his men across open grassland, but Warren was not. No night attack was considered and an opportunistic attack on the right flank was called off. Warren decided instead on a four-day bombardment of the ridge and asked Buller for more artillery and the long-range naval guns. Buller responded that he could have artillery, but not the naval guns. Without Buller expressly directing Warren to take Tabanyama regardless, the man's elastic reasoning simply snapped back into the position it had occupied days ago: if Warren didn't have the naval guns necessary to menace Spion Kop from Tabanyama, he believed he would have to assault Spion Kop rather than Tabanyama.

The Battle of Spion Kop

After seemingly an age of preamble, the Battle of Spion Kop (January 23-24, 1900) began with a pre-dawn raid in heavy mist. The entire 2nd The Lancashire Fusiliers, six companies of the 2nd The King's Own (Royal Lancaster Regiment), and two companies of the 1st The Prince of Wales's Volunteers (South Lancashire Regiment) under Maj Gen Sir Edward Woodgate stormed the hill. A detachment of unmounted Mounted Infantry under Lt Col Alexander Thorneycroft - like Baden-Powell, a British regular on special service - led the way, driving off the panicked Boer pickets.

As the light began to break and the mist began to thin, Woodgate discovered they had dug in on the lowest corner of Spion Kop and were overlooked on three sides by deeply entrenched Boers. Viewed from only one angle during the previous day's reconnaissance, Warren and his staff had completely missed the three higher summits of Aloe Knoll and Twin Peaks which were now crawling with enemy reinforcements.

There were no instructions from either Buller or Warren as to what the Lancashires should do when they 'successfully' reached the summit, nor had any thought been given to what the rest of the force should be doing at the same time. Lt Col Charles à Court, acting as in the no-doubt frustrating role of liaison between ➤➤

Reitz wrote: "The English troops lay so near to us that we could have tossed a biscuit tin in among them, and whilst the losses which they were causing us were only too evident, we on our side did not know we were inflicting even greater damage upon them. Our own casualties lay hideously amongst us but theirs were screened from view behind the breastwork so that the comfort of knowing we were giving worse than received was denied to us."

The *Manchester Guardian* correspondent John Atkins - who dubbed Spion Kop "an acre of massacre" - reported: "I saw three shells strike a certain trench within a minute; each struck it full in the face, and the brown dust rose and drifted away with the white smoke. The trench was toothed into a rampart. Another shell struck it, and then—heavens! —the trench rose up and moved forward. The trench was men; the teeth against the sky were men. They ran forward bending their bodies into a curve—they looked like a cornfield with

LEFT *A shallow British trench and sanger (low barrier of heaped of stones) on Spion Kop, filled with the dead.*

ABOVE *Ten days after the Battle of Spion Kop, the unburied British dead are still visible on the hilltop despite Gen Louis Botha having agreed to bury them.*
Zuid-Afrika Huis

the two generals, wrote: "Some 1,700 men were to assault a hill [...] and the rest of Buller's 20,000 men were to look on and do nothing."

By 8.30am the hills were alive with the sound of Mausers. Fire was being poured down from so many different angles - soon followed by the krump of Krupp from the Boer positions on Tabanyama - that many of the poor bloody sods under Woodgate's command were later found with entry wounds on the sides of their heads. Woodgate himself fell at 8.45, a shell splinter shattering his eye socket, and the Lancashires responded as best they could in the murderous close-quarter firefight, charging the Boer positions again and again.

In his memoir *Commando* (1929), Deneys

The Complicated Business of Blame

"The officers, with some few exceptions, are ignorant of everything an officer should know. The operations (?) of Sir Charles Warren, Lord Methuen, and Sir Redvers Buller seem to be a sort of competition of lunatics," wrote the anonymous French author of *Ten Months in the Field with the Boers* (1901).

Even without the benefit of hindsight, the number of ways in which the Battle of Spion Kop might have been turned was obvious. The Mounted Brigade's early move on Tabanyama and the Ladysmith road was entirely consistent with Buller's original battle plan, whilst the success of the 3rd King's Royal Rifle Corps in reaching Twin Peaks from unfavourable approach revealed just how overstretched the Boers were on the summit and should have made it obvious that they were incapable of resisting on multiple fronts. Lt Gen Warren was unfit for battlefield command and Gen Buller, who clearly felt as much, should have taken charge and corrected the situation.

Buller wasted no time in distancing himself from the debacle. His first report to Lord Roberts talked about Warren's force as if he had not been present, whilst Warren's report blamed Lt Col Thorneycroft for abandoning the position that he himself had abandoned him on. Lord Roberts wasn't so easily led, he bluntly told Buller that responsibility ultimately rested with him and informed Lord Lansdowne: "Whatever faults Sir Charles Warren may have committed, the failure must also be ascribed to the disinclination of the officer in supreme command to assert his authority." Lansdowne clearly agreed, but despite the scale of the blunder, Buller was too popular to be ousted and so steps were taken to test that popularity. To the horror of the Prime Minister, the Queen and Parliament who felt that the army's dirty laundry was best left under the bed, Lansdowne decided to release the damning dispatches to the press. This decision seems bizarre and self-defeating in the context of the day - the press, largely a patriotic and gung-ho bunch, were appalled by the leak (to use a modern phrase) as were the public - and Lansdowne back pedalled back on his earlier suggestion that Lord Roberts sack Buller, writing: "With a large section of the Army he is very popular, and in the eyes of the public he represents the dogged soldier who in face of very great difficulties has persevered and succeeded." Roberts concurred: "Personally, I should be very glad to see both Buller and Warren leave the country, but it is not easy to get rid of them without a storm being raised."

Following the relief of Ladysmith, Sergeant W. C. Mitchell of the 2nd The Devonshire Regiment wrote home to offer the view on his general from the front: "I hear they are making severe remarks about him at home. But I for one would go with him anywhere, and there is not a soldier in South Africa but has full confidence in him."

ABOVE *Sir Redvers Buller in the uniform of a colonel, 1882.*   Courtesy of the Royal Collections Trust

a heavy wind sweeping over it from behind."

From his headquarters on Three Tree Hill, Warren could see little of what was going on - partly because of the limited view but also because he was near-sighted - and so he answered each request for reinforcements obligingly enough, adding: "Mind, no surrender." Buller, who had a better view from his position (in both senses), made no effort to act on it beyond offering a steady stream of commentary. At one point Warren informed Maj Gen John Coke who was heading up to the

cluster of dusty and sweat-streaked Lancashires who were by now unable to find an officer that they recognised. As the Boers moved in to disarm them, the Mounted Infantry protested and fetched their boss. Thorneycroft, who had twisted his knee, limped over in a fury bellowing: "I am in command here! Take your men back to hell, sir! I allow no surrender!"

His argument was rejected by the Boers and some of his men, and 167 demoralised soldiers were led away. Thorneycroft fought on for another half-hour with the remaining

Lancashires, bolstered by the Middlesex and Cameronians sent up by Coke, before another wave of capitulation swept through the exhausted, dehydrated British. The will to fight was leaving the Boers too. Unable to see how close the British were to collapse and how many khaki-clad corpses lined the trenches, they knew only their own suffering. The boy soldier Deneys Reitz recalled: "We were holding the blood-splattered ledge with a mere handful of rifles."

Maj Gen Lyttelton, who had crossed Potgieter's Drift and run out of orders from Buller, assailed Twin Peaks from the right out of frustration at the slaughter he was being forced to witness. Gallantly, the 3rd The King's Royal Rifle Corps managed against all odds to fight their way up the sheer slopes and drive the Boers back when Buller ordered Lyttelton to withdraw from his near victory. The valiant Lt Col Robert Buchanan-Riddell fell at the summit, just one of the 17 Riflemen killed and 61 wounded on Twin Peaks for no gain.

In the end, it was the dogged and dutiful Thorneycroft who relinquished Spion Kop. He had received no messages from Warren since his promotion (which had taken hours and three messengers to reach him) and had driven his men to fight on since the early hours without food or water under the blazing sun. He had no idea what Warren or Buller were doing to ease the situation, no idea that Coke was on the hillside below him with the rest of the Cameronians and the Middlesex, or that a column of fresh reinforcements were

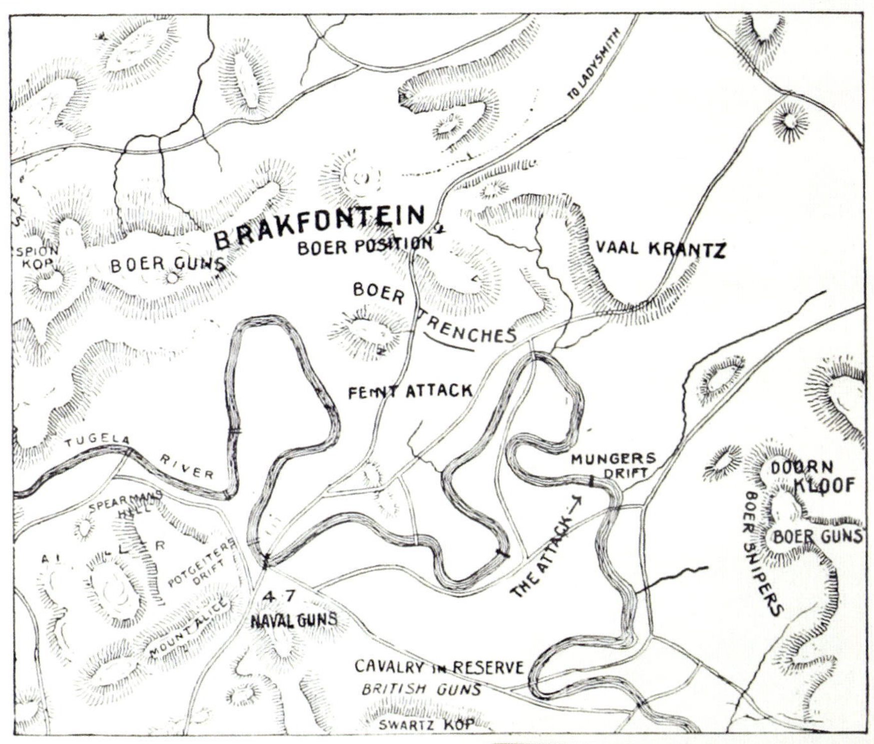

LEFT *A simplified map of the aborted action at Vaal Krantz.*

hill with the 2nd The Cameronians (Scottish Rifles) and 2nd Duke of Cambridge's Own (Middlesex Regiment), that he was to take over from the fallen Maj Gen Woodgate. Then at Buller's suggestion, Warren sent a messenger to Lt Col Thorneycroft to let him know that he was in command and was now promoted to brigadier general. Neither man encountered the other and throughout the day they both believed they were in charge.

The chaos was absolute and after hours of horror, a wave of surrender swept through a

ABOVE *British cavalry water their mounts on the Tugela, 1900.*

LEFT *A stereoscopic photograph showing a long trench grave marked by two crosses and a line of stones.*

finally moving up, and no idea of the sally made by the 3rd KRRC against Twin Peaks. All he knew was exhaustion and the continued presence of the Boers above him and the constant hammering of their artillery

RIGHT *Members of the 1st or 2nd Royal Dublin Fusiliers, both part of the 5th (Irish) Brigade, January 1900.*

from Tabanyama. As he descended the hill with his weary men, he met the long-overdue reinforcements and supplies coming the other way but refused to turn back.

The Battle of Vaal Krantz

The Boers withdrew from Spion Kop at nightfall. Unaware that both sides had now vacated the hill that 322 British soldiers had been killed and another 585 wounded on, Buller pulled back across the river. As dawn broke on January 24, the baffled Boers discovered that somehow, they had won. They had begun this war with their leaders asking them to trust in God and there would now have been few unbelievers on the veldt.

"We stand where we did 10 days ago, with a licking thrown in," growled Brigade

"Buller's confidence was ebbing and flowing like a tidal pool..."

Major Henry Wilson in his diary. Despite the setback, conditions had again grown more favourable for the relief of Ladysmith: Gen Botha returned to his farm to take care of some personal business, and larger numbers of the commandos likewise drifted home believing that Buller was finished, leaving little more than 4,000 on the Tugela. Restlessly, Buller decided to attempt a third crossing and push again on the Boer defences.

The hill of Vaal Krantz was five miles east of Spion Kop, the furthest forward of three - the others being Brakfontein and the taller Doornkop - which guarded the plain before Ladysmith. The Battle of Vaal Krantz (February 5-7, 1900) began with a feint against Brakfontein, which Buller intended to pivot to a genuine attack against Vaal Krantz with Maj Gen Lyttelton's 4th Brigade. However, Buller's confidence was ebbing and flowing like a tidal pool and he changed

ABOVE *Boer defenders pose for the cameras on the hill of Vaal Krantz, February 17, 1900.* Zuid-Afrika Huis

BELOW *A Boer commando in positions near Colenso which they had held in strength since December 1899.* Zuid-Afrika Huis

his mind until Lyttelton talked him round to continuing the offensive, promising that the kopje could be taken before nightfall. With the same boldness that he had directed against Twin Peaks, Lyttelton sent forward the 1st Durham Light Infantry, who crossed at Munger's Drift and taking the Boers by surprise, occupied Vaal Krantz despite heavy fire from the surrounding hills.

According to the original plan, Maj Gen Henry Hildyard's 2nd Brigade was supposed to follow the 4th Brigade across the Tugela and occupy the smaller Green Hill, which lay between Vaal Krantz and Doornkop, then the cavalry would gallop forward through the gap and into the Ladysmith plain, levering the way clear. Unfortunately, after Lyttelton advanced, Buller's cold feet returned and Hildyard was not prepared to warm them. Buller ordered Lyttelton to withdraw, and Lyttelton ignored him, stayed on the hill and hoped his commander would quickly come to his senses. By the morning of February 6, the Boers had managed to bring up more artillery from which to pummel the 4th Brigade. Having now depleted even Lyttelton's determination, Buller decided to dodge his responsibilities further. He telegraphed Lord Roberts, explaining

what was happening and asked if Ladysmith was worth the risk of the 2,000 or 3,000 (!?) casualties he expected to incur. Roberts, having become wise to both Buller's defeatism and his wild calculations, insisted he continue with the offensive. This clearly was not the response Buller was hoping for. Downplaying Roberts' instructions and overcooking the potential catastrophe, he called a war council of his generals and asked their opinions. Only Hart, who would hold his sabre aloft and charge a brick wall if ordered, was strongly in favour of continuing come what may, and Warren - a dreadful general but clearly a competent Royal Engineer surveyor - suggested they return to Colenso and try for Hlangwane Hill.

Retreating by the cover of night with an estimated 50 dead and 300 wounded, Buller remarked on how well executed their nocturnal crossing had been. "Yes sir," replied a staff officer dryly. "We've practised it twice."

The Battle of Tugela Heights

By the end of the month, the tone of the war drastically changed. Under the energetic direction of Lord Roberts, Kimberley had been cracked open on February 15, and the Battle of Paardeberg (February 18-27, 1900)

ABOVE *A map showing General Buller's final operation in the Relief of Ladysmith, starting with the taking of Hussar Hill at the very bottom of the illustration.*

had trapped Gen Piet Cronjé and over 4,000 Boers within their wagon laager. Orange Free State was on the verge of capitulation, and Buller - who was now being mocked as 'Sir Reverse' and 'The Ferryman of the Tugela' for his repeated river crossings - readied his army to march on Ladysmith where he believed the Boers would simply melt away before him.

The Battle of Tugela Heights (February 14-28, 1900) was in fact a series of actions in the vicinity of Colenso, where the Boers had now entrenched south of the river as well as above it. Barely a week after the abandonment of Vaal Krantz, Buller's forces began to move on Hlangwane, beginning with Hussar Hill which offered a view of the new Boer lines, a

Artillery wagons race across a pontoon bridge over the Tugela during the third and final crossing, from the painting by Georges Bertin Scott, 1900.

line of kopjes extending east of Hlangwane. On February 12, Lord Dundonald's Mounted Brigade was finally unleashed and with support from the 1st The Royal Welsh Fusiliers and 64th Battery, RFA drove the Boers from Hussar Hill. The line began with the 544-foot Hlangwane, followed by Naval Hill, Fuzzy Hill, Clump Hill, the two hills of Monte Cristo and the smaller Cingolo which connected by a nek, and finally Green Hill. Only Monte Cristo was taller than Hlangwane and it was clear from Hussar Hill that each would have to be pacified in turn.

Its job done for now, Hussar Hill was evacuated under the cover of the 64th Battery guns, and Buller outlined his new plan: Hussar Hill would be retaken and then used as an artillery platform for pounding Hlangwane and Monte Cristo, whilst the infantry swept methodically east from hill to hill. Once secured, pontoon bridges would be opened under the cover of artillery.

The bit between his teeth, Dundonald reclaimed Hussar Hill and the heavy naval guns moved in. Now occupied in strength, Buller had one of his now regular fits of self-doubt and for almost a week no action was taken other than the digging of trenches and the throwing up of cover. Fortunately, Gen Botha had been taken sick and the line south of the Tugela was held by Gen Christiaan Fourie who lacked his ingenuity, lacked the confidence of the commandos, and rarely left his dug-out.

On February 17, under the cover of an immerse diversionary rain of shells and shrapnel, Hildyard's 2nd Brigade attacked the northwestern corner of Cingolo, the 1st Rifle Brigade (Prince Consort's Own) CO Col Charles Norcott (replacing Lyttelton, who was temporarily commanding the division) took the 4th Brigade to the nek, whilst Barton's 6th (Fusiliers) Brigade and Dundonald's Mounted Brigade moved in support. The 150 Boer defenders were unable to hold whilst Fourie ignored pleas for reinforcements and with Dundonald gleefully grasping the opportunity to ascend Cingolo himself, they found themselves being pressed on two sides. By 2pm, Cingolo was in British hands and the defenders had retreated to Monte Cristo. The momentum finally on their side and with clear, quantifiable objectives, over each successive day one hill after another toppled like chess pieces into Buller's palms. ➡

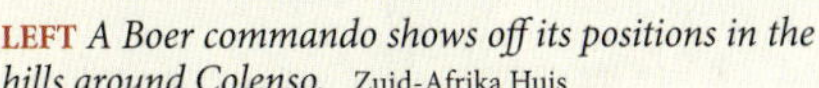

LEFT *A Boer commando shows off its positions in the hills around Colenso.* Zuid-Afrika Huis

The Rough Road to Ladysmith

Gen Botha had returned to the field just in time to fling reinforcements at Hlangwane but to little avail. Once the hill had been seized, he was forced to withdraw from Colenso and by February 20, the southern bank of the Tugela had been successfully occupied with Buller's naval guns entrenched on Monte Cristo. Over the first six days of the battle, only four British lives had been lost and 26 wounded, but the north bank would be another matter entirely.

Buller had hoped to assemble a pontoon bridge under the watchful eye of Monte Cristo, but the Royal Engineers hemmed and hawed and confessed that this was impossible. Instead, he was forced to cross closer to Colenso: under the protective shield of his guns on Hlangwane but into the positions which the Boers had held in strength since December 1899. Crossing the river on February 21 and securing the hills in the immediate vicinity, Maj Gen Hart reverted to type and on February 23 assaulted what became known as Hart's Hill piecemeal, throwing the 5th (Irish) Brigade straight into the fray as soon as fresh men moved up. This absurdity cost his brigade 500 casualties, with the 2nd Royal Inniskilling Fusiliers accounting for half of the losses.

"Our fellows were falling as thick as mist," wrote Private Hugh Coffie, 2nd Inniskillings. "It was terrible. We lost all our officers but four. They were all crying for water. Some of our fellows were riddled with bullets. There was some blood spilled that day."

Whilst the operations south of the Tugela had been planned carefully and methodically, once he crossed the river Buller locked onto the idea that he was facing Botha's rear-guard as opposed to the same bloody minded hill-by-hill defence. He was treating the battle as already won, whilst for Botha the battle was still very much raging. In the four days on

ABOVE *The view over Ladysmith from one of the surrounding hills. The low, flat country town had suffered greatly during the siege.*

the northern bank, over a thousand casualties had been counted and Buller had flung so many men across the river and into the hills that even he had to admit the situation had spiralled massively out of control. On February 25, he negotiated an armistice so that the wounded could be recovered and so he could quietly consolidate his jumbled Natal Field Force. As Maj Gen Lyttelton wandered around the battlefield during the ceasefire, he exchanged words with one Burgher, telling him: "A rough time? I suppose so. But for us, it is nothing. We are used to it and are paid for it. This is what we are paid for."

With the armistice allowing him time to collect his thoughts, Buller set upon a second crossing where the Tugela passed through a gorge and floated the pontoon bridge further upriver. Lt Gen Warren, now entrusted with a brigade rather than an army, crossed out of sight to attack the Boer left flank. The hills were raked in an artillery barrage so fierce that the dead were said to be discoloured yellow from lyddite fumes. This assault represented a level of artillery-infantry co-ordination that prefigured the 'creeping barrage' of World War One, with

the massed British artillery shelling the enemy trenches and then as the infantry moved forward, extending the barrage beyond the Boer trench line to avoid hitting them but to induce the Boers to keep their heads down. Not a true creeping barrage, but a similar principle.

After months of costly frontal attacks, Buller had finally succeeded in blindsiding Botha and after six hours of bitter fighting the British clambered atop Pieter's Hill overlooking the road to Ladysmith where the Boers could be seen in full retreat. In a final miscalculation, Buller neglected to order them to be run down by Dundonald or shelled by the artillery. Denys Reitz wrote: "Had the British fired a single gun at this surging mob everything on wheels would have fallen into their hands."

For the fighting men - and the emaciated citizens of Ladysmith - this was the furthest thing from their minds. Just before sunset on February 28, Major Hubert Gough, 16th Lancers, led his column through streets riddled with starvation, enteric fever, and typhoid, but loud with cheers. The 118-day Siege of Ladysmith was over.

BELOW *'My Brave Irish', copy of the 1901 painting by Richard Caton Woodville depicting the final offensive against Peter's Hill.*

DUNKIRK

Playing to Win

Roberts' First Campaign, February 11 - March 13, 1900

Field Marshal Frederick Roberts 1st Baron Roberts arrived in Cape Town on January 10, 1900 to find only one piece of good news waiting for him on the quayside.

Whilst the Natal Field Force flung itself against the northern banks of the Tugela again and again, the rest of the 1st Army Corps in Cape Colony switched from trying to relieve Kimberley, to fighting a desperate rear-guard. A siege was no place for an aggressive cavalry commander and Major General John French, last seen at the Battle of Elandslaagte, had escaped Ladysmith just before the Boer vice clamped around it. From November 1899, French had been pushing into the enemy positions around Colesberg where local Cape Afrikaners had thrown in with the forces of Orange Free State. Accompanied by a handful of British regulars and mounted South African and Australian irregulars, French was the only strong link in a chain of defeat, with Lieutenant Generals Paul Methuen, 3rd Baron Methuen on one side and Sir William Gatacre on the other.

The contrast could not have been greater, the aristocratic Methuen and Gatacre were licking their wounds, whilst French - a cavalry colonel who only five years earlier had been unable to afford his own horse - was causing the Free Staters so much anxiety with his outnumbered

BELOW *Field Marshal Frederick Roberts, 1st Earl Roberts takes the surrender of Orange Free State's General Piet Cronjé on February 27, 1900. Oil by Fritz Neumann.*

scratch force of colonials that they failed to advance any further into northern Cape Colony.

Letting it be put about that he intended to advance from the vicinity of Colesburg, Roberts concentrated his forces on the Modder River, even drawing French back for the big push. Despite being an 'African', French's talent was impossible for the 'Indian' chief to ignore and the general realised - as Buller had, in fairness - that the mobility of the mounted Boers gave them an edge against slow-moving columns of British infantry. He set about drawing together every mounted unit that could be found in South Africa, and with all the horses that could be spared pressed regular soldiers into the role of mounted infantry. They were nicknamed 'Ikonas', an Afrikaner word of isiZulu origin and complex meaning which perhaps refers to their inexperience (one MI confessed that he did not know whether to feed his mount beef or mutton). After witnessing them at work in his role as a war correspondent, Rudyard Kipling composed '*M. I. (Mounted Infantry of the Line)*' in 1901:

ABOVE *Lord Roberts in South Africa. Notice his unadorned tunic, with only his cap and Sam Browne belt marking him out as an officer.* Zuid-Afrikahuis

ABOVE *Cecil Rhodes (in white trousers), former Cape Colony prime minister and perhaps the wealthiest man in the British Empire, with his retinue in 'Fort Rhodes'.* Zuid-Afrika Huis

LEFT *A pair of ration ticket for four pints of soup and for the purchase of 14 loaves of bread, issued during the Siege of Kimberley.*

BELOW *The Orange Free State Staatsartillerie and signals section with heliographs (a tripod-mounted mirror with shutter) outside of Colesberg.* Zuid-Afrika Huis

"That is what we are known as - we are the push you require
For outposts all night under freezin', an' rearguard all day under fire.
Anything 'ot or unwholesome? Anything dusty or dry?
Borrow a bunch of Ikonas! Trot out the M. I.!"

The Great Flank March

With warnings from Kimberley that the diamond town's defenders were mere days from capitulation, Roberts made his move on February 11, with some issues of supply still unresolved and many units still arriving. The Great Flank March, as history has ➤

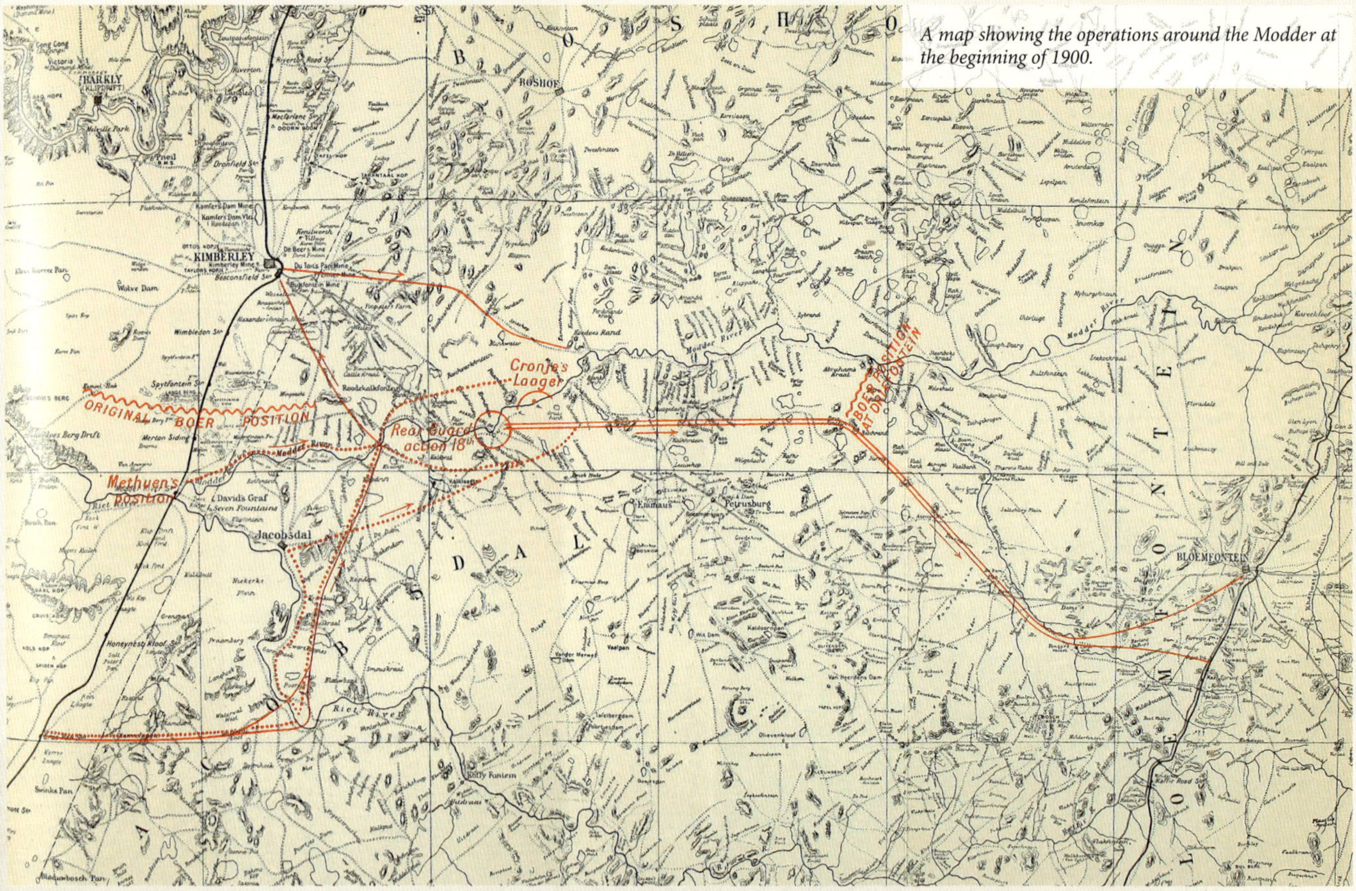

A map showing the operations around the Modder at the beginning of 1900.

"A force 5,000-strong was left on the Modder River under Lord Methuen to make a feint towards the trenches and barbed wire of Magersfontein..."

remembered the bold and arduous endeavour, was to leave the shade of the railway entirely and sweep widely around the Boer line at Magersfontein.

A force 5,000-strong was left on the Modder River under Lord Methuen to make a feint towards the trenches and barbed wire of Magersfontein, whilst 18,000 infantry and 7,795 mounted troops (although only 5,000 would ride with French in his three brigades) would undertake the main action. Roberts's real target was not Kimberley, but the Orange Free State capital Bloemfontein - the relief of Kimberley would be a by-product of a manoeuvre that would throw the Boers back on their heels. As French cleared each drift, the infantry would follow, cutting off the enemy army in the field.

By now, General Piet Cronjé was convinced of the British propensity for a frontal assault and their dependency on rail so he interpreted the first fleeting reports of the Great Flank March as signs of a diversion and sent only a few commandos to feel them out. Amongst them was his second-in-command Gen Christiaan de Wet.

Riding hard over the hot and dusty veldt at the height of summer where temperatures climbed as high as 120 degrees, 500 horses dropped through exhaustion or dehydration in the first 48 hours alone. On February 13, the Cavalry Division seized the Modder crossing at Klip Drift, five miles east of the Boer laager at Jacobsdal, where the startled defenders retreated in such haste that their supplies were left as sorely-needed bounty for men and mount alike. Whilst the Cavalry Division watered and rested, Gen Cronjé - still not grasping the scale of the threat - detached a force of 800 Boers to retake the crossing. Rather than attack the Cavalry Division, which although exhausted was larger than expected,

Cecil Rhodes (in white trousers) poses with the defenders of Kimberley in front of the tower-mounted spotlight used for signalling. State Library of Queensland

LEFT Lord Roberts and his staff enter Kimberley to cheering crowds. Cecil Rhodes having exaggerated the situation, the townsfolk looked considerably better fed than the men who were delivering them.

BELOW General Christiaan Rudolf de Wet served in the First Boer War but came to fame in the Second as one of Orange Free State's greatest guerrilla commanders. Zuid-Afrika Huis

similar attack at Aldershot, we should certainly have all been put out of action, and have been looked upon as idiots."

However, for the Boers in the hills, the charge of some 5,000 horses was a terrifying spectacle. The clouds of dust were like an approaching storm into which shells disappeared seemingly without impact, and by the time the Cavalry Division was in rifle range, many of the Boers had already fled. Only two men were killed and 17 wounded, and in June 1900 the *London Evening News* enthused:

"'E's a daisy, e's a brick, and e's up to every trick,
And 'e moves amazin' quick, don't yer French?"

Now some 30 miles from Kimberley, the besieging Boers had already begun to withdraw towards Bloemfontein, dragging their formidable Long Toms along with them. Gen Cronjé too was totally deflated and led his army along the Modder and through a gap in Roberts' lines. By early afternoon, French was close enough to Kimberley to signal the defenders - although it took an hour to convince the heliograph operators that this wasn't some Boer deception - and by early evening the weary Cavalry Division marched into the town.

"A large body of horsemen was seen away in the distance tearing across the long sloping plain that stretches towards Jacobsdal," wrote one of Kimberley's civilian defenders, John Mackenzie. "At first we thought it was Boers [...] but when they came nearer we could see it was regiments of cavalry in echelon formation riding to us - the long-looked-for column. The Boers evidently saw them, too, for all of a sudden the firing ceased, and they crawled like snakes on the ground and scooted for all they were worth."

Having covered over 100 miles in four days, the parched, dust-draped troopers dropped from their horses and into the embrace of enthusiastic townsfolk, who plied them with fresh bread and warm handshakes. Maj Gen French, who no doubt longed for the mattress, was whisked off to the Sanatorium Hotel where Cecil Rhodes had uncorked his champagne reserves and laid on a spread.

they took up positions in the hills which barred the way to Kimberley.

Resuming their dash on February 15, the British were only a few miles along the road from Klip Drift when Boer artillery opened up from the ridges which lined the road. To the disbelief of some of his staff officers, French ordered them to take the road at a gallop in three lines, each 500 yards apart, five batteries of Royal Horse Artillery firing on the Boer positions and then limbering up quickly to fall into the final line.

An anonymous cavalry officer recalled: "The enterprise appeared to us at first as quite hopeless; we believed that only a few of us would come out of it alive, and, had we made a

ABOVE *The hard-riding Cavalry Division - now down to only 1,200 men due to exhaustion - catch up with General Piet Cronjé's retreating force at Koodoosrand Drift. Watercolour by Arthur Gough, 1900.*

RIGHT *Stereoscopic photograph showing the men of Lieutenant General Thomas Kelly-Kenny's 6th Division paused for a drink on the road to Paardeberg Drift.*

BELOW RIGHT *Major General Herbert Kitchener, 1st Earl Kitchener was Lord Roberts' chief of staff, and had served with distinction in Egypt and Sudan. However, South Africa was his first war against a white enemy.*

Chasing Cronjé

For all under Roberts' command, February 15 proved to be an eventful day. The infantry followed roughly the same route as the cavalry, with the 7th Division peeling off to ransack Jacobsdal and keep its commando from harassing the army's flanks.

The three miles of heavily laden supply wagons and oxen had meanwhile slowed to a halt on the Riet by the broken banks and the deep mud of Waterval Drift. Roberts left the 3,000 oxen to recuperate on the northern bank under an escort of 500 men, but it was not long before the marauding Gen Christiaan de Wet found them. Stylishly attired in a waistcoat and broad-brimmed felt hat, a pair of binoculars slung from his neck, and sat astride a gleaming white Arabian called Fleur, he scarcely fitted the British conception of the Boer as a barely-civilised mountain man but he fought like one, striking as opportunity dictated. Hiding his artillery and Maxim guns in the hills overlooking the Riet, Wet poured fire into the chaotic mess of cattle and carts.

Roberts had to weigh up the cost of turning back - effectively losing the momentum of an offensive that depended exclusively on it - against the cost of some 150 wagons of 30,000 forage and 150,000 meal rations, scores of medical supplies and ammunition, and all 3,000 oxen. Condemning his army to

with the sun: the Boers were unable to retrieve their oxen from under the guns of the Royal Horse Artillery or cross the river, but 5,000 armed Boers were too many to be taken head-on by French's outnumbered troopers.

The Battle of Paardeberg

Time proved to be no friend to Gen Cronjé. If only they had realised just how diminished the force opposing them was, they would have been easily able to fight their way free. Cronjé was confident of reinforcement from Ferreira, Wet or Bloemfontein, and he decided to hold fast. The Boers formed a wagon laager and began digging trenches east and west along the Modder either side and around the laager like a bandage. Eventually, they would even hollow out shelters in the Modder's high banks to protect themselves from bombardment. It was the turn of the Boers to come under siege

"Kitchener tossed battalion after battalion into the deeply entrenched Boer lines."

half-rations, Roberts decided to abandon the supply train.

After months on the Modder where the Burghers had grown altogether too comfortable, Gen Cronjé's army was more of travelling city. Women, children, and oxen, as well as fighting men, shambled towards Bloemfontein in a five-mile column. On February 17, only 1,200 men of the Cavalry Division could be made fit enough for another day of fighting, but the indefatigable French set off from Kimberley, covering some 40 miles in pursuit of Cronjé. Thinking they had breathing space from the British pursuit, the Boers had unlimbered their wagons and were watering their oxen in the Modder at Koodoosrand Drift when French swept in from the north and scattered shrapnel amongst the panicked Burghers.

The Cavalry Division fought amongst the hills with the tenacity they had learnt around Colesberg, scrabbling over the kopjes with carbines raised to deny Cronjé any opportunity to turn their flanks. A tense stalemate settled

Tethered balloons inflated by coal gas had been used by the Confederate forces for surveying and directing artillery during the American Civil War (1861-1865), but the unlikely pioneer of British military aviation was the enthusiastic amateur balloonist and militia officer, Captain James Templer. Templer established the Royal Engineers Balloon School with his personal hot air balloon, 'Crusader', as its first recruit. Hydrogen, rather than coal gas, was considered more suitable for military use. It had a greater lift, so a smaller balloon could ascend to a much greater height, which in turn presented a smaller target to the enemy. The balloon school spent the end of the 19th-century wrestling with the problems of finding a durable enough fabric and finding a way to safely transport hydrogen in the field.

The most suitable fabric was discovered to be 'goldbeaters' skin', made from the lining of cow intestines and used in the production of gold leaf. Cow intestines, however, are generally not large enough to hoist a basket skywards and the intensely time-consuming process of sewing strips of goldbeater's skin together was a trade secret known only to a family of Jewish artisans resident in London's East End. Eventually, Templer - who was constantly digging into his own pockets to support the project - persuaded the family to share their technique with two Royal Engineers.

Steel tanks capable of storing 100-cubic feet of compressed hydrogen gas were designed and mounted on wagons 44 at a time. Each one could be turned on independently through a 'junction' at the back of the wagon, which released the gas into a hose of goldbeater's skin. Templer's balloons were tested in the field in Bechuanaland (now Botswana) in 1884 and Sudan in 1885. The Bechuanaland expedition (at Mafeking) turned out to be vital for the use of balloons in the Second Boer War, as it was discovered that the existing 10,000 cubic foot design was too small to obtain sufficient lift in the hot, lighter air of the veldt.

Two new balloons were designed, the 'A' class (13,000 cubic feet) and 'B' class (11,500 cubic feet), both of which saw use in South Africa. Following a successful demonstration at the 1890 Summer Manoeuvres, British military aviation left the experimental phase and became a reality with the creation of the Balloon Section, Royal Engineers and the relocation of the Balloon School to Aldershot, where an on-site plant manufactured hydrogen.

Three balloon sections saw action in South Africa, each consisting of three officers, 34 NCOs and men, and seven wagons: one for the balloons, four for gas tubes, and two for stores and supplies. The 2nd Balloon Section, RE was besieged in Ladysmith, where it was put to good use in the first month until its hydrogen ran out. The 1st Balloon Section, RE accompanied Lieutenant General Lord Methuen's column as it attempted to relieve Kimberley, but Methuen made little use of it. They then joined General Sir Redvers Buller where they came of age at the Battle of Tugela Heights, directing the artillery as Lt Gen Sir Charles Warren made his decisive flanking attack. The 3rd Balloon Section, RE arrived in Cape Town in March 1900 and joined Lord Roberts.

ABOVE *A balloon on its wagon accompanies Lord Roberts to Johannesburg, 1901. They could remain inflated for days at a time.*

RIGHT *An illustration of an observation balloon in action, directing the advance on Potgieter's Drift during the disastrous Battle of Spion Kop.*

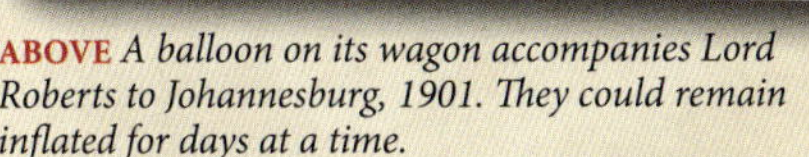

as Lt Gen Thomas Kelly-Kenny's 6th Division moved up past Paardeberg Drift to the east, followed by Lt Gen Sir Henry Colville's 9th Division and the Mounted Infantry.

Lord Roberts, who was shivering in his sheets in Jacobsdal with fever, placed his chief-of-staff in command, making it clear that Maj Gen Herbert Kitchener, 1st Earl Kitchener, spoke with his voice. Despite his seniority,

Kelly-Kenny, who advocated placing artillery on all the surrounding hills and shelling them into submission, was overruled by the younger Lord Kitchener who had built his legend on the use of sudden overwhelming force.

"It is now seven o'clock," observed Kitchener at the start of what became known as 'Bloody Sunday'. "We shall be in the laager at half-past ten." Whilst Roberts had learnt his lessons from the reports of 'Black Week', it seemed Kitchener needed to experience them first-hand. The first day of the Battle of Paardeberg (February 18-27, 1900) ended at a cost of 324 dead and 924 wounded as Kitchener tossed battalion after battalion into the deeply entrenched Boer lines. As they had at the Battle of the Modder River (November 28, 1899), the 3rd (Highland) Brigade took the Boer trenches head-on and then found themselves lying flat in the dirt as fire poured over them. Colville, who watched

them in part admiration and part horror, wrote: "I never hope to see or read of anything grander than the advance of that thin line across the coverless plain, under a hail of lead from their invisible enemy in the river banks. Thinner and thinner it grew and thicker and thicker the brown patches on the grass behind it. What men are able to do the Highlanders did but there seems to be some law which fixes the exact amount of thinning that a civilised body of men can stand."

Having undertaken no reconnaissance, the British were fighting completely blind. Kitchener galloped around personally delivering orders as they occurred to him to brigades as he encountered them. Maj Gen Horace Smith-Dorrien of the 19th Brigade recalled: "I was in a complete fog as to what was happening and knew nothing of the situation either of our own troops, or of the Boers, beyond what I could see, or infer, myself."

After limping back from a failed assault by his unmounted mounted infantry, Colonel ➤

LEFT *Men of the 1st or 2nd Gordon Highlanders take breakfast during the siege.*

O. C. Hannay, 1st (Princess Louise's) Argyll and Sutherland Highlanders was sent back in - on horseback this time: "Time has come for a final effort [...] Gallop up, if necessary, and fire into the laager." Incapable of refusing a direct order and resigned to his fate, Hannay led three officers and 50 men to their deaths, the colonel himself falling only 200 yards from the trenches. Whilst some accounts credit Hannay's sacrifice with persuading Kitchener of his folly, the depressing truth is that it did nothing of the sort and the bloody battle continued for another two or three hours in much the same manner as it had begun.

ABOVE *Lt Gen Thomas Kelly-Kenny's 6th Division creep forward towards the Boer positions at Dreifontein, the final roadblock on the way to Bloemfontein.*

LEFT *Stereoscopic photographs showing the bedraggled Boer prisoners of war taken after the Battle of Paadeberg.*

Kitchener's Kopje and Roberts's Return

Shortly after 5pm, just as the battle was winding down for the day, Gen de Wet launched a sudden attack on what the British would later dub Kitchener's Kopje. Held by barely a hundred goldfield irregulars of Kitchener's Horse, the Burghers quickly moved in and disarmed the Uitlanders. Whilst Ferreira had been spooked by Maj Gen French's swift interception (and was later shot dead by one of his own sentries), Wet was made of sterner stuff and drove a salient across the plain south of the Modder where he hoped Cronjé would attempt to force a breakout.

Kitchener's final order for the day was for all units to dig in where they were, but it reached so few of the widely dispersed brigades that the majority simply dribbled back into the camp. In one respect, Kitchener's day of carnage had been a success: so much ordnance had been poured into the Boer lines that the number of pack animals slain hobbled any hope Cronjé had of escape. The single costliest day of the war drove Roberts from his sickbed and on the morning of February 19, he resumed command, although he never publicly criticised Kitchener's performance, nor did Kitchener ever break faith with his mentor. In a letter written a month later, Kitchener remained blasé about the cost he had run up: "I hope the authorities keep their hair on [...] War

means risks, and you cannot play the game and always win." Kitchener urged an immediate resumption of the attack, but Roberts resolved instead to besiege the laager, shelling and starving the Boers into capitulation.

The British dug in, but the loss of their stores at Waterval Drift took its toll. Men slept in rain-sodden blankets and lost weight rapidly on half rations, and the Modder was so choked with dead animals that the men sent to draw water called it 'dead horse soup'. The Royal Army Medical Corps worked in the open with only the surgical kit they carried, unable to sterilise their blades effectively. Conditions within the laager were worse. Young children huddled together in their muddy boltholes on the riverbank, unable to escape the overpowering smell of dead and decaying animals, silence the sound of buzzing flies and distant thud of the guns, or scrub the sickly yellow lyddite from their clothes. The war correspondent H. F. P. Battersby wrote: "No human soul could have grown used to the reek of that slaughterhouse. It was appalling. Shrapnel had scattered the bodies of beasts; lyddite had turned them inside out. Cattle, twisted out of the likeness of kine, stripped to a red and skinless horror, rent into mounds of broken pieces, lay on every hand and had lain there for weeks under a sun that turns meat sour almost between plate and mouth."

Wet stubbornly held Kitchener's Kopje for three days - and around 100 Boers slipped out of the laager to join him - but Cronjé refused to withdraw and he was forced to leave the old Burgher to his fate when the ammunition began to dwindle. Cronjé initially asked for an armistice so that they could bury their dead, but Roberts refused and the old Burgher replied: "If you are so uncharitable as to refuse me a truce as requested, then you may do as you please. I shall not surrender alive. Bombard as you will." Later, when the field marshal discovered that the laager contained women and children, Roberts offered them safe passage through the British lines but this time it was Cronjé who declined. Despite the general's grim determination, the will to resist amongst his fighting men was beginning to ebb.

In the early hours of February 27 - chosen as it was the anniversary of the Battle of Majuba Hill (1881) - Roberts began to tighten the cordon around the laager. Under the cover of darkness 2nd Royal Canadian Regiment of Infantry and sappers from No 7 Company, Royal Engineers moved up to dig in right under the Boers' noses. While the first rank gave covering fire, the second rank hacked out trenches in the earth. Mistakenly someone yelled out "Retire!" but two companies held fast - men from the rugged Maritime Provinces of Nova Scotia, New Brunswick and Prince Edward Island - and as dawn broke the Boers discovered the Canadians were as close as 65 yards in places and able to fire directly into their own trenches. It was the final straw. White flags began to appear along the enemy line and unable to ignore the collapsing resolve of his army, a couple of hours later Gen Cronjé emerged to offer Lord Roberts his hand and his surrender.

The Gates of Bloemfontein

Cronjé's defeat - on the anniversary of the great Boer victory at Majuba - was effectively the end of large-scale resistance, at least on the battlefield. Boer heartbreak was mirrored by British exultation - crowds in London trilled 'God Save the Queen' and Madame Tussaud's swiftly created a wax scene of Cronjé and Roberts.

If manpower rather than morale won wars, the shrinking frontline had at least gifted Orange Free State with a significant number of fighting men who could be concentrated before the capital. With the British advance having halted for long enough for Wet to gather around 5,000 Boers to his banner, they dug in on the hills near Poplar Grove ten miles to the east along the road to Bloemfontein.

Eager to restore momentum to his war of manoeuvre, Lord Roberts planned an envelopment by which two divisions of infantry would move on Poplar Grove from the south and southwest, whilst Maj Gen French swept around the southern flank and cut off their retreat. In the end, there was no Battle of Poplar Grove (March 7, 1900) as either Roberts or Wet had imagined. With news that the British were closing in on them, the defenders melted away and Transvaal President Paul Kruger who had that very minute arrived to pump them full of patriotism was bundled unceremoniously back into his carriage.

French, however, was not where he was supposed to be. Temperamental in the extreme, his relationship with Roberts had taken a blow when he was given a dressing down in front of his subordinates for apparently overdrawing the forage rations. It transpired the field marshal's chief supply officer had made his estimates based on active horses, forgetting the many invalided mounts that the division also needed to care

BELOW *The horrific scene of death and devastation inside Cronjé's laager.* Zuid-Afrika Huis

for. Although the largely static weeks around Paardeberg Drift afforded the horses rest, they had no hope of recovering their strength without proper feed.

Feeling particularly hard done by, French greeted the Poplar Grove plan with a mixture of petulance and defeatism. He was supposed to depart in the early hours but suspecting a night march on a moonless night would end in many lame horses, he waited for dawn to arrive. Additionally, the planned route had not given the Cavalry Division a wide enough berth so that their manoeuvre to the south of the Boer lines was clearly observed for what it was. In the end, French's tentative attacks were easily seen off by the rear guard.

Dismayed by the stream of retreating Burghers, Kruger managed to rally at least enough of them from his pulpit to attempt another stand at the Battle of Driefontein (March 10, 1900), but the delaying action was wasted. Orange Free State President Martinus Steyn boarded a train for the new war capital at Kroonstadt with as many government papers as he could stuff into his baggage, whilst Wet summoned a krygsraad and

voted for a defiant last stand at Bloemfontein. Despite the belligerence of their commanders, the Burghers voted with their feet and there was to be no blaze of glory.

On the morning of March 13, three eager war correspondents rode into the Orange capital unchallenged and found the mayor and other civic leaders debating what to do. Asked their opinion, the newsmen advised their surrender and later that afternoon Lord Roberts formally entered Bloemfontein. For many, on both sides, it felt as though the war was as good as over.

President Steyn later reflected: "No one who had not personally witnessed the despondency that existed after the taking of Bloemfontein can realise how great and deep it was. There was no courage and no wish to carry on the fight by the Burghers. The Transvaalers left in great numbers, and the Free Staters had turned their faces to their homes [...] The road to Pretoria was practically open for Lord Roberts."

BELOW *Staff officers on the surrounding hills watch the shells fall amid the laager during the first day of the Battle of Paardeberg.*

Bullets and Bacteria

Medical Care in the Great Boer War

It was obvious by the time the army entered Bloemfontein that it needed rest and resupply, but for many, the dusty Orange Free State capital was where their journey ended rather than paused. The peacetime population of 4,000 grew tenfold over the first month of occupation, pushing the infrastructure to breaking point. Lord Roberts' supply lines stretched down 750 miles of train track - the final furlough of which was a single narrow-gauge line - to his headquarters in Cape Town and 400 miles to the closest saltwater port, Port Elizabeth.

By 1900, typhoid - also known as enteric fever - was no longer one of the pestilent horsemen of the Victorian apocalypse. Spread by the contamination of drinking water by faeces from infected persons, large-scale civil engineering projects had resulted in elaborate networks of sewers and reservoirs that deposited Britain's waste far from its drinking water. South Africa was not Britain. The towns of the interior drew their water from rivers, streams and, less often, shallow wells, making the summer rains a catalyst for regular typhoid outbreaks as cesspits flooded and waste was washed off the veldt. The situation worsened considerably when large numbers of thirsty and filthy British soldiers pitched up.

Officially, all water was supposed to be boiled and then filtered before being drunk, with ceramic Berkefeld filters provided for

BELOW: *A haunting wash showing medics inspecting the dead and wounded and hauling the survivors into an ambulance wagon.* Wellcome Collection CC BY 4.0

this purpose, but the muddy waters of the Modder - what the fighting men called 'dead horse soup' - quickly choked the filters with slime. The Royal Engineers tried to blast wells through the rock, but were largely unsuccessful, and latrines likewise lay too close to the surface. As the post-war Elgin Commission put it: "Regarding sanitation and hygiene, Tommy doesn't understand it and his officers regard it just as a fad."

Bloemingtyphoidtein

During the last two decades of the 19th century, military medics began to lead in the treatment of infectious disease, with some of its earliest discoveries being the confirmation in 1897 by garrison surgeon Ronald Ross of the Indian Medical Service that malaria was transmitted by mosquitoes (which earned him a Nobel Prize), and the successful identification of the bacterium behind the so-called 'Malta fever' (later named

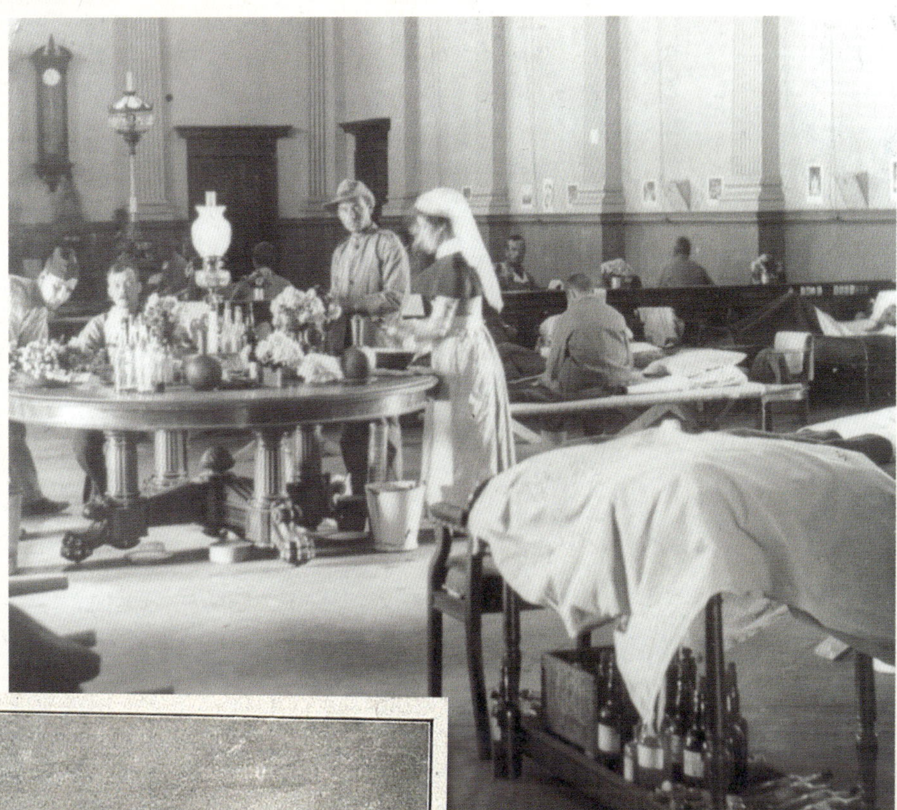

ABOVE *The grand interior of the Bloemfontein council chamber, the Raadzaal, used as a field hospital during the typhoid outbreak.*

LEFT *Indian stretcher bearers recover the wounded from the scene of the terrible bloodshed atop Spion Kop.* Wellcome Collection CC BY 4.0

brucellosis) by surgeon captain David Bruce in 1886. Dispatched to South Africa in 1894 to study disease in cattle, Bruce was promoted to surgeon major and found himself facing the Second Boer War's first typhoid outbreak during the Siege of Ladysmith (November 2, 1899 - February 28, 1900). His wife and clinical collaborator, the microbiologist Mary Elizabeth Bruce, served as the sister in charge of the operating theatre and was later awarded an OBE for her contributions to science. Despite using a dismounted railway engine to boil water, it simply was not enough to keep people from the fetid river and in contrast to the 59 inhabitants of Ladysmith killed by shelling, 465 were killed by disease. The civilian surgeon Sir Frederick Treves wrote in his memoir, *The Tale of a Field Hospital* (1900): "The wretchedness of the place was not mitigated by the horrible smells which greeted one at every corner, nor by the miserable, dirty river which crawled slimily through the place."

Following Sir Waldemar Haffkine's 1892 success using cultured cholera bacillus as a vaccine, Sir Almroth Wright, the Army Medical School's eccentric professor of pathology, developed a typhoid vaccine in 1896. Wright tested variable doses on soldiers stationed in India, but the side-effects ➡

were so punitive that he failed to convince the army of its value. Wright's vaccine was offered to soldiers departing for South Africa on a voluntary basis and the uptake was only 5%. As Wright had a deeply felt hostility towards statistics, too few records were kept for either this or the Indian experiment to be useful and 'Sir Almost Right' resigned from the Army Medical School in 1902. Anecdotally, many of those who received the vaccine were convinced of its benefits and in 1905, the dosage was tweaked and made compulsory.

With an incubation period of two to three weeks, diseases swallowed on the road flowered in Bloemfontein and soon as many as 6,000 soldiers lay shivering in almost every available public space, schools, churches and even the palatial assembly hall, the Raadzaal. Over the course of the conflict, 57,684 British soldiers were recorded to have contracted typhoid, of whom 8,225 died - nearly a thousand more than those killed by enemy action. So widespread was sickness that it defined the shared experience in Rudyard Kipling's 'The Parting of the Columns' (1903):

"Our blood 'as truly mixed with yours—all down the Red Cross train,
We've bit the same thermometer in Bloemingtyphoidtein.

We've 'ad the same old temp'rature—the same relapses too,
The same old saw-backed fever-chart. Good-bye—good luck to you!"

The Corps on the Frontline

The Royal Army Medical Corps was only a year old when the Second Boer War began. It was born through a merger of the Army Medical Department (doctors and military administrators) and the Army Hospital Corps (orderlies and NCOs), and it placed medical officers (MOs) firmly within the army hierarchy - much to the disdain of many generals, including Sir Garnet Wolseley.

ABOVE An army doctor tends to a fallen infantryman in the heat of battle. Wellcome Collection CC BY 4.0

LEFT A casualty of the Battle of Modder River is loaded into an ambulance cart in this stereoscopic photograph. Wellcome Collection CC BY 4.0

BELOW The wounded from Ladysmith disembark from a hospital train at Durban. Watercolour by Frank Dadd for The Graphic, 1899. Wellcome Collection CC BY 4.0

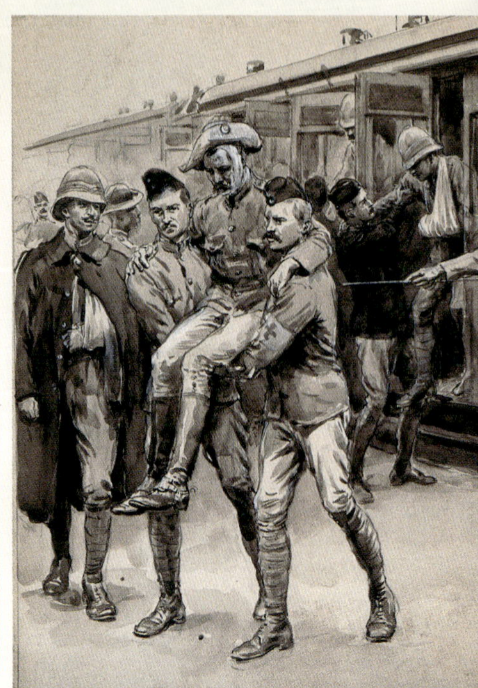

The impetus for the professionalisation of military medicine had come from the civilian world and with the corps still in its infancy, understanding of the RAMC's role by the wider army hierarchy varied hugely.

The distinguished surgeon general Sir William Wilson was appointed principal medical officer (PMO) in South Africa but found himself struggling to be heard. It was not that Lord Roberts had any particular disdain for medical men - his wife, Nora Henrietta Roberts, had founded a nursing corps for the British Indian Army - it was simply that administration wasn't one of his talents. When

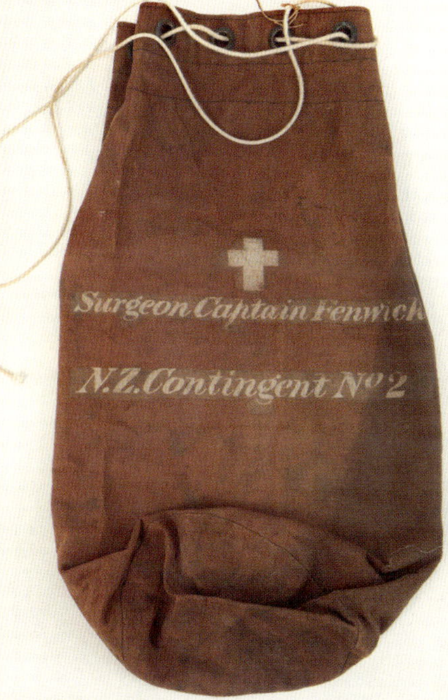

ABOVE *The Boer War kit bag of Surgeon-Captain Percy Fenwick of the NZ Volunteer Medical Staff, attached to the 2nd New Zealand Mounted Rifles.*
© Auckland Museum CC BY

Gandi's War: The Indian Ambulance Corps

ABOVE *Mahatma Gandhi (third from the right, middle row) with the Natal Indian Ambulance Corps. To his right is Dr L. P. Booth.*

RIGHT *A heroic illustration of defiant Indian stretcher-bearers coming under fire as they rescue a fallen soldier.*

Towards the end of 1899, parties of volunteer stretcher-bearers were raised in both Natal and the Cape to respond to the threat of Boer invasion and to supplement the meagre medical presence already garrisoned in South Africa.

Despite the insistence of Cape Governor Sir Henry Milner that this was to be strictly a 'white man's war', the patriotic young lawyer Mahatma Gandhi pushed for the local Indian community to be able to contribute. Gandhi wrote in his 1927 autobiography: "The average Englishman believed that the Indian was a coward, incapable of taking risks or looking beyond his immediate self-interest."

Determined to prove them wrong, the Natal Volunteer Indian Ambulance Corps was formed from a mixture of free Indians and indentured labourers, many of whom had fled Transvaal where they feared retaliation from the Boers as British subjects. As the majority were Christians, they appealed to Reverend Dr L. P. Booth, Superintendent of St Aidan's Mission Hospital and Diocesan Superintendent of Indian Missions in Natal, who had devoted his life to the education and healing of Natal's Indian poor. With Booth as their MO and first aid instructor, the Indians served with Buller at the bloody Battles of Spion Kop (January 23-24, 1900) and Vaal Krantz (February 5-7, 1900) before being honourably disbanded when medical staff arrived from Britain. For Gandhi, who formed a similar corps to aid the British against the Zulu in the 1906 Bambatha Rebellion, the war proved a great leveller between race and religion. He later recalled: "Human nature shows itself at it's best in moments of trial [...] Everyone was thirsting for water. There was a tiny brook on the way where we could slake our thirst. But who was to drink first? We had proposed to come in after the Tommies had finished. But they would not begin first and urged us to do so, and for a while, a pleasant competition went on for giving precedence to one another."

"Boer doctors treated fallen British soldiers with the same tenderness as their own men and the RAMC returned the sentiment."

the time came for his Great Flank March, Roberts neglected to inform Wilson of his plans and the RAMC was as wrongfooted as the enemy and left unprepared for a gruelling trek across the veldt in high summer. The field marshal's casual attitude towards his supply lines left medical supplies as stretched as rations and drinking water, and once the army returned to the comforting embrace of the railway, the operational needs of Roberts's campaign - food, ammunition and remounts - took precedence over the pleading of the PMO.

The basic unit of the RAMC on the frontline was the stretcher bearer company. This consisted of three officers and 58 other ranks divided between eight stretcher squads of four men apiece, a dressing station party, and ten orderlies for the ten ambulance wagons. They were charged with bringing the wounded to the regimental aid post (run by a regimental medical officer or RMO). At the RAP, the bloodied field dressing might be changed, and wounds cleaned before the patients were either returned fighting fit or moved further down the line to the field hospital. Stretcher bearers - and medical staff generally - were protected in their duties by the terms of the 1864 Geneva Convention, but poor understanding of the codes of European warfare meant that inexperienced or jumpy Boers were often likely to fire upon medics. Rushing towards the sound of guns or creeping through the darkness ➤➤

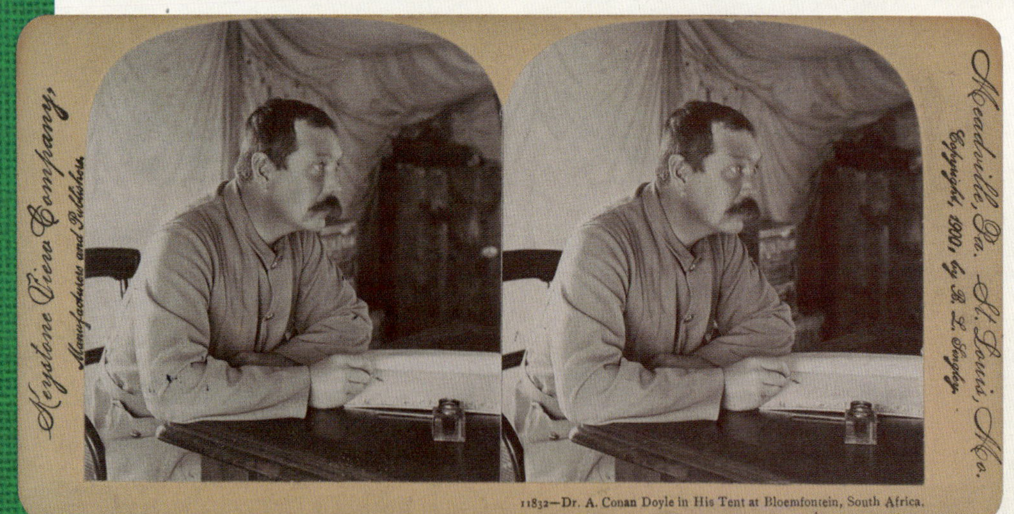

ABOVE *Sherlock Holmes author and retired ophthalmologist Dr Arthur Conan-Doyle at his writing desk at the Langman Field Hospital, Bloemfontein.*

RIGHT *An X-ray radiograph showing a bullet wound in the hand of Major William Scott-Moncrieff, 2nd Duke of Cambridge's Own (Middlesex Regiment), presumably incurred at the Battle of Spion Kop.* Wellcome Collection CC BY 4.0

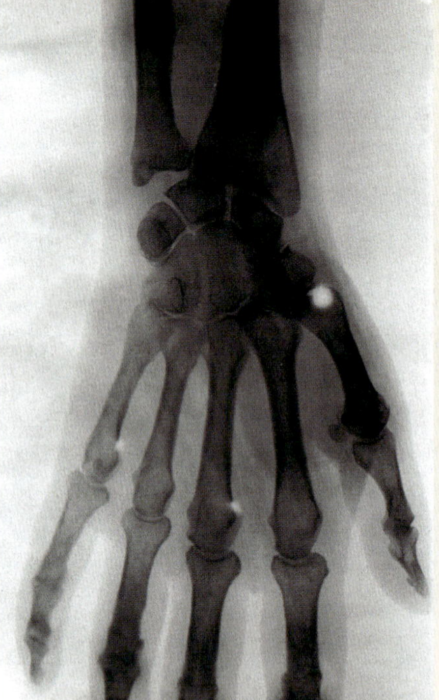

Fortunately for the Treasury, few prestigious Harley Street surgeons could afford to be away from their practises for more than a couple of months at a time. This company included Sir William MacCormak, the sitting president of the Royal College of Surgeons, surgeon-in-ordinary to the Prince of Wales, and renowned authority on the treatment of gunshot wounds, Sir William Stokes, a former president of the Irish Royal College of Surgeons and surgeon-in-ordinary to Queen Victoria, and the previously mentioned memoirist, Sir Frederick Treves, surgeon extraordinary to the Queen, pioneer of the appendectomy, and benefactor of Joseph Merrick, the 'Elephant Man'.

Also, among their number was the one-time ophthalmologist Dr Arthur Conan-Doyle, who had retired from medicine when literature's most famous crimefighter proved more lucrative. Using his medical knowledge, first-hand experience, and talent for persuasive writing, Conan-Doyle filed numerous reports for the *British Medical Journal* and *The Lancet* advocating mandatory

to follow the moans of the fallen without the comfort of a sidearm was not a task for the weak of heart. Sometimes, medical officers were forced to negotiate with - or in some cases, browbeat - the enemy for the recovery of the wounded who, as they had been left in the field, were considered prisoners of war. For the most part, decency prevailed, and stretcher-bearers could return with their charges, Boer doctors treated fallen British soldiers with the same tenderness as their own men and the RAMC returned the sentiment.

The field hospital was a travelling circus of five officers and 34 other ranks, and assorted ox wagons and bell tents which packed up and followed the frontline as the fortunes of war dictated. The stated capacity was '100 beds', but these 'beds' were rarely more than a ground sheet to lie upon and the capacity was however many men needed attention. From field hospitals, the wounded were either discharged back to their units or moved along the chain to a stationary hospital. These were sited at 20-mile intervals along the major arteries of road or rail and again had a capacity of 100, then a general hospital in a major town and perhaps from there to Britain by hospital ship. As the army moved, stationary hospitals moved up the line like a millipede of soiled sheets and discarded dressings.

Reserves and Volunteers

The infant RAMC could call on 840 doctors and 2,700 orderlies and other staff in 1899, and with the outbreak of typhoid found itself overwhelmed and understaffed with fewer medics per fighting men than the British Army in the Crimea, popularly considered the lowest watermark in military medicine. A

vital pool of reinforcements was drawn from the Volunteer Medical Staff Corps, which had been formed with much fanfare in 1885 by the Scottish surgeon James Cantlie with a gaggle of students from London's Charing Cross Hospital medical school. Universities across Britain soon followed and by 1892, there were 14 companies of 100 personnel each. Writing to the medical department of King's College, London at the end of 1899, surgeon and volunteer colonel Valentine Matthews praised the "technical knowledge and superior education and intelligence, added to the training [the medical student] receives" in the VMSC.

The St John Ambulance Brigade, a religious charity which had traditionally laid on first aid duties to the militia, also sent around 1,800 'Johnnies' for service as hospital orderlies. An estimated 500 society doctors, pharmacists and surgeons were also recruited for consultant roles, lured to South Africa by a £5,000 annual salary - nearly £400,000 in modern money.

ABOVE *Lady Randolph Spencer Churchill with her second son, Lieutenant Jack Churchill of the South African Light Horse, then recovering from an ankle wound aboard RFA Maine.* Wellcome Collection CC BY 4.0

inoculations for soldiers, practical means of boiling water in the field, and harsh punishments for those who didn't.

Surgery, Radiology and Recovery

Aseptic (germ free) surgery had been pioneered by Joseph Lister in the 1860s and by Robert Koch in the 1870s. Battlefield surgery followed suit with the issue of rubber aprons and nail brushes to ensure that hygiene began with the surgeon himself. It was on surgical grounds that the kilt was finally retired from the combat dress of the Scottish Highland regiments, as fibres of soiled plaid proved difficult to dig out and were an enthusiastic ally to infection.

From 1884, first field dressing had been issued to each soldier to enable them to guard their wounds from environmental dangers - in South Africa, the swirling dust, and buzzing flies - immediately. It consisted of a packet with instructions printed on the side: a pad of wool and gauze was clamped over the wound, then bound in place with a bandage, and until early 1900 when it was discontinued, a waterproof cover was then applied. Major Frederick Porter, RAMC explained: "I noticed today that these wounds which came in with a first field dressing on, and over which the piece of waterproof material had been applied, were quite moist and smelt offensively. Others on which the waterproof had not been applied, were quite sweet, dry, and scabbed. The idea of a dry dressing is to make all discharges dry up at once and leave nothing for the germs to live in."

Surgery was performed as soon as possible and therefore as close to the front as possible, but difficulties in securing clean water made sterilisation of surgical steel difficult. Sir Frederick Treves wrote of a field hospital: "The floor of the tent is much-trodden grass, and, indeed, much-stained grass, for what drips upon it cannot be wiped up. There are no bright brass water-taps, but there is a brave display of buckets and tin basins. Water is precious, more precious than any other necessity, for every drop has to be brought by train from Frere."

Once treated, they were quickly moved but it was soon discovered that after surgery - particularly amputation - the trauma of their

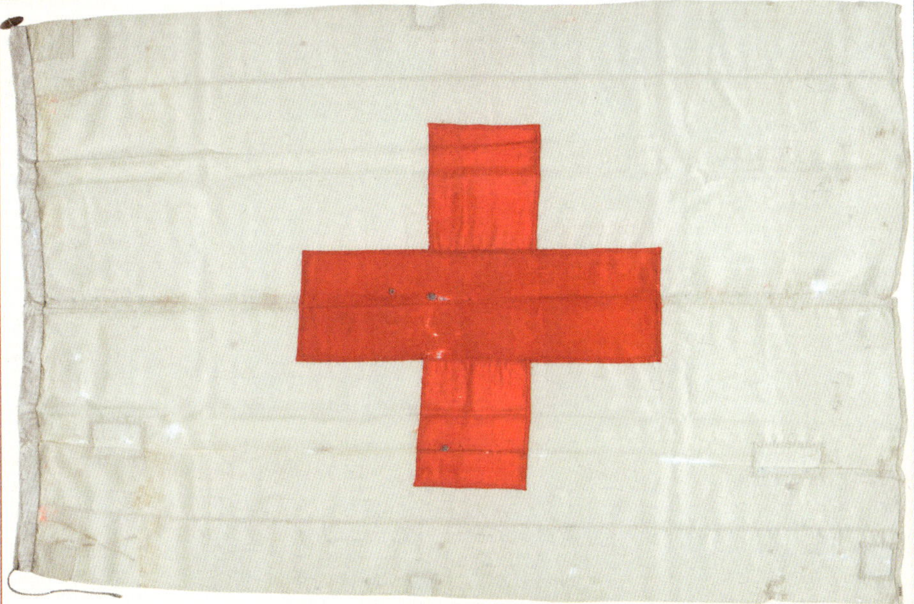

evacuation over broken ground led to wounds being opened, sepsis, further amputation and even death. It then became standard practise for the wounded to remain at the field hospital for several weeks following surgery until they were deemed well enough to travel. This was not always possible and if the field hospital was ordered to advance - as with Lord Roberts' unexpected Great Flank March - the RAMC was forced to send its charges down the line prematurely. MP William Burdett-Coutts visited South Africa and exposed the disastrous consequences of the Great Flank March to the press: "They were lifted out of their tents and put into rough ox-wagons - all typhoids and many of them dangerously ill- and then jolted across the veldt, which in this place is much broken by spruits and gullies. One case was in a state of 'haemorrhage' when moved. The order had come to evacuate the hospital; the medical officer had no choice but to obey; there were no ambulances. In three days four of these 20 were dead men."

Surgery was guided using Röntgen rays - or X-rays - to find bullets or shrapnel fragments in the body. A recent innovation, ten X-ray machines - cumbersome contraptions of valves and coils mounted on a frame - were carried to South Africa for use in base hospitals, general hospitals, and hospital ships. Dr John Hall-Edwards became the first to use X-rays in clinical conditions in 1896, as with many other leading lights in British medicine, he went to South Africa in 1900 to serve as chief radiologist at the Imperial Yeomanry Hospital in Deelfontein and then Pretoria. Sadly, Hall-Edwards was already losing the use of his left hand from repeated exposure to radiation and by 1908, his X-ray dermatitis was so agonising that he had his left forearm and the fingers of his right hand amputated. It was, he wrote, "as if bones were being gnawed away by rats."

Sisters and Society Darlings

Whilst nursing was firmly the domain of women, it was generally agreed that nurses were too delicate to lay eyes upon the battlefield, save from the windows of a hospital train, and for the most part the Army Nursing Service - formed in 1881 - had been left at fewer than a hundred staff, curiosities in crinoline who provided sisters to military hospitals of certain size. With no more than ten per general hospital at the start of the war, they were outnumbered by male orderlies who often lacked anything but the most basic medical knowledge.

Sister Kate Luard wrote on July 7, 1900: "We were pretty busy all the morning as the➡

Just Say No: Confessions of a Cordite Eater

Challenges that few military medics could have prepared themselves for, however, were the long-term effects of what became known as 'cordite eating'.

A shortage of matches led to soldiers extracting the highly combustible cordite from their rifle cartridges to ignite their pipes or cigarettes. Cordite contains nitro-glycerine, which is a vasodilator and is still in use for the treatment of angina. Vasodilators work by relaxing the blood vessels which increases the flow of blood and oxygen to the heart, meaning that the heart no longer has to work as hard. For servicemen who sought an escape from their sweltering misery and could not wrangle any opiates out of the doctor, this was just the ticket.

Cordite use led to an intense headache, slight yellowing of the skin, constipation, thirst, occasional fever, listlessness, and then deep sleep, with alcohol, opium or cocaine (used as a local anaesthetic) the 'pick me up' of choice amongst the hardened cordite eaters. Major J. W. Jennings, RAMC reported in the corps' journal of October 1, 1903: "As an experiment, I tried one-fourth of a strand from a Lee-Metford cartridge, which I kept in my mouth and sucked for two minutes. I then took it out. Its diminution in size was scarcely appreciable, and yet I experienced the most racking, splitting headache that I ever felt in my life, together with hammering and ringing noises in my ears; the headache lasted quite 36 hours [...] Its physiological action is similar to, but slower than, amyl nitrite, viz., throbbing headache, flushing of the face, visible carotid pulsation, giddiness and disordered action of the heart."

Jennings wrote about one cordite eater ('Trooper R') who could not be woken without being punched, slapped or shaken, and would shrug off his unresponsive stupor after "a few ounces of spirit of a few pints of beer," which is really solving one problem with a new problem. When taken as a solution with tea or water, the cordite appeared to result in a burst of hyperactivity before the coming sleep, whilst imbibing it in beer made 'Trooper R' "as mad as a man can get, without becoming absolutely a raving lunatic."

Despite the obvious issues of discipline, Maj Jennings appeared to conclude that the matter of cordite eating would sort itself out: "The symptoms and effects produced by cordite are sufficiently forcible and unpleasant to prevent any but the most depraved resorting to it."

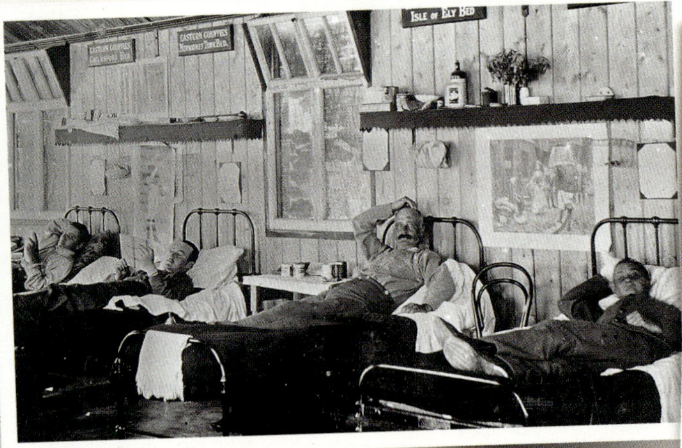

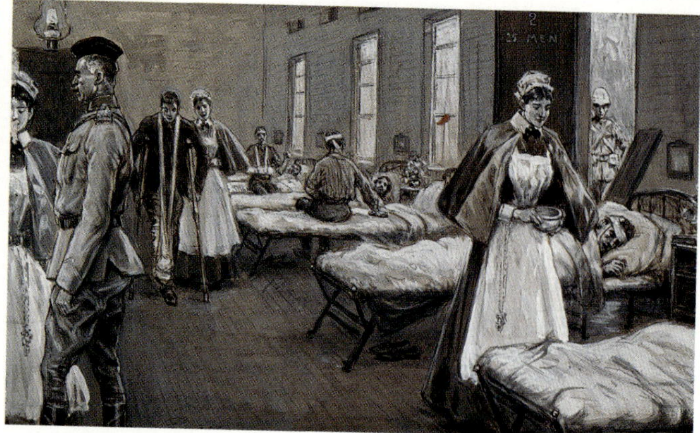

ABOVE *Men recline in their beds in the 'Eastern Counties ward' - so called because the beds were donated by towns in the south east - of the Imperial Yeomanry Hospital, Deelfontein.* Wellcome Collection CC BY 4.0

ABOVE RIGHT *Nurses tend to the wounded at a ward in the military hospital at Wynberg. Pen and ink drawing by P. Spence, 1900.* Wellcome Collection CC BY 4.0

RIGHT *Queen Alexandra presenting medals to the nurses who served at the Imperial Yeomanry Hospital by Oliver Paque, 1902.* Wellcome Collection CC BY 4.0

orderlies want so much looking after: they are a very scratch lot and perfect boys most of them: all the first class orderlies are up at the front. They are very willing and say, 'Very good Sister' to whatever you tell them."

Princess Christian's Army Nursing Service (Reserve) was formed in 1897 to try and bolster the numbers, but by 1899 it had only another 100 or so nurses on strength, having hit the same institutional barriers as the ANS. As a result of the Second Boer War, both bodies would be absorbed by a new permanent nursing staff, Queen Alexandra's Imperial Military Nursing Service, but for now an immediate recruitment drive was needed.

Intense patriotism was by no means the exclusive preserve of men and in terms of their background, many PCANS(R) volunteers acted as the mirror image of the predominantly middle-class Imperial Yeomanry. They were supposed to have nursing experience, with character references required from their matron and testimonies from doctors. Many were massively inexperienced, and the higher their social standing the more likely that they would have a family friend sign them off for a steamer to the Cape.

One frustrated sister wrote to the *Taunton Courier and Western Advertiser* of May 1900: "When society women, with no technical training, take these posts they fill posts which ought to be filled by certificated nurses. Real nurses, as consequence, are too few and terribly overworked by doing their own and the amateurs' duties. No end of trouble has been caused by these masquerade nurses to doctors, nurses, and poor, sick, wounded Tommies. They get in everybody's way and have no intention of working. Their idea is to take posts of authority and 'boss' the trained nurses who have borne the heat and burden of many years in hospital. We don't grudge them going round the wards in fancy dress, distributing flowers, and petting Tommy Atkins."

Nonetheless, many women of ability answered the call. Emily Jane Wood kept a diary of her time at No.8 General Hospital in Bloemfontein caring for typhoid patients. She wrote on June 21, 1900 of her duties: "Each of the five bad cases have Temp. Pulse and Resp. taken every four hours, if over 102.5 to be sponged with tepid water, that pretty frequently. Stimulants given every two, three or four hrs. Mixtures every four hrs. One is almost wholly unconscious, and three others take turns of it. Tea and arrowroot have to be made, milk and beef tea warmed."

Those who lacked nursing experience but had family in the field and a surplus of social influence put their efforts into helping from home. Lady Beatrice Chesham and Lady Georgiana Curzon raised funds to establish the Imperial Yeomanry Hospital, and Theodosia 'Dosia' Bagot and Olivia, Lady Henry Cavendish-Bentinck, established the Portland Hospital at Bloemfontein. The US-born society heiress and mother of Winston, Jennie, Lady Randolph Spencer Churchill, galvanised Americans sympathetic to the British cause to finance the hospital ship *RFA Maine*. The National Society for Aid to the Sick and Wounded in War (which became the British Red Cross Society in 1905) also purchased and fitted two hospital trains and a hospital ship from donations estimated at over £500,000 - nearly £40 million in modern terms.

The Royal Red Cross - instituted in 1884 as the first military honour exclusively for women - was awarded to nurses who showed exceptional bravery or devotion to duty during the Boer War.

In an obituary for a sister lost to typhoid, the Scottish nurse and suffragist Ethel Bedford Fenwick proclaimed: "The obligations of empire are incumbent upon women as well as men, and they claim their right to face danger and death in the discharge of their duty." It is estimated that 2,000 women served in South Africa, mostly with Princess Christian's Army Nursing Service (Reserve) and of that number, 47 lost their lives.

Pretoria & Prey

Roberts' Second Campaign, March 29 - June 5, 1900

Though raging typhoid forced a halt, Field Marshal Frederick Roberts, 1st Baron Roberts was keen to continue his offensive as soon as possible. The Natal Field Force of General Sir Redvers Buller was still around 50,000-men strong but no amount of pleading stirred the sullen warhorse into action. After two months of fruitless and frustrating telegrams back and forth, Roberts gave up and stripped Buller's command for parts, helping himself to an entire division, a handful of promising officers, and the veteran Imperial Light Horse. Why Roberts didn't simply order Buller across the rugged Drakensberg escarpment and into Transvaal is as difficult to decode as Buller's decision to let Lieutenant General Sir Charles Warren run wild at Spion Kop (January 23-24, 1900).

The Second Boer War hadn't exactly showered him in glory, but in one respect Buller's jitters were well-founded. Occupying Bloemfontein was not the checkmate that Roberts believed it to be, nor would occupying Pretoria be.

"Time has not yet glorified the seat of government with a halo of sentiment," Buller wrote. "To every [Boer] his own home is the capital. Hence there is no commanding centre by the occupation of which the whole country or even a whole district can be brought into subjugation; no vital spot at which a single blow can be struck that will paralyse every member of the body."

As Buller had foreseen, the government of the Orange Free State – safely reconstituted in Kroonstad - voted unanimously to continue the war. The sting of defeat had hardened President Martinus Steyn and the defiant individualism of the Boers was finally curtailed: deserters were to be punished, the foreign volunteers were organised into a single professional Uitlander Korps, and wagon-loads of women and children were discouraged from following their patriarchs to the front.

Finally, with Gen Piet Cronjé now languishing in captivity, Gen Christiaan de Wet was appointed commander-in-chief of the Free State forces. Putting pen to paper to win back the Boers who had laid down their arms, Wet hinted at the shape his renewed war

ABOVE: *Brigadier General George Broadwood served under Lord Kitchener in Sudan leading the Egyptian cavalry at the Battle of Omdurman (September 2, 1898).*
RIGHT: *A jingoistic cover of the satirical magazine Puck from March 1900 shows the British lion charging towards Pretoria whilst the Boer generals scramble for safety.*

One of the concealed crossings near Sanna's Post, a perfect spot for an ambush.

"Defeat had hardened President Martinus Steyn and the defiant individualism of the Boers was finally curtailed."

would take: "We need not be downhearted, as the most wonderful acts which God has done for us before, and also in this war, were accomplished by small bodies."

Though Roberts was forced to cling to Bloemfontein by matters of sickness and supply, Boer forces remained at large in the immediate vicinity and a series of limited actions were necessary to secure their lines of communication and prevent the army from being bottled up in the capital.

A force of 9,000 - the 7th Division, two cavalry brigades and a brigade of Mounted Infantry - drove Gen 'Koos' de la Rey from his position on the railway at the Battle of Karee Siding (March 29, 1900), 12 miles north of Bloemfontein. The scrap is notable mainly for Lieutenant General John French receiving another drubbing and for having Rudyard Kipling bussed up as part of a gaggle of war correspondents. French had occupied Dewetsdorp and was on his way to occupy Thaba 'Nchu when he was recalled, covering 40 miles in a single day before executing two flanking manoeuvres on the Boers. Major Douglas Haig, French's subordinate and creditor (an awkward combination, he had recently loaned French £2,500), wrote to his sister, Henrietta, scathingly: "Whenever there is an alarm, Lord R[oberts] at once orders out French and the cavalry. I don't know what we'll do for horses; only wretched beasts of Argentine ponies are arriving and very few of them."

Just northeast of Kimberley, two battalions of Imperial Yeomanry bloodied themselves in their first engagement at the Battle of Boshof (April 5, 1900), which made a short-lived experiment of the Uitlander Korps, who were left to fight on when the Burghers bolted. Of the 75 volunteers, 11 were killed, including the experienced French colonial commander Major General George de Villebois-Mareuil and the Georgian playboy and aristocrat Prince Niko Bagrationi, and the remainder were taken captive. Another well-connected foreign fighter, the 32-year old Cornelius van Gogh - youngest brother of the impressionist painter Vincent van Gogh - committed suicide on April 12, 1900, at the Dutch Red Cross hospital in Brandfort where he had been swallowed up by fever. By date and geography, he is likely another casualty of Boshof.

The Battle of Sanna's Post

It was Gen de Wet's actions that were the ones to watch. Leading 1,600 Burghers out from Brandfort and setting out northeast, Wet suddenly swung south under the cover of darkness with designs on the pumping station which fed Bloemfontein's beleaguered water supply from the southern bank of the Modder, just east of the confluence with the Kroonspruit. A small British garrison was holding the waterworks from a cluster of buildings called Sanna's Post which nestled between the Kroonspruit and the Modder, but as he neared his target Wet became aware of a British mounted column advancing along the road.

Before his thankless race to Karee Siding, French had detached Brigadier General George Broadwood, 1,800 of his men (a mixture of regular and irregular cavalry, mounted infantry and Royal Horse Artillery) and the bulk of his baggage, and sent them on to Thaba 'Nchu, a restive frontier town on the border with - and originally stolen from - Basutoland ➤➤

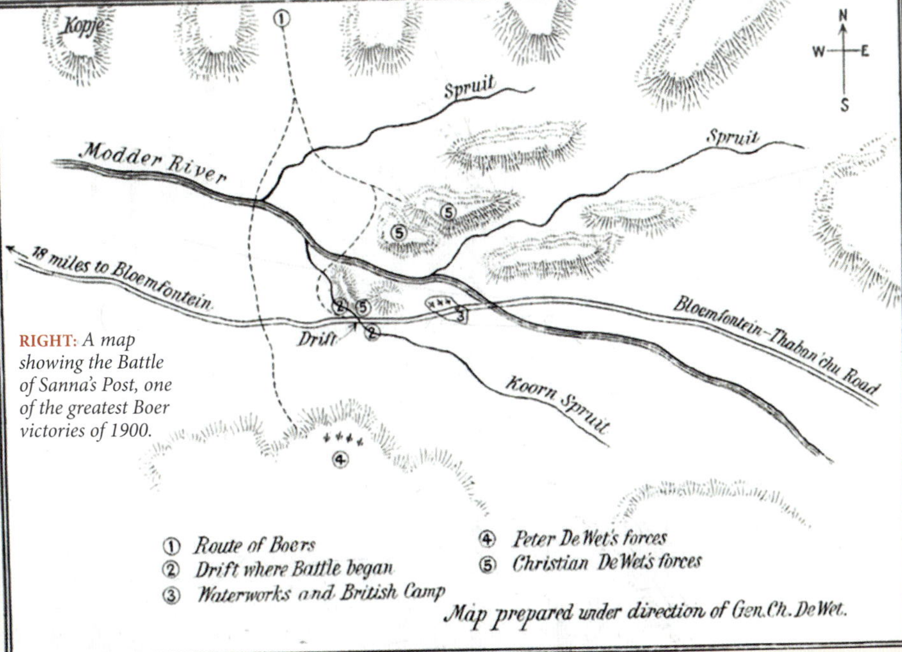

RIGHT: A map showing the Battle of Sanna's Post, one of the greatest Boer victories of 1900.

Q Battery, Royal Horse Artillery gallop to safety.

"Major Edmund Phipps-Hornby ordered his guns smartly about and they opened fire at 250 yards"

(now Lesotho). After a week at Thaba 'Nchu with little action, Broadwood was ordered back to the safety of Bloemfontein. Following an incomplete railway line, he crossed the Modder on March 30 and spent the night bivouacked at Sanna's Post. The rivers of South Africa were ideal spots for an ambush, they lay at the bottom of small canyons carved out by the torrential summer rains, and they curved wickedly through the undulating landscape. Wet placed the bulk of his men, his three Krupp guns and his two Maxim-Nordfeldt 'Pom-Pom' guns on the hills north of the Modder, facing the waterworks, and concealed a further 350 men in the drift over the Kroonspruit. Broadwood was woken at dawn on the morning of March 31, 1900 by the Boer artillery opening up. With one hand, the startled Broadwood ordered his 12-pdrs to return fire and with the other, hitched the supply wagons and sent them scrambling towards Kroonspruit Drift. As the panicked wagoneers descended the steep banks, they found Mausers levelled at them from both sides. To the column all appeared as it should: one by one each wagon dropped from view where they were hijacked and then reappeared on the other side of the spruit, their drivers now held at gunpoint.

In his haste, Broadwood had failed to send a patrol ahead of the wagons, but he had not sent it without escort and two batteries of Royal Horse Artillery rattled towards the canyon. As U Battery descended, they were held at gunpoint like the civilians before them and disarmed but in the chaos, one of the field guns and its crew managed to slip back the way they had come and warn Q Battery which followed on their heels.

ABOVE: *Lieutenant Colonel Edmund Henry Dalgety, the British-born CO of the prestigious Cape Mounted Rifles.*
RIGHT: *2nd The Royal Warwickshire Regiment skirmish with General Christiaan de Wet's rear-guard as they race to relieve the bitter Siege of Wepener.*

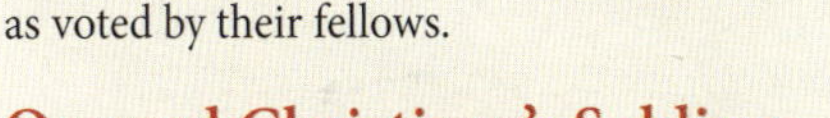

ABOVE: *The Railway Pioneer Regiment undergo a kit inspection. They were raised in 1899 to assist the Royal Engineers with the protection and repair of South Africa's vulnerable rail links and were vital to Roberts' rapid advance.*
BELOW: *Field Marshal Frederick Roberts, 1st Baron Roberts leads his staff up the north bank of the Zand River and on to Kroonstad.*

The jig now up, the Boers rushed up in pursuit and Major Edmund Phipps-Hornby ordered his guns smartly about and they opened fire at 250 yards with bullets striking all about them. As the ammunition began to run out, Q Battery (and the survivors of U Battery) withdrew towards Sanna's Post where the Mounted Infantry cowered under the shadow of the railway siding. "It was an awful sight—dead and wounded all around," wrote one anonymous Q Battery gunner in *The Black & White Budget* of April 14, 1900, "and the poor horses all smothered in blood and struggling about. I captured an MI horse but could not ride owing to the bullet in my hip. I have been in several scraps, but they were all picnics to this turn-out."

Just as the battle was dying down and Wet was beginning to withdraw, an infantry division arrived at around 11 am from Bloemfontein. Though superbly placed to cut off Wet's escape, Lt Gen Sir Henry Colville instead instructed Broadwood to extract himself from the battle he was fighting and report in person. Broadwood rightly refused to trek back and forth across the veldt and instead urged the general to move up immediately. Colville, evidently not used to having the lesser orders ignore his requests, waited until the next morning when the Boers had cleared out completely before he sent the 9th Division up to take possession of the battlefield. Any residue of confidence Broadwood had for Colville was firmly swept away when he refused Maj Gen Horace Smith-Dorrien and his 19th Brigade permission to evacuate the 87 wounded MIs

that the Boers had left behind rather than take prisoner, explaining that the cavalry's fallen was the business of the cavalry. Smith-Dorrien, in possession of a functioning moral compass, ignored the order and escorted the casualties to safety.

The Battle of Sanna's Post cost the British 159 casualties and 421 men taken captive, along with the loss of seven field guns and 83 supply wagons. Desperate to snatch some good news from the jaws of humiliation, the unusual step was taken to issue four Victoria Crosses to Q Battery, RHA for their collective valour in saving their guns and keeping the ambushing Boers at bay. The VCs were awarded to a man each of the commissioned officers, one NCO, and two gunners or drivers, as voted by their fellows.

Onward Christiaan's Soldiers

Whilst recriminations took flight from Sanna's Post, Wet's force rode for Dewetsdorp (incidentally founded by his father, Jacobus de Wet) some 40 miles south where a token garrison of 500 men under Captain William McWhinnie had been left by Lt Gen Sir ➤

ABOVE: *The Royal standard is raised in Bloemfontein in a formal ceremony to mark the annexation of Orange Free State as Britain's newest territory, the Orange River Colony. Wash by Frank Dadd, 1900.*

ABOVE: *British troops march into Johannesburg to a warm reception from the diamond town's remaining Uitlanders.* Zuid-Afrika Huis

William Gatacre. Lord Roberts had instructed that the town be occupied but had left the details entirely to Gatacre. When he discovered on April 1 the paucity of defenders, he ordered McWhinnie back to Bloemfontein.

Gatacre passed on the order but without warning him that Wet was closing in. Unable to outrun the mounted Boers with two companies of 2nd Royal Irish Rifles on foot, McWhinnie was forced off the road to dig in for a battle he had no hope of winning without food, water, artillery or rescue. The Battle of Mostert's Hoek (April 3-4, 1900) ended with McWhinnie's positions being overrun by the dawn of day two and Gatacre's overdue disgrace. When news reached Lord Roberts of the column's plight, he ordered Gatacre to clean up the mess his "grave want of judgement" had created. The 3rd Division marched as far as Reddersburg - five miles from the sound of gunfire - before withdrawing smartly, suddenly fearful of Burghers behind every bush. Furious, Lord Roberts ordered Gatacre back into Reddersburg and by the time they reached Mostert's Hoek, the battle was over. Ten British

had been killed, 37 wounded - McWhinnie mortally so -and 470 were taken prisoner. Gatacre was relieved of his command and was sent back to Britain.

The prospect of General de Wet continuing to circle Bloemfontein with impunity caused huge concern for Lord Roberts. The defeats inflicted by de Wet had underscored just how vulnerable the isolated British patrols and garrisons were. Maj Gen Herbert Kitchener, 1st Earl Kitchener had been busying himself repairing and securing the long line of sleepers, steam and steel that linked the army to Cape Colony. This was in part chastisement for his mishandling of Paardeburg's first day (February 18, 1900), but it also suited Kitchener's no-nonsense manner and his experiences in Sudan. He was reunited with his old friend, the energetic and charismatic French-Canadian Lieutenant Colonel Percy Girouard, Royal Engineers, as the newly appointed Director of Imperial Military Railways. In 1897, Girouard had driven a track 250 miles across the Nubian Desert at a mile a day and had the rare ability to address Kitchener frankly without unleashing the prickly peer's ire.

The army needed two train-loads of rations a day and after seven weeks of tireless exhortation from Kitchener and Giroud, six trains a day were running to Bloemfontein - escorted by armoured trains bristling with guns - and bringing up enough surplus and stores to establish a forward depot.

All this required time and ultimately it was Wet, rather than any strategic masterstroke from Lord Roberts, that secured it. Allowing his heart to countermand his head, Wet descended upon Lt Col E. H. Dalgety's colonial irregulars at the town of Wepener for what was effectively a family feud. Dalgety's force, consisting of his own Cape Mounted Rifles, 1st and 2nd Brabant's Horse, the Kaffrarian Rifles and a few smaller 'regiments', were predominantly Cape Afrikaners and their presence incensed the Boers. Wet managed to muster a force of almost 6,000 men to punish the 'traitors' and opened up the fruitless Siege of Wepener (April 6-25, 1900). These sorts of operations had never played to the Boer strengths and the situation was worsened by their quarry. A veteran of numerous frontier conflicts, Dalgety knew as well as the hoariest Burgher how best to use the terrain to his advantage and the colonials dug in on a cluster of hills by Jammerberg Drift on the Caledon River. The assault was so fierce that the defenders could only pass out their rations by cover of night. An unnamed officer wrote: "My men have been ten days in their trenches without leaving them, wet to the skin oftener than not, and day and night exposed to shrapnel, not able to raise their hand above without getting a bullet through them, and yet not a grumble is heard." Eventually Wet was forced to withdraw by an approaching relief column. Though a costly engagement for the colonials - 33 dead and 133 wounded, with the Cape Mounted Rifles bearing the brunt - Wet had thrown away the initiative.

The Thin Khaki Line

On May 3, 1900, Lord Roberts led 38,000 men and 100 guns in three columns along the railway north to Transvaal, his right flank protected by French and his left by the Mounted Infantry, detached from the Cavalry Division under the newly promoted Lt Gen Sir Ian Hamilton. Bolstered by the Imperial Yeomanry and the Mounted Infantry, Roberts had ten times the cavalry that Buller had been able to field and they turned every flank on every muddy brown river where the Boers chose to stand.

General Louis Botha's defensive line was overcome at the Battle of Zand River (May 10, 1900), better remembered in the Commonwealth than in the mother country, for the key role played by the 2nd Royal Canadian Regiment of Infantry. Botha concentrated his artillery around the railway bridge (artfully sabotaged by the 'Wreckers

Corps' of Irish volunteers), but the British crossed the river four miles upstream and Botha struggled to reposition his guns accordingly. Once across, wrote an unnamed old boy to *The Radleian* in July 1900: "The fight then proceeded as usual; heavy shellfire, and then our infantry advanced with flanking cavalry and mounted infantry. The position was taken about 4pm, and very cheaply too, as the Boers were present in great numbers (7,000) and the position was undeniably strong."

Private E. D. Curran, an American volunteer with Kitchener's Horse, told *The New York Times*: "We had been fighting all day from behind shelter, neither side doing much damage. I was lying alongside the 5th Lancers, and I heard them get permission to charge. Out

they went with their long pikes, and I scurried along behind them. They went through the Boers in horrible fashion, spearing them like pigs. I saw one man on the Boer side drop his gun, and getting on his knees before a lancer, he yelled: 'For God's sake, don't strike. I'm an Englishman.' 'You are not an Englishman now,' said the lancer, and he ran the man through."

The acting capital Kroonstad was taken on May 12 with little fight, President Steyn having already retreated further north to Heilbron. There the army rested for ten days, allowing time for the long tail of supplies, remounts, and reinforcements to catch up. The 128 miles of rail from Bloemfontein to Kroonstad had been cut in 17 places by means of ripping up hundreds of yards of track, demolition

of bridges and other acts of sabotage by the retreating guerrillas. Victory seemed inevitable as the long Siege of Mafeking was finally relieved on May 17 - its defender, the inventive and indefatigable imperial adventurer Colonel Robert Baden-Powell, now a national hero - and on May 24, French's scouts splashed through the Vaal River which marked the border with the South African Republic. As it was Queen Victoria's birthday on May 28, Roberts issued a proclamation formally annexing the Orange Free State to Britain as the Orange River Colony. Events to his rear exposed this as wishful thinking. Behind the relentless hammer-blows of Roberts's advance, divisions swept the veldt for resistance and found it. ➤➤

RIGHT: *A British guard post in occupied Johannesburg, July 1900.* Zuid-Afrika Huis.
BELOW: *A Maxim gun position on the walls of the fort.* Zuid-Afrika Huis.

"The loss of so many bluebloods caused a scandal...."

Lt Gen Colville - courting comeuppance for his conduct at Sanna's Post - was instructed by Kitchener to rendezvous with his reinforcements, 13th (Irish) Battalion, Imperial Yeomanry on May 24, before moving up to Lindley on May 26 and then Heilbron on May 29. When the citizen soldiers were nowhere to be found, Colville moved on to keep to his schedule. Owing to delays in being issued forage, Lt Col B. E. Spragge's 13th (Irish) were running late and they raced to catch up with Colville. The 13th (Irish) was a prestigious group, recruited in part from Irish hunt regulars such as Captain Thomas Pakenham, 5th Earl of Longford and Lieutenant Richard Hare, Viscount Ennismore, or from the Protestant gentry

such as 2nd Lt Charles Clements, 5th Earl of Leitrim and the wealthy whiskey barons, Lt James Craig and Lt Sir John Power. They had to purchase their own arms and mounts and donated their wages to charity. They reached Lindley to discover that Colville was a distant column of dust and that the Boers had taken up positions in the hills and immediately fired on the isolated cavalry.

Trapped outside the town and with only two days-worth of rations, they dug in on what became known as Yeomanry Hill where Spragge believed he could hold out for as long as it took to be rescued. He fired off a desperate dispatch to Colville pleading: "I want help to get out without great loss." Colville decided that his primary objective

was his schedule and after four days of defiance, Spragge was forced to surrender. The loss of so many bluebloods caused a scandal, Colville was relieved of his command and later pressured to resign his commission entirely.

Double-time through Transvaal

General Buller's view about the Boers and their capitals had its adherents on Roberts's staff, but despite the regular evidence that the so-called Orange River Colony was far from annexed, the field marshal could not be swayed. Major Colin Mackenzie, director of Military Intelligence to Roberts, circulated a report that Pretoria would only be lightly defended and that like President Steyn before him, the rheumy President Paul Kruger would simply fight on from deep in the high veldt.

Gen de Wet was still very much at large, along with an estimated 7,000 Boers, but Roberts wanted the war over and in his impatience clung to the belief that Pretoria was the key to victory. He drove on relentlessly into the Transvaal.

The Johannesburg forts had been erected at great expense and similarly Roberts had spared no little outlay in preparing to confront them - bringing up siege guns and howitzers for a set piece battle. When it came down to it, the Burghers preferred freedom of manoeuvre to being locked up in a fortified fastness, and the unmanned Maginot Line of South Africa was taken without struggle. Though the diamond city lay open, it was still home to a defiant cadre of local Burghers who were prepared to fight tooth and nail. Roberts fretted for the safety of the mines and Johannesburg's governor Dr Fritz Krause fretted for safety of the population, so Krause agreed to usher the refuseniks out and guarantee the mines remained intact, so long

ABOVE: *Stephanus Johannes Paulus 'Paul' Kruger, president of the South African Republic (Transvaal), and his second wife Gezina sitting on the porch of their Pretoria home. By mid-1900, both were in considerably ill-health.* Zuid-Afrika Huis

as the British delayed their entrance. Roberts obliged and on May 31 to a warm reception from the few Uitlanders who had chosen to wait out the war, he paraded his grimy rows of infantry to the town hall where the red, white and blue was duly raised.

The Transvaal government had already vacated Pretoria. The most established of the Boer communities, it was Afrikaner Jerusalem - the heart of their way of life - and President Kruger's decision to depart on May 29 plunged him into defeatism and despair. He left his frail wife Gezina in the care of their daughter and next-door neighbour, Elsie Eloff, and left the equally frail republic in the care of the state attorney general, Jan Smuts. As all that remained of civil authority, Smuts could do little to halt the looting and unrest, and the steady stream of retreating Boers scattered ahead of Roberts' column discovered desolate scenes. Smuts wrote: "They found scarcely anything to eat and thousands passed with sad hearts and empty stomachs through the ungrateful capital."

Kruger wrote to his Orange counterpart proposing they surrender, but it was President Steyn's turn to play the role of the diehard. He responded: "Only a small part of the Transvaal is in the hands of the enemy; nearly all of our land lies under his heel [...] We must fight to the bitter end."

After some talk of a bloody last stand - the armoury was emptied, and rifles handed out - Pretoria capitulated just as bloodlessly as Johannesburg. On June 5, 1900, Lord Roberts marched ahead of a column of 25,000 men into a city of stony silence and set jaws, onlookers wearing Vierkleur (Transvaal flag) ribbons in mute defiance. In his exhaustion and relief, one soldier dropped to his knees and cried out: "Thank God, the war is over."

The 22-year old Johanna van Warmelo hissed in reply: "Tommy Atkins, the war has just begun."

ABOVE: *Lord Roberts enters Pretoria as the Union flag is raised above the Raadsaal, the Transvaal government building. Painting by Harry Payne, 1900.*
BELOW: *The triumphant flag-raising ceremony in front of the Raadsaal on Pretoria's Church Square. A second capital conquered without resistance.* State Library of Queensland

Churchill and Company

War Correspondents in South Africa

ABOVE *A group photograph of some of the best-known war correspondents in South Africa, taken at sea. Second from the left in the middle row is Winston Spencer Churchill representing The Morning Post.*

Winston Spencer Churchill, wearing even as a 25-year old the sullen pout and heavy scowl that would define his public image later in life, gazes back from a photograph of British POWs surrounded by curious Boers. He stands apart from the men in Khaki, a uniquely high-profile captive with a uniquely high-profile destiny.

Like many young men of means - he was the son of former Chancellor of the Exchequer Lord Randolph Churchill and the American heiress Jeannie Jerome - Churchill joined the army. Commissioned into the 4th Queen's Own Hussars in 1895, Churchill took up journalism to sustain the absurdly high costs demanded from a cavalry officer. Securing transfers to war zones, commissions from newspapers, and most-likely permission from his superior officers, courtesy of his influential family, he resigned his commission in 1898 to run for Parliament. When he failed to win a seat, he was free of ties for an all-expenses paid South African assignment for *The Morning Post*.

Desperate to get as close to the fighting as he could, Churchill joined the armoured train 'Hairy Mary' which was pushing up the track to the town of Frere. The exact circumstances of their capture are somewhat murky, but it appears as though the officer commanding the scouting mission, Captain Aylmer Haldane, was persuaded by Churchill to move onto Chieveley which was well beyond the scope of their orders. They soon came under fire from the Boers who had blocked the line with rocks, trapping the train like a butterfly under a pin. Blurring the lines between correspondent and combatant, the hot-headed Churchill cleared the track and brought the wounded to safety. Staying in the field, however, assured his capture with Haldane and half of his command, and the daredevil reporter found himself languishing in a POW camp in Pretoria. It wasn't somewhere that Churchill planned on sitting out the war and he immediately set

ABOVE *Winston Spencer Churchill, the rising star of the Second Boer War, poses by the entrance to his tent outside of Bloemfontein, 1900.*

RIGHT *An illustration of Churchill's daring escape from the POW camp in Pretoria, an adventure which made him a household name.*

about getting away.

The escape party of Churchill and Haldane were joined by an abrasive Irishman, Sergeant Major Adam Brockie, a fluent speaker of Afrikaans and isiZulu. When the night came, Churchill alone cleared the perimeter wall by scaling the latrine roof. Haldane was spotted and ducked back into cover. Churchill - who did not want to wander around Transvaal without Brockie's local knowledge - asked him to send the Irishman anyway. Haldane decided not to.

Haldane nursed a grudge against Churchill for abandoning him, Brockie nursed a grudge against Haldane for holding him back, and Churchill became a national hero. He detailed his colourful adventures crossing the 300 miles of veldt to neutral Delagoa Bay in his book, *London to Ladysmith via Pretoria* (1900). Churchill promptly rejoined the war for General Sir Redvers Buller's relief of Ladysmith and then accepted a commission in the South African Light Horse where he continued to file copy (and write another book) on a war that he was cheerfully waging himself.

BELOW *The armoured train 'Hairy Mary', so-called because of the layer of dangling ropes which served to absorb the detonation of shells.* Museums Victoria CC BY 4

Write Place at the Write Time

Wars had consumed headlines hungrily long before 1899, but the Second Boer War was arguably the first 'media war'. It was Britain's longest and largest armed engagement in almost a century, the first overseas conflict fought by Canada, New Zealand and the colonies of Australia, and for the latter the reports of their countrymen were used to underwrite a newly confident national identity.

Technology was up to the challenge of reporting on such a complex conflict unfolding over a large area. The mass-market Kodak box camera and cheaper models which followed

in the late 1800s allowed correspondents to spice up their content with context - although the established Victorian war artists such as R. Canton Woodville and Melton Prior also went out in order to depict the action scenes that the camera couldn't.

Reuters, the largest news organisation active in South Africa, also ran the commercial telegraph operation that allowed missives to make London in time for the next morning's papers. The introduction of the rotary press which ran papers between two cylinders rather than printing onto flat sheets made the process cheaper and faster, and it emboldened

publishers to experiment with luxuriously illustrated supplements such as the *Daily Mail*'s weekly *With the Flag to Pretoria*. Launched to target the newly literate working class, the *Daily Mail* was only three years old in 1899 and its publisher, the energetic Alfred Harmsworth, threw it feet first into coverage of the conflict.

There was little objectivity as it would be recognised now. The press of the day was not typically in the business of propaganda, but British correspondents - as well as those from Australia, New Zealand, and Canada - were broadly sympathetic to the British cause. Correspondents were not

above criticising the conduct of the war if it needlessly endangered or dishonoured their countrymen, and Lord Roberts was attuned to public opinion in a way that was very much ahead of his time. The press was not uniformly pro-war by any means, however. J. A. Hobson of the *Manchester Guardian* was one of the most dedicatedly pro-Boer British correspondents, he reported from both sides of the lines and eventually concluded that British foreign policy was the plaything of powerful mine owners and businessmen. This position was set down in three texts, *War in South Africa* (1900), *Psychology of Jingoism* (1901) and the influential *Imperialism* (1902), which despite its antisemitic undercurrent counted amongst its admirers Vladimir Lenin and Leon Trotsky.

For writers to favour one side over another was the natural order of things and after the war 149 journalists were awarded the Queen's South African Medal as if they had been a branch of the armed forces.

Over the course of the conflict at least 276 journalists reported from the British side and an unknown number from the Boer lines, including one German photographer who was found piling up British dead for a photograph at Spion Kop and was shot dead by an appalled British scout. Many British and colonial correspondents paid the price for their eagerness to chase the story or ➤➤

for their closeness to the fighting men, such as the *Melbourne Argus*'s W. J. Lambie and the *Daily News*' A. A. G. Hales, both of whom were wearing British uniforms and riding with an Australian patrol. During a Boer ambush, both correspondents were shot and Lambie was killed outright. Hale recovered from his head wound in a Boer POW camp and used the opportunity to interview President Martinus Steyn.

BELOW *The Australian correspondents W. J. Lambie and A. A. G. Hales come under fire during a Boer ambush.*

ABOVE *The resting place of G. W. Steevens in Natal. One of the most famous of the Victorian correspondents, Steevens reported from within the Siege of Ladysmith for the Daily Mail and died of typhoid on January 15, 1900.*

In total 15 journalists were killed in the Second Boer War - including the *Daily Mail*'s star reporter G. W. Steevens who contracted typhoid during the Siege of Ladysmith - and 37 were wounded or captured.

Gentlemen of the Press

For those with a gift for prose, the Great Boer War was a place where reputations could be made and embellished. With war reporting as a concept very much in its infancy, these were a colourful bunch - a mixture of professional newsmen, established writers of celebrity, and correspondents of convenience, well-to-do men and women who found themselves in the right place at the right time. Present were the leading newspaper correspondents of the day, including the tireless American Richard Harding Davis, who covered the Spanish-American War and almost single-handedly frothed up the legend of Theodore Roosevelt and the Rough Riders, the campaigning journalist Henry Nevinson, and the fearless Scottish veteran of the US Civil War, Bennet Burleigh.

Amongst the best known of the celebrity writers were, of course, Rudyard Kipling and Dr Arthur Conan Doyle. The *Sherlock Holmes* novelist had volunteered at first for the army, then the Imperial Yeomanry, and only when his advanced years threatened his dreams of grand imperial adventure, did he remember that

ABOVE *Rudyard Kipling, circa 1900.*

he was also a medical doctor. Conan Doyle's contemporary history of the conflict's first two years, *The Great Boer War* (1900), is still a vital document, although its publication proved premature.

Kipling, whilst often thought of as being the chief propagandist of Victorian imperialism,

was in a dark place and that was reflected in his collection *The Five Nations* (1903). In 1899 pneumonia struck, forcing Kipling to his bed, and killing his eldest child, the six-year old Josephine. Writing was one way of soothing the pain in his heart, but for every gung-ho recruiting anthem like 'The Absent-Minded Beggar' - published in the *Daily Mail* to raise money for the Soldiers' Families' Fund - is a verse cutting enough in places to rival anything produced during World War One. Kipling's disillusionment is clear in 'Stellenbosch (Composite Columns)', the sleepy Cape Colony town of the title was notorious as the destination for disgraced senior staff:

"An' it all went into the laundry,
But it never came out in the wash.
We were sugared about by the old men
(Panicky, perishin' old men)
That 'amper an' 'inder an' scold men
For fear o' Stellenbosch!"

A national hero in his native Australia and second only to Kipling in sales, the bush

BELOW *The heavy Biograph movie camera which printed images at 30 frames a second, taking the first newsreel footage of war. The action sequences were staged and intercut with genuine documentary of soldiers on the march.*

poet A. B. 'Banjo' Paterson - best known for 'Waltzing Matilda' (1895) and 'The Man From Snowy River' (1890) - also covered the conflict for the *Sydney Morning Herald* and *Melbourne Argus*.

Our Lady Reporter

"A lady journalist, it is reported, has been informing an interviewer that she makes by her profession, and by working no more than an hour and a half every day, the very respectable income of a thousand pounds a year [...] A thousand pounds a year! Hark! Do you hear? It is the frou of a hundred thousand skirts, the rush of two thousand feet, the cry of a hundred thousand tongues," wrote Walter Besant in an issue of *The Author*, 1893. Like many male writers circling their desks in the masculine space of the newsroom, he was by equal measure intimidated and disdainful of the increasingly confident, self-reliant, and highly educated middle-class women who began to find their voices in print.

The crude caricatures drawn of Besant and his ilk dismissed the reality of a growing female readership for newspapers, but the market did not. An increase in periodicals aimed at women and greater emphasis on 'women's subjects', such as family and housekeeping, drove an increase in female correspondents. Domestic affairs were the unquestionable domain of women, and this

ABOVE Frontispiece to The Absent-Minded Beggar score by Sir Arthur Sullivan (of 'Gilbert and…').

was extended to include other 'soft subjects' such as writing short fiction and interviewing authors.

War, suffice to say, was absolutely not the place for a 'lady journalist' and the majority of those who did report from South Africa found themselves in the theatre for other purposes, most often nurses like the Irish-born Australian Sister Agnes Macready who also filed copy for the *Catholic Press*. While supportive of the troops themselves, the paper - which was established by Irish immigrants - was hostile to the British Empire and Macready wrote of the commonalities between the hardy, freedom-loving frontiersmen of both veldt and bush. "If war came to Australia," she asked, "wouldn't Australians fight to keep their country the same as these Boers are?"

Another nurse-turned-writer deserving of mention is the African explorer and critic of imperialism Mary Kingsley. She travelled to Cape Colony under her own steam to volunteer as a nurse in Simonstown where she tended to Boer POWs. Possessing incredible self-reliance and intense moral certainty, she was approached by the editor of the *Morning Post* to cover the war, but the spread of typhoid claimed all her energies and eventually her life. She died on June 3, 1900, aged 37 and in accordance with her wishes was buried at sea. A similar potent force for good (and journalist second) was the feminist and welfare activist Emily Hobhouse, secretary for the women's section of the anti-war South African Conciliation Committee. After learning of the plight of refugees, she arrived in Cape Town on January 24, 1901 with a shipment of aid for displaced Boer women and children, and wrote a number of letters to the *Manchester Guardian* to raise awareness of their suffering in Britain's concentration camps.

The first cousin once removed of Winston Churchill and daughter of the Duke of Marlborough, Lady Sarah Wilson, née Spencer-Churchill, filed her dispatches from within the Siege of Mafeking, where her husband, Lieutenant Colonel Gordon Chesney Wilson was second in command. Originally evacuated with the other civilians, she baffled the Boers by trying to break back into the siege and made such a nuisance of herself as a POW that they were overjoyed with the opportunity to trade her back. When the *Daily Mail* correspondent Ralph Hellawell was killed trying to smuggle his reports through the Boer lines, she stepped in as their regular

ABOVE A. B. 'Banjo' Paterson, the best known of the Australian bush poets, circa 1890.

correspondent.

Her missives were typical of her social class. Cheerful and condescending - preferring to focus on the defenders' larks and the 'shabbiness' of the Boers - she played no small role in investing the British public in the Siege of Mafeking and its defender, Colonel Robert Baden-Powell.

The most remarkable female correspondent of the Second Boer War was the only woman actually sent to South Africa in that capacity. Although Wilson had been appointed earlier, she had found herself in the role by chance. The British-born Edith Dickenson arrived in March 1900 to cover the conflict 'from a woman's standpoint' for Australia's *Adelaide Advertiser* and over three visits to South Africa focused on the effects that the war had on the people of Natal and Orange River Colony, as well as publicising the horrific conditions of Boer women and children held in the British concentration camps. Her family connections opened doors across the theatre - her brother was a major in the Imperial Yeomanry, her sons were serving on General Sir George White's staff, and her father had been a colonel in the 10th Hussars - and she was the only woman given a pass to enter Ladysmith in the ➡

ABOVE The campaigning journalist Henry Nevinson, pictured around 1915. Nevinson exposed the illegal slave trade in Angola for Harper's Monthly Magazine and reported on the Second Boer War for the Manchester Guardian.

ABOVE *Lady Sarah Wilson, kitted out for adventure, circa 1909.*

immediate aftermath of the siege. It did not however make her blind to the army's failings and Dickenson reported on unpopular officers being shot by their subordinates and one who was wounded and dumped into the Modder River by the stretcher party. She wrote: "Too many of the young British officers are in the style of those in the [musical comedy] *Gaiety Girl*, who when asked what they do reply, 'Oh, we play polo.'"

Censors and Sensibility

Management of the press was the duty of the War Office's Department of Military Intelligence which exorcised variable influence out in the field. Field Marshal Frederick Roberts, 1st Baron Roberts had his own intelligence staff, as did General Buller, and it was Lieutenant Colonel George Henderson - at the head of Roberts's six-man intelligence corps - who dealt with journalists. His duties included censoring press reports as well as gleaning intelligence from intercepted enemy letters. This process could have been made a lot easier with a little consideration early, but as with much of the British Army's infrastructure, the further a function was seen to be from the bloody business of warfighting, the less attention and funding it was given.

In theory, war reporters intending to work from the British lines were issued a correspondent's license by the War Office and there was supposedly a fixed number that each outlet was entitled to. Plenty of journalists appeared in the Cape without official approval, along with those reporters of circumstance who had been drawn to the Boer War by some other means and found themselves filing copy on the side. Additionally, much coverage of the conflict came in the form of 'personal letters' from men and women at the front, often

uncensored and sometimes anonymous.

Not that it seemed to matter much: no British request for a correspondent's license was ever refused, and despite concerns about issuing them to foreign nationals and worries that it might be a cover for espionage, no central register of active war correspondents was ever kept. The business of verifying the motives and credentials of journalists then became an additional nightmare dropped onto the head of the minuscule intelligence operation at the front.

ABOVE *Explorer and ethnographer Mary Kingsley, author of Travels in West Africa (1897) and West African Studies (1899).* Wellcome Collection CC BY 4.0

ABOVE *A mobile print shop operated by the Royal Engineers mainly for the publication of official notices. It was also used for running off copies of the Ladysmith Lyre, a newspaper produced during the siege and edited by Steevens of the Daily Mail.*

Censorship in the name of operational security had been a concern of Buller's whilst he was serving as the army's adjutant general - and had been enthusiastically taken up by Lord Worsley, then commander-in-chief - but the government paled at curbing civil liberties and the proposal was shelved.

On the outbreak of war, Natal Colony was placed under martial law but in the more robust civil administration of Cape Colony life went on as usual until 1902 when censorship was finally introduced.

From his seat in Natal, Buller attempted to roll out his 1889 proposals, published as *Revised Rules for Newspaper Correspondents at the Seat of War*, which included refusing licenses for papers with low circulation, showing preference to correspondents who had served in the army, and restructuring licenses to one per outlet. Attempts to extend this to Cape Colony were quashed when Lord Roberts arrived and replaced Buller at the top. Roberts had a recent bestseller under his belt - *Forty-One Years in India: From Sub-Altern to Commander-in-Chief* (1897) - and preferred courting public opinion over coercing it. He organised photoshoots of his triumphant flag ceremonies in Pretoria and Johannesburg, made a great show of exempting the letters of war correspondents from censorship (as it

ABOVE *The editorial team of the Bloemfontein Friend, an army newspaper with Lord Roberts as its editor-in-chief. Kipling sits on the desk to the right.*

happened, patriotic newspaper owners did the job of censor for him), and even launched his own newspaper, the *Bloemfontein Friend*. For operational reasons, the South African press was a different matter. Without the bodyguard of vast distance, British troop movements could be published in Cape Town the next morning and telegraphed to the Boers by sympathetic Cape Afrikaners by lunchtime. Publication of local newspapers was subject to a three-week delay.

Major General Sir GW Nicholson, director of Military Intelligence in London, journeyed out to South Africa later in the war and noted approvingly in a letter to his wife: "I send you a *Johannesburg Star*, by glancing over which you will perceive how very little information or comment is allowed to leak out here. Not a single word has transpired in the local papers about Lord Methuen's operations of late."

Scorched Earth

The Guerrilla War, June 1900 - May 1902

The fall of Pretoria was followed by a series of engagements intended to mop up resistance, conducted as if British victory had already been earned. Rather than marking the end of the war as many believed, these engagements marked the death rattle of conventional warfare by the Boers.

A week after the capital's capitulation, Field Marshal Frederick Roberts, 1st Baron Roberts closed in on the minority Transvaal government which conducted its business from railway carriages on the line to Delagoa Bay. Roberts led some 14,000 men out from Pretoria where they were met in the field by Generals J. H. 'Koos' de la Ray of the Free State and Louis Botha of Transvaal. The Battle of Diamond Hill (June 11-12, 1900) was fought with a lack of conviction by both sides. Boer enthusiasm for meeting the British in the field had dwindled, and Roberts had impressed upon his subordinates the need to avoid unnecessary casualties. They sparred inconclusively for two days before the Boers simply melted away at the cost of 28 British dead, including the dashing Lieutenant Colonel David Ogilvy, 11th Earl of Airlie commanding the 12th Lancers. According to Dr Arthur Conan Doyle, Airlie's final words - characteristic of his breeding - were a rebuke to a foul-mouthed NCO.

In response to Lord Roberts's offer of amnesty, between March and July, 5,940 Boers of the Orange River Colony and 7,960 from Transvaal surrendered their arms and took an oath of neutrality. Committed to a future in which a partnership between Afrikaners, British settlers and (to a lesser extent) black Africans could raise up a loyal, unified and self-governing South Africa as the continent's Canada, the idea of neutrality played to Boer sensibilities: they would be left alone if they took no further part in the conflict. For many Afrikaners who had no conception of the increasingly anachronistic honour codes of European warfare, this was a cheerful fiction that allowed them to smile, nod, and ride off to rejoin their commando.

Boer resistance in the new Orange River Colony was headquartered in the verdant Brandwater Basin, east of the contested town of Lindley. A formidable natural citadel 75-miles across, the depression was ringed by a horseshoe of mountains nestled against the Caledon River and accessible to wagons only at six points. President Martinus Steyn and Gen Christiaan de Wet had led the remainder of the Free State forces to this Eden but the rapid approach of Lieutenant General Sir Archibald Hunter was making them reconsider. Tasked with pacifying the wild east, Hunter had advanced rapidly through Lindley and Bethlehem, his command swelling with reinforcements until it included the 12th, 20th and 21st Brigades, the 2nd and 3rd Cavalry Brigades, a brigade of Mounted Infantry, and the entire 8th Division and Colonial Division. ➤➤

'All that Was Left of Them' by the Victorian artist Richard Caton Woodville, showing the 17th Lancers making their valiant defence at the Battle of Elands River.

Humiliation at Brandwater Basin

On July 15, Wet and Steyn slipped away via Slabbert's Nek and headed north for the relative safety of the Transvaal. They were pursued by Brigadier General Robert Broadwood's 2nd Cavalry Brigade - thirsty for revenge after Sanna's Post, perhaps - in what was later known as 'The First de Wet Hunt'. Broadwood drew blood at Lindley on July 19 and then the two faced off in a mutually costly skirmish near Vredefort on July 24 that stripped the Boers of five of their supply wagons. By the slimmest margin, Wet and Steyn eventually slipped through the cordon that Major General Herbert Kitchener, 1st Earl Kitchener had flung up and made their way into Transvaal.

The holdouts at Brandwater Basin were under the command of the young Gen Paul Roux, a preacher of the Dutch Reformed Church, and had been ordered to attempt a breakout once Steyn and Wet were clear. Without the cool-headed influence of their leaders, the Burghers followed their instincts and embarked upon a time-consuming election to replace Roux with the elderly Gen Martinus Prinsloo. This carnival of democracy cost the Boers three weeks, by which time four of the six passes had passed into Hunter's hands.

The 8th Division took Commando's Nek and Generaal's Nek with little resistance, but Slabbet's Nek was more doggedly defended with the Boers dug in along a four-mile front. Only on the second day did Brabant's Horse discover that the enemy rifle pits on the far left of the Boer defensive positions were unoccupied and from their vantage

point offered a view down the entire line. The positions were taken on July 24 and the defenders were forced to withdraw. The same day, Hunter himself led the Highlanders onto Retief's Nek, having drawn some of the defenders away with a feint, and they too were forced from the pass. In the third action of July 24, elements of the 21st Brigade and the 3rd (Highland) Brigade took Naauwpoort Nek.

With their paradise looking increasingly like their prison, the Burghers continued to debate among themselves. They even approached Hunter with a request for a six-day armistice so that they might bicker in peace, but he had little need to accept and eventually Prinsloo decided to surrender. This was interrupted by another leadership election which returned Gen Roux to the top spot and he galloped off

to Hunter's field HQ to rescind the surrender, but it was too late. That night 1,500 diehards made for the Golden Gate pass, hauling their wagons and artillery up the sheer incline and along the narrow mountain path to freedom and the next morning the surrenders began. Over a week 4,314 Boers - amongst them, three generals - laid down their arms to Hunter, surrendering with them 2,800 cattle, 4,000 sheep, 6,000 horses, two million rounds of ammunition and the U Battery guns seized at the Battle of Sanna's Post (March 31, 1900).

The Job Half Done

In the northwest of Transvaal, Lord Roberts - his numbers bolstered by the release of the British POWs from the camp outside Pretoria - launched his final offensive against President

"This carnival of democracy cost the Boers three weeks..."

Troopers of the Johannesburg ZARP (Zuid-Afrikaansche Republiek Politie or South African Republic Police) in their dark blue tunics pose for the cameras earlier in the war. Zuid-Afrika Huis

Paul Kruger's travelling government-in-exile, which trundled up and down the line from Middelburg to Komatipoort. Middleburg was taken on July 27 and after finally pushing out of Natal, General Sir Redvers Buller joined Roberts for what they believed would be the conflict's coup de grâce.

Knowing that Roberts would attack his flanks, Gen Botha weakened his centre to bolster where he expected the British to strike. The Battle of Bergendal (August 21-27, 1900) was to be the last set-piece battle of the Great Boer War and was a victory by accident rather than design. Directed into the left flank - as Botha had foreseen - Buller instead discovered a salient in the centre caused by Botha's withdrawal of men. With his scouts unable to see any more enemy positions (as Roberts had already stripped him of some of his best cavalry), he reasonably assumed that this was the flank and attacked with overwhelming force. A forward position of 74 uniformed ZARP (Zuid-Afrikaansche Republiek Politie, South African Republic Police) found themselves cowering under perhaps the single heaviest bombardment of the war as for three solid hours Buller's 42 guns hammered their positions before 1,500 men of the Natal Field Force fixed bayonets and overran their positions in fierce close-quarter combat. With the centre levered open, Botha's lines crumbled. Witnesses of the Battle of Bergendal were struck not just by the apocalyptic intensity of the artillery, but by the coolness of the ZARP under fire.

The problem was that not since the Battle of Paardeberg (February 18 - 27, 1900) had the Transvaalers been prevented from retreating almost intact. Defeats had been inflicted, but the fighting men themselves simply moved on to fight another day. On September 1, Lord Roberts proclaimed the annexation of Transvaal and shortly afterwards the near-blind President Kruger left for Europe, ostensibly to seek allies but more likely to deny the British his capture. He would never return from his diplomatic tour. Gen Botha was now de facto leader of the Transvaal Boers and he formed new commandos, each one around 300-strong, and consisting of only the best men. Their commandants were appointed by Botha and these new guerrilla commandos were scattered across the highveldt, to continue the fight closer to their homes and families. The remainder - 3,000 unreliable, unwell or unwilling Afrikaners - were left at Komatipoort where they decided to destroy their ammunition and locomotives and limp across the border to Portuguese Mozambique.

The war to date had seen 4,185 British and colonials killed in combat and another 6,493 killed by typhoid, dysentery and other diseases. Another 34,499 combatants had been invalided home, although many with minor wounds as it was assumed the war would be over before they were healthy. The press had long since lost interest in South Africa, with Roberts's recent triumphs generating a fraction of the newsprint now being given over to the unfolding Boxer Rebellion in China.

In the apathetic 'Khaki Election' of October 24, 1900 - the low turnout generally empowered those who held strong feelings about the war - the government increased its majority by two and returned the returning hero Winston Spencer Churchill as MP for Oldham. Finally, on December 11, Lord Roberts and his family - pausing for a moment of contemplation at Colenso where the young Lt Frederick Roberts had fallen in battle - began their journey home, followed shortly afterwards by Buller. Both were greeted by cheering crowds, but Buller by conspicuously little official fanfare. The dominance of the 'Wolseley Circle' in the general staff and the bitter rivalry between 'Africans' and 'Indians' was ended. The increasingly marginalised and discredited figure of Field Marshal Sir Garnet Wolseley - only two years shy of a full half-century in the British Army - was replaced as commander-in-chief by the further ennobled 1st Earl Roberts.

On October 8, Sir Alfred Milner, High Commissioner for South Africa, was appointed administrator of the two new colonies, and with the departure of Buller and Roberts, the indefatigable Lord Kitchener was placed in charge of putting down what his mentor referred to dismissively as "unrest." ❱❱

ABOVE: *Boer POWs who have taken the oath of neutrality gather in Pretoria, waiting to be issued passes to return to their homes. Stereograph from 1901.*

ABOVE: *A suitably regal portrait of General Louis Botha, the senior most commander of the Transvaal Boers after the flight of President Paul Kruger to Europe.* Zuid-Afrika Huis

ABOVE: *The ruins of General Christiaan de Wet's farm, destroyed by order of Field Marshal Frederick Roberts, 1st Baron Roberts.*

Bitter Seeds

There was no coordinated masterplan between the Boer resistance, known as 'bitter-enders' in contrast to the 'hands-uppers' who stuck by their oaths of neutrality ('bittereinders' and 'henssoppers' in Afrikaans). The Second Boer War was now in the hands of disparate bands of the most hardened and experienced guerrillas, who struck at the long stretches of railway, bringing down bridges, cutting the track and derailing trains, ambushing patrols and isolating unwary garrisons. They were commanded by some of the most aggressive of the Boer leaders - men like Christiaan de Wet, J.H. 'Koos' de la Rey and Louis Botha who had replaced the old guard over the course of the conflict, and men like Jan Smuts who were shortly about to.

Between October 1900 and September 1901, the railway was severed on nearly 200 occasions and the British response to what they saw as banditry escalated tensions considerably. Lord Roberts had made much of his fairness but his final few months in the field foreshadowed the direction his protegee would pursue. Much blame has been levelled at the feet of Lady Nora Roberts, who followed her husband to Pretoria in August 1900. Her grief at the death of their only son had curdled into hatred and her arrival marked a hardening in Roberts' attitude to the Boers.

On June 7, 1900, Gen de Wet made three simultaneous attacks along the Rhenoster River at positions held by the 4th The Sherwood Foresters (Derbyshire) Regiment, a militia battalion drafted in for the most basic of tasks. They fought more fiercely than their commanders might have hoped, taking 36 dead and 104 wounded before they dropped their weapons, allowing the commando to destroy the railway bridge and then move on to ransack the supply depot at Roodewal Station, liberating winter clothing and ammunition, and tearing through 1,500 sacks of personal mail for cigarettes and chocolate. To their discredit, some of the POWs were unable to restrain themselves and joined in. Wet buried 600 crates of ammunition for later recovery and set the rest ablaze, before making off with 800 prisoners.

Roberts had been initially opposed to the burning of farms - he had seen it breed only resentment and resistance in British India's restive northwest frontier - but in response to the Rhenoster raids, he sanctioned the torching of farms nearest the railway. This he justified on the basis that the guerrillas could not have struck without the 'knowledge and connivance' of nearby farmers.

To make a point, he ordered them to begin with Wet's own property. Under Lord Kitchener's direction, the burning of farms became widespread policy wherever guerrillas were deemed to be active. Neutral Afrikaners were placed in an impossible position - those who refused to support the commandos were seen as traitors by their neighbours and driven out - whilst even the most inconclusive suggestion of sympathy to the bitter-enders elicited the destruction of their property and the seizure or slaughter of their herds.

Reverend Father Francis Timoney, chaplain of the mounted New South Wales Citizens Bushmen, wrote on October 14, 1900: "Then began the most diabolical work I have yet witnessed. Every home in the valley, probably 20 in all, was burned to the ground. Women and children stood in groups, the children rending the air with their cries. They were allowed to move their furniture before the match was put to the building. The women were admirable. Not a tear bedimmed their eyes. [...] The wisecracks say that this vandalism will terminate the war. My opinion, shared by every intelligent man, is that it will prolong the war indefinitely."

This was by even contemporary standards a war crime. It represented the deliberate destruction and intimidation of a civilian population in defiance of the Brussels Declaration of 1874 and the Hague Convention of 1899. Martial law was finally extended to even Cape Colony in January 1901 - the autonomy of the Cape government crudely trampled by its British counterpart - passes were required for travel, curfews were enforced, horses not required for farm work

ABOVE: *Major General Herbert Kitchener, 1st Earl Kitchener, pictured in South Africa. Appointed commander-in-chief in South Africa in late 1900, he directed the British response to the guerrilla war.*
Zuid-Afrika Huis

were seized, and stockpiling of any goods which could be used to supply commandos in the field - tobacco, blankets, horseshoes and so on - was prohibited.

The policy birthed by Roberts and raised to adulthood by Kitchener resulted in the destruction of an estimated 30,000 farms and 40 entire towns, and from June 1901, the controversial and catastrophic crowding of enormous numbers of civilian Afrikaners - mostly women, children and the elderly - and their black servants into a network of concentration camps.

Africa's Most Wanted

The guerrilla war made little difference to the way that Gen de Wet fought. He had always kept his own counsel and allowed himself to be guided by the two corps of professional scouts. What did govern his movements was the growing pressure from Kitchener's 'flying columns', especially after the Battle of Bothaville (November 6, 1900) when he was forced to abandon his remaining artillery to a surprise attack by 600 men of the 5th and 8th Mounted Infantry under Lieutenant Colonel P. W. J. Le Gallais.

Mostly made up of irregulars with knowledge of the veldt and local languages, the flying columns travelled light for speed and tracked the guerrillas by day, whilst a second column attacked the Boers by cover of darkness where they would struggle to escape. Few were as successful as Lt Col George Elliot Benson's notorious No. 3 Flying Column. Disciplined and driven, Benson was able to cover enormous distances under cover of darkness with help from his black guides, and testament to his reputation is Botha's own desire to bring him down. He got his chance at

ABOVE: *A cheery stereoscopic photograph of the irregular Rimington's Scouts (or Rimington's Tigers from their tiger skin hatband) taking tea in a destroyed Boer home.* Museums Victoria

the Battle of Bakenlaagte (October 30, 1901) by using Benson's bogged-down supply column as bait and ambushing the colonel himself in the drizzle.

Playing cat and mouse with Kitchener alone would not bring Britain to the negotiating table so Wet decided to dispatch commandos to Cape Colony and in doing so push Kitchener to extend his repressive policies on the colony.

Gen Pieter Kritzinger crossed the Orange River on three occasions to rampage through the Cape, but during his third attempt he was shot, wounded, and captured trying to rescue fallen comrades from a British ambush. Another prominent guerrilla leader, the former Free State supreme court judge Gen J. B. M. Hertzog - addressed even in war as 'Judge Hertzog' - drove 150 miles deep into Cape Colony and, unlike Kritzinger, evaded capture.

The most impressive of the new Boer commanders, however, was the 30-year-old Jan Smuts. The former Transvaal attorney general attached himself to 'Koos' de la Rey after Pretoria fell and on June 20, 1901, was ➤➤

"The wisecracks say this vandalism will terminate the war."

"Burning farmhouses for treachery." Lord Kitchener's 'scorched earth' strategy at work in Cape Colony.

placed at the head of a 362-man commando and pointed towards the Cape. It was a gristly affair from the outset, with six of his men killed by a freak bolt of lightning before they even set off, with another 30 lost to one of Kitchener's sweeps as they crossed the Orange River. Their fodder froze solid and their coats were soaked with rain, they finally found success at the Battle of Elands River (September 17, 1901), using the heavy morning mist to encircle C Squadron of the 17th Lancers who had been entrusted with the pass at Elands River Poort. Of the 130-man squadron, 29 were killed and 41 wounded making it the worst day in the regiment's history, eclipsing even the Charge of the Light Brigade at the Battle of Balaclava (October 25, 1854). The Boers rearmed, resupplied and - with fatal consequences for many of their number - swapped their sodden rags for crisp new British uniforms. Now they were able to take British patrols unawares by posing as the very men they had butchered, but it also left them open to summary execution if captured.

It was the trial of the 22-year old Com Gideon Scheepers that stirred the outrage of not just Afrikaners, but of the British public. Wrongly sentenced to death for treason on the assumption that he was a Cape Afrikaner, he was in fact born in Transvaal. Scheepers came to Wet's notice as one of his scouts before being elected commandant and sent into the Cape to raise hell. Burning out those Afrikaners he

Commandant Piet Kritzinger as a prisoner of the British at Graaff-Reinet. He was later tried by the Graaff-Reinet Military Tribunal and narrowly escaped the death sentence. Zuid-Afrika Huis

"Now they were able to take British patrols unawares..."

The great guerrilla commander General Christiaan de Wet and his staff. Wet himself is third from the right. Zuid-Afrika Huis

ABOVE: *An illustration showing the alleged cruelty of the Boers towards black Africans at Klerksdorp in the southern Transvaal.*

one of Kitchener's drives in a letter to his sister, Maud: "A line of mounted men, their right on the railway and stretching away to the horizon, advancing at a slow canter, with the wretched band of terrified Boers hustled along in front, with five armoured trains keeping pace with them and helping them along with a liberal hail of bullets and 6-pdr shells [...] They made a sort of stand outside Wolverhoek, but of course had no chance at all, and all soon surrendered."

Forts had first been erected along railway lines from June 1900 as part of Roberts' reaction to the Rheonoster raid. These were fortified positions, usually, trenches or rifle pits with walls of sandbags or sangers of heaped stones and surrounded by a tangle of wire. In late 1900 when it became clear that railways - particularly bridges and junctions - were the focal point of guerrilla hit-and-runs, Kitchener ordered the construction of three-storey stone blockhouses based on a design by Colonel Elliot Wood, Royal Engineers.

Wood's design had a low corrugated iron roof and steel-rimmed firing holes on each floor, two steel boxes jutting out from opposite corners to provide crossfire, and the ground floor - which mostly consisted of a water tank - could only be accessed from the first floor. The entrance to the blockhouse was set above ground level on the first floor so that the ladder could be pulled up for additional security. As guerrilla attacks increased in both frequency and range, spreading well into ➤➤

regarded as collaborators and executing blacks he suspected were spying for the British, he was pursued relentlessly for months before he grew too ill with abdominal pain to ride. Left behind by the commando, Scheepers was captured on October 12, 1901, and executed by firing squad on January 18, 1902. Young, handsome, and ostensibly fighting for freedom, his plight moved US President Theodore Roosevelt to implore Britain to: "set aside the sentence in the interest of humanity." It was already too late, but the American reaction helped bring an end to the executions of captured Boer leaders.

The Fox and Hounds

Like a pheasant shoot, Kitchener's co-ordinated flying columns acted as beaters, sweeping the veldt area by area in a line, driving the Boers towards infantry pickets and fixed positions. These great tangles of barbed wire punctuated every couple of miles by fortified posts which bristled with rifle barrels crosshatched the veldt, often following the major railway arteries from town to town and coast to coast. In contrast to the 'hunt', these were described as 'drives'.

The aristocratic Second Lieutenant the Honourable John 'Jack' Lyttelton, 7th Rifle Brigade (Prince Consort's Own), described

ABOVE: *A posed photograph of a group of Boer guerrillas picking out a distant British patrol from the cover of a railway siding.*

Cape Colony, stone blockhouses were deemed too costly and time-consuming and Wood's model was replaced by a simpler construction devised by his fellow sapper, Major Spring Rice. The Rice blockhouse consisted of a single corrugated iron cylinder with a second cylinder inside and the void filled with stones or earth, and these could be built in six hours by only six men. They were less durable, but after the mass surrender at Brandwater Basin and the scattering of the Transvaalers at Komatipoort, the Boers had little heavy ordnance left and it took something like an improvised hand grenade - rigged up from blasting dynamite - to crack one open. Yet, as Lt Lyttleton wrote, they attacked them anyway: "The Boers would crawl up to within 50 yards [...] make themselves comfortable behind some rocks and begin sniping the sentry; of course the men inside the blockhouse begin shooting all round a few hundred rounds, during which time the Boer sits snugly behind his rock and when the firing stops, begins hurrying off at dawn. Neither of them, blockhouse or [Boer], ever hit a man doing this so it doesn't matter much, and helps keep the sentry awake."

By mid-1901 a network of around 9,000 blockhouses covered some 5,000 miles of track, and at its greatest extent required 56,000 to stand sentry, a tedious and anxiety-inducing duty. Men played cards and smoked

ABOVE: *Commandant Gideon Scheepers is driven to his place of execution in an ambulance. His wrongful conviction by the Graaff-Reinet Military Tribunal on grounds he was a British subject shocked the world.* Zuid-Afrika Huis
LEFT: *A formidable Colonel Elliot Wood-designed blockhouse on the Modder River, from the collection of Sister Mabel Warner, Princess Christian's Army Nursing Service (Reserve).* Museums Victoria
BELOW: *Gen de Wet breaks through the blockhouse line by driving a herd of cattle through the gap in this melodramatic painting by Fritz Neumann.*

endlessly, scanning the horizon for saboteurs, and straining to hear the warnings of their tripwires rattling an empty mess tin. A typical blockhouse was held by a junior NCO and six men, a lieutenant would be in charge of three to four blockhouses and a captain between ten and 12, allowing a single battalion to occupy around 60 blockhouses and stand watch over a distance of perhaps 90 miles.

Down to the Wire

Gen de Wet bullishly dismissed Kitchener's blockhouse strategy as the "the policy of the blockhead" and with good reason, it tied down enormous numbers of British soldiers and whilst it gave him momentary pause, Wet was able to slip the net on February 6, 1901, by cutting the wire and driving a herd of cattle through the gap.

The strain placed on British manpower encouraged Kitchener to re-arm around 5,000 Boer 'hands-uppers' who had previously fought against him - even approaching the veteran Gen Piet Cronjé to lead them. These National Scouts, as they were officially known - many British preferred 'tame Boers' - were despised by the guerrillas who took no prisoners when it came to traitors. Kitchener also enlisted Bantu as armed sentries for the overstretched blockhouses and turned a blind eye to their use as scouts by his flying columns. Whilst Roberts had consented to using Africans as dispatch riders so long as they weren't armed or in uniform, Kitchener had no such qualms and in July 1901, Gen Kritzinger warned that any black auxiliary, whether he bore arms or not, would be shot if he fell into the hands of the Boers.

Both recruitment of blacks and hands-uppers were guaranteed to further antagonise, as if feelings could possibly reach any greater fury after the trials, executions, drives and concentration camps. Whilst Lord Roberts had trodden carefully in the hope that South Africa could be rebuilt as a prosperous and self-governing part of the empire, Kitchener appeared to be pursuing a policy of widening division.

He repeatedly dodged the War Office's queries about the number of blacks he had in service, finally offering the total of 10,053 in March 1902 - a figure that his critics in Parliament believed far closer to 30,000. Though Wet denied it, Kitchener's strategy of blockhouses, concentration camps and scorched earth choked the resistance of even the bitterest of the bitter-enders. It cost them food and fodder, shelter, and supply, and it forced them to either attack the lines and breakout or wait to be driven into them by the periodic sweep of the British mounted columns. Men like Wet, Rey, Botha and Smuts were increasingly confined to the frontier fiefdoms they had managed to drive British patrols from, but blockhouse by blockhouse Kitchener's grip around these remote safe havens tightened also.

ABOVE: *The Second Contingent of the South Australian Mounted Rifles, October 1899. Trooper Harry Harbord 'Breaker' Morant is third from the left.*

On January 1, 1901, the colonies of Australia federated into a single state. Many of the men who went out to South Africa as Tasmanians or Queenslanders found themselves returning simply as Australians. After World War One and especially after World War Two, which saw Australia grow even more divided and disillusioned with the 'leadership' of Great Britain, the Boer War increasingly meant not sacrifice and duty, but betrayal - a betrayal personified by the trial and execution of Lt Harry Harbord 'Breaker' Morant. This narrative was kept alive by Bruce Beresford's 1980 film *Breaker Morant*, starring Edward Woodward in the title role, which is considered a classic of the Australian New Wave of cinema.

Born in Britain as Edwin Henry Murrant, almost everything about Morant's life is contested by design. He claimed aristocratic origins - and to be the estranged son of a British admiral - but he was born to a workhouse master and matron, and for 15 years he drifted around rural Queensland as a drover and horse-breaker, and allegedly a gambler and womaniser, and earned fame in the outback successfully riding Dargin's Grey, a notorious buck-jumper. He also wrote bush-poetry under the name of 'The Horsebreaker' or 'The Breaker', which was published in the nationalist magazine *The Bulletin* whose now unpalatable masthead read 'Australia for the White Man'. In short, it might have been built on falsehood and self-aggrandisement, but the life and death of Breaker Morant was exactly how Australia liked to see itself at a time when its collective identity was still being sculpted.

Morant sailed for South Africa with the South Australian Mounted Rifles and later joined the Bushveldt Carbineers, one of the highly mobile battalions of mounted irregulars raised for the guerrilla war. After their commanding officer, Captain Percy Hunt, was killed and according to Morant (but nobody else) mutilated, the remaining officers went on a rampage. Not all the Carbineers approved. One, a justice of the peace in his civilian life, wrote a letter detailing the crimes and sent it to the senior British officer in the district. Trooper Robert Mitchell Cochrane's statement - co-signed by 15 of his fellow Carbineers - detailed six incidents in which prisoners, both combatants and civilians, were murdered. At least three of these incidents directly implicated Morant.

The toll of these crimes was the murder of 11 Boer prisoners of war, four Dutch schoolteachers, a German missionary, four Boer children, and one of their own comrades, Tpr B. J. van Buuren who objected to the killings and told the victims' families what had happened. On one occasion, a father and his two sons were made to dig their own graves by Morant who then ordered them shot. Although the numbers were not recorded by Cochrane, at least four black Africans were also killed in these encounters as potential witnesses.

At a court of inquiry, Morant, Lt Peter Handcock and Lt George Witton were sentenced to death. Witton was granted a reprieve by Kitchener, who believed he had been under the influence of Handcock and Morant, and he was released in 1904. Bitter, unwell, and still carrying the stain of his conviction, Witton set down his version of events in a book entitled *Scapegoats of the Empire* (1907), which maintained that Morant and his comrades were nothing more than victims of British hypocrisy. Witton's account was so persuasive that throughout World War One, the Australian government refused British courts-martial any jurisdiction over the Australian Imperial Force (AIF). Witton's assertion that the prosecution of the Carbineers was politically motivated, both to appease the Boers before peace talks and to satisfy critics at home, is likely true, but multiple accounts attest to the crimes as well as the role of Lt Harry Harbord Morant in carrying them out.

Perhaps his death was not fair, but it was arguably just.

ABOVE: *A group photograph of Second Contingent NCOs, circa 1900. Then Corporal Morant is second left in the middle row.*

Methods of Barbarism

Concentration Camps in South Africa

Of all the acts of inhumanity and the terrible losses of life during the Great Boer War - from the dreadful slaughter of Spion Kop to the needless waste of life during the typhoid epidemic at Bloemfontein - nothing has endured like the memory of the British concentration camps.

From late 1900 when the first camps were erected, to 1902 when the war ended, between 18,000 and 28,000 Boers died in epidemics caused by the miserable conditions, with 80% of their victims being children. Perhaps as many black victims also perished, their numbers sadly unrecorded. In war it is almost inevitable that the innocent bear the heaviest burden, but part of the tragedy of the British concentration camps in South Africa is that they began as an act of unthinking largesse. In September 1900, the first Boer refugees - families whose men had taken an oath of neutrality and had been burned out of their homes by guerrillas - began to cluster around Bloemfontein and Pretoria seeking the protection of British bayonets. By the time Field Marshal Frederick Roberts,

1st Baron Roberts handed over control to his protegee and began his journey back to Britain, there were nine camps.

These were opened as refugee camps. They were a humanitarian response to the thousands of displaced Afrikaner and black families fleeing from the war. The Boers were housed in army tents with little provision for sanitation or supply. Just as the febrile infrastructure of Bloemfontein had buckled under the weight of the British Army in the middle of 1900, it would do so again under the weight of thousands of displaced Boers.

On October 17, 1900, one unnamed woman quoted by the campaigner Emily Hobhouse wrote: "We are half an hour from Bloemfontein, in a camp; they call it the refugee camp. There are 23 families in the camp. We are placed 12 in one tent, and your mother is cook, for we were forbidden to bring servants [...] There are no cattle here, and we have to use mule dung to light the fire with."

The phrase 'concentration camp' in relation to events in South Africa was first uttered in

Parliament in reference to the Reconcentrados established by the Spanish during their ugly colonial wars in Cuba (1895-1898) and the Philippines (1896-1898). Over a century later it invites unhelpful comparisons to the system set up by the Third Reich during the Holocaust, but without wishing to minimise the immense suffering and needless loss of life, the British concentration camps were not intended to kill and their purpose was not collective punishment, although both of those things happened regardless.

Kitchener's Catastrophe

On December 21, 1900, Major General Herbert Kitchener, 1st Earl Kitchener announced an enormous expansion of the camp system to not just house refugees but to create them: "Of the various methods suggested for the accomplishment of this object (ending the guerrilla war), one which has been

BELOW *Refugees were first accommodated in Johannesburg in December 1900 before being moved to the Turffontein racecourse and then finally into army tents.*

strongly recommended and has lately been successfully tried on a small scale, is the removal of all men, women, and children and natives from the district which the enemy's bands persistently occupy."

Whether they left willingly or unwillingly no longer mattered as the ends justified the means. He also created a system of privilege and want: Hands-uppers and their families were given preferential treatment, better rations, and better accommodation, whilst the families of Boers still in the field were second class citizens. Rations consisted of

flour, sugar, coffee, salt, condensed milk, and meat, with far smaller portions and no meat at all issued to the families of men on commando. There was a complete absence of fresh fruit and vegetables of any kind - the best the Boers could do was scavenge for roots in the veldt - and fresh milk, which was reserved for camp hospitals and infants. Often the meat issued had already started to rot, and the Boers - used to fresh meat and vegetables - were wary of the tinned meat supplied by the British Army.

The supply chains which had proved so deadly for so many British soldiers during the typhoid epidemic were no more able to handle the tent cities filled with demoralised families, elderly and infants which had sprung up in their shadow. Their populations grew enormously over the first few months of 1901 after peace talks between Kitchener and Gen Louis Botha, representing the Transvaal bitter-enders, disintegrated. Insisting that Botha left him little choice, Kitchener escalated what he himself described as the "very unpleasant and repugnant" business of burning farms and deporting their owners. Tents were without groundsheets or cot beds, there were no building materials for hospitals or latrines, medical supplies were lacking and medics almost entirely volunteers, and there were no clothes or blankets. What sanitation arrangements had

been dug or supplies of clean water that existed were soon swamped and disease flourished.

In theory, each camp had a doctor, but the shortage of medical personnel meant that many had to make do with periodic visits from the nearest available military doctor or a district health officer. Not all of those who did have a medical staff fared better. At

Bethulie - one of the most infamous in the system - their first doctor was dismissed after assaulting patients, whilst the second was an incompetent and a drunk. Typhoid, dysentery, scarlet fever, pneumonia, and measles raged largely unchecked. Amongst the children who made up an estimated 60% of the population of the camps - their immune systems ravaged by malnutrition and starvation - measles proved especially fatal.

An inhabitant of Volksrust camp in Natal, Elizabeth Neethling wrote: "Bad food, bad sanitation, bad shelter, wet floors, insufficient covering in the severe weather, are amongst the causes. Disease itself would not have claimed so many victims, but when disease came,

ABOVE *The school at Norvalspont was made compulsory for all school-aged children in the camp.*

RIGHT *Suffragist, pacifist, and campaigner Emily Hobhouse, by the Australian portrait photographer Henry Walter Barnett.*

their constitutions had been undermined by hardships suffered since falling into the hands of their enemies; and when patients did pass the crisis and become convalescent, there was nothing they could digest, not to speak of tempting the appetite. So, after all, cruel though it seems to say so, the great majority died of actual starvation."

Black refugees, many miners driven from the goldfields, labourers on farms which had been put to the flame, or servants who had followed their Boer masters, were also placed in camps. Unlike their white counterparts, they were expected to fend for themselves. They were able to work to improve their lot and there was plenty of work going, although an arrangement that concentrated cheap labour on the outskirts of major towns was always going to benefit the employer more than the employee.

At Kitchener's urging, the Army Labour Department was rearranged by the Canadian Major Henri-Gustave Joly de Lotbinière into the Department of Native Refugees (DNR), whose first order of business was re-opening the gold mines. In Transvaal, Lotbinière closed some camps and dumped their inhabitants onto empty farms with the expectation that they would feed the British Army and themselves. The remaining DNR camps - 38 in Orange River Colony and 28 in Transvaal - were run almost exclusively as labour camps, with Lotbinière's staff subcontracting workers out to various branches of the army. Though few first-hand accounts exist and few white do-gooders paid heed, the conditions in the black camps were worse than those of their white counterparts with no medical facilities, little sanitation, and little or no food issued by the authorities. One medical report dated March 31, 1901, read: "Much sickness in refugees in camp Heidelberg. There are 600 coloured people in the camp here. Many suffering from the fever aggravated by want of proper food [...] They are mostly living on the carcasses of animals dead of lung sickness."

That Bloody Woman

From the very beginning, Kitchener had proven evasive about his scorched earth strategy, prompting St John Brodrick, Lord Lansdowne's successor as Secretary of State for War, to grumble: "Why does Kitchener never tell us anything except the record of every Boer cow his troops have caught by the hind leg?"

He first reported on the camps to Brodrick in December 1901 - a full six months after they had been opened - and even then, neglected to mention that he was driving Boers to them by force. Having created the problem, Kitchener - who was no more interested in administration than Roberts - attempted to offload it as quickly as possible. Whilst the DNR camps remained exclusively military, he turned over most of the Boer camps to Sir Henry Milner, the high commissioner for South Africa, who represented the civilian administration. Milner went on a recruitment drive for medical volunteers and appointed civilian superintendents.

Although the man at the top of each camp no longer wore Khaki, they continued to be managed - insomuch as they had been managed - by the army. This was particularly the case in the unstable Transvaal where Major George Goodwin was appointed general superintendent, able to overrule the civilian superintendents and answering to Transvaal's military governor rather than Milner.

In January 1901, Britain was forced to

BELOW *Bantu labourers hoisting railway lines for the Department of Native Refugees (DNR). It was paid work, but not by much.*

ABOVE *The black refugees at Kimberley camp who were expected to feed themselves. When the Department of Native Refugees (DNR) took over, the inmates were put to work farming.*

gaze upon the unfolding horror by the life-long radical Emily Hobhouse who filed the first of her reports from South Africa to the *Manchester Guardian*. A suffragist and pacifist, she campaigned against the Second Boer War as chair of the women's section of the South African Conciliation Committee, and when war was waged regardless of her objections, she founded the South African Women and Children Distress Fund to raise money for struggling Boer families. In December 1900, armed with letters of introduction from prominent Liberal MPs, she pitched up in South Africa to distribute alms and to see the situation for herself. Milner, impressed by her credentials, arranged for her to see whatever she wanted to see.

Hobhouse immediately made her presence felt, not just handing out blankets and writing scathing dispatches, but challenging camp authorities. Thanks to Hobhouse, soap was taken off the list of luxuries, and kettles were made more readily available for the sterilisation of water. She also documented everything she saw in heart-breaking detail, writing of the camp at Aliwal North where up to 25 people a day died from disease: "The full realisation of the position dawned on me - it was a death rate such as had never been known except in the times of the Great Plagues. The whole talk was of death - who died yesterday, who lay dying today, and who would be dead tomorrow."

Hobhouse's *Report of a Visit to the Camps of Women and Children in the Cape and Orange River Colonies* (1901) lit a fire under the Liberal Party, who aside from a few outraged outliers had been rather muted on the matter. Opposition leader, Sir Henry Campbell-Bannerman exploded into life at a banquet on June 14, 1901, to thunder: "When is a war not a war? When it is carried out by methods of barbarism in South Africa." Another prominent Liberal peacemaker (and another future Prime Minister), David Lloyd George, described it in the Commons as "a policy of extermination against children."

Reform without Blame

The government, which had been wrongfooted by Kitchener's misleading missives, charged another leading light in the women's suffrage movement, Millicent Fawcett, to investigate at the head of a six-woman commission. The Fawcett Commission visited all the Boer camps but one and like Hobhouse failed to visit any of the black camps.

The government got what it wanted out of the Fawcett Commission. Unlike Hobhouse, Fawcett made no mention of the farm burnings, the mass theft of livestock, or the forced deportations, and instead viewed the camps as a necessary answer to the ravages of war. Regardless of their divergent conclusions, there was no difference in their recommendations. Conditions began to improve, mortality rates began to decline and in November 1901, Kitchener ordered that no more Boers be rounded up.

Supplies of disinfectant, timber and galvanised steel buckets arrived to enable the construction and maintenance of proper latrines at a ratio of one per every ten people. By 1902, each camp employed an engineer to monitor water quality, lay pipes and bore wells. Clean water meant not just reduced contamination, but the ability to sterilise surgical implements, cooking pots, and soiled clothing, and thereby reduce disease.

Ration scales were improved - although supply did not always meet demand - to reverse the horrendous mortality rates which had claimed the lives of one in every four Boer children behind the wire. By the end of the war, frozen meat was being imported from Australia and the rations for under-fives consisted of milk, flour, oats, sugar, syrup, butter salt, soap, and vegetables.

Young Boer women called 'probationers' were appointed as nursing aids and by 1902 every camp had 20 probationers working in its hospital. More than just providing direly needed personnel, the probationers were vital in building the trust of the Boer mothers who were wary of the British staff and preferred to nurse their own children.

The Grave of Two Republics

The End of the Great Boer War

The war ended because it had to. The British were weary, and the Boers had no cards left to play. The fighting showed no sign of winding down and whilst the bitter-enders believed passionately in the principles they were fighting for it was not clear how they were going to make them a reality.

On March 7, 1902 in the wild western Transvaal where Kitchener's blockhouse system had yet to intrude, a British column attempting to pin down General 'Koos' de la Rey became itself prey, attacked by the Boers in the rear and on the right flank. The Battle of Tweebosch was a final embarrassment for Britain, and amongst the 68 killed, 121 wounded, and 205 prisoners was Lieutenant General Paul Methuen, 3rd Baron Methuen. As he rode to rally his men, a bullet passed through his thigh and killed his horse, breaking the general's leg in the fall. With the medical care available to the Boers so rudimentary, Rey organised a wagon to take Methuen back to British lines with his belongings to receive treatment. Lord Methuen walked with a cane for the rest of his life, but he made a firm friend of Gen Rey. Was reconciliation really so impossible?

Despite the undeniable cruelty of his scorched earth policy, Kitchener was not necessarily a cruel man, he simply gave little thought to anything other than the most direct possible route to his objective. In February 1901, he met Gen Louis Botha at Middleburg for a tentative conference. Botha protested the farm clearances, the deportations, and the executions of Cape rebels. Kitchener was perfectly happy to ease off on all counts and made it clear that although both former republics would become British Crown colonies, they would in time receive autonomy. It's unclear whether Botha had the authority to negotiate on behalf of the Transvaal Boers, but it was a moot point - as soon as the High Commissioner arrived he refused to relent on the prosecution of Cape rebels with the fullest sentence available to traitors. Kitchener wrote to the Secretary of State for War, St John Brodrick complaining that: "[Sir Alfred] Milner's views may be strictly just, but to my mind they are vindictive." Not that he seemed outraged by the 'vindictiveness' of his own farm burnings or concentration camps but capturing the intricacy of Lord Kitchener's moral compass would tax the skills of even the most surrealistic artist.

BELOW: *The capture of Lieutenant General Paul Methuen, 3rd Baron Methuen at the Battle of Tweebosch by Fritz Neumann.*

ABOVE: *When the War is Over' by Udo Keppler, 1900 shows Britannia promising a wounded Boer and racist caricature of an African the benefits of British government: trade, schools, mines, railways, and democracy.*

Kitchener's Compromises

The same day as Methuen's capture at Tweebosch, Kitchener made passive-aggressive overtures to the Boers. The Dutch government had approached London with a proposal to mediate between the warring parties, and Kitchener had been copied in on the response: "The quickest and most satisfactory means of arranging a settlement would be by direct communication between the leaders of the Boer forces in South Africa and the commander-in-chief of His Majesty's Force." (It should be noted that Queen Victoria had died in January 1901, and the British Empire's reigning monarch was now her son, King Edward VII.) Kitchener passed this without comment, but the subtext was clear: well, go on then, give it another go.

Armed with guarantees of safe-passage, six Boer leaders - acting president Schalk Burger, and Generals Louis Botha and 'Koos' de la Rey representing the Transvaalers, and President Martinus Steyn, and Generals Christiaan de Wet and J. B. 'Judge' Hertzog representing the Free Staters - met to discuss their options. They voted to parlay and on April 12, 1902, the six leading bitter-enders travelled to Pretoria to meet Kitchener. The starting point was not auspicious: Burger opened the proceedings by reading out a laborious proposal that answered the gripes of 1899 - votes for the Uitlanders, for example - but refused to acknowledge that the Boer republics now consisted of a few wretched stretches of bandit country. Kitchener cabled London with this absurd return to the status quo and London said ➤➤

ABOVE: *General Louis Botha (centre left) and Major General Herbert Kitchener, 1st Earl Kitchener (centre right) at Middleburg in February 1901. The British representatives wear black armbands to mourn the passing of Queen Victoria on January 22.* Zuid-Afrika Haus

ABOVE: *Alfred Milner, 1st Baron Milner British High Commissioner for South Africa and Governor of Cape Colony, pictured on a visit to London in 1901.*

town of Vereeniging southeast of Johannesburg, where 60 delegates - 30 from each republic - were accommodated and a marquee was erected for their talking shop. Each delegate was given a pass to guarantee their safety as they transited British lines and they were permitted to bring an aide and an orderly. Kitchener had no interest in the political or diplomatic ramifications, only bringing an end to the fighting. The voices of the neutral hands-uppers - representing the majority of Afrikaners in the former republics - weren't heard, nor were the voices of the black population - the traditional owners of the land who continued to outnumber both the Boers and British by a significant margin. Neither were the opinions of the 'coloured' population - the Indians, the Malays and those of mixed-heritage - deemed worthy of consideration.

no. The conference met again on April 14, this time with Milner - now Baron Milner - in attendance. No more conciliatory than he had been at Middleburg, Milner's starting point - not unreasonably - was that British rule over the former republics was an established fact.

The schism between military and civilian approaches to peace was answered on the Boer side by the marked differences between the Transvaalers and the Free Staters. Botha and Schalk were eager for a settlement at almost any cost, but Steyn and Wet had fought so hard and lost so much, and all they had left was their dignity and anything short of independence was unacceptable. They could speak for their Burghers, but decisions of this scale could not be made without their consent. An armistice was proposed to give the bitter-enders time to meet, but Kitchener refused - time, after all, was on the side of attrition. Instead, Kitchener arranged a meeting on the Transvaal/Orange border at the

ABOVE: *A pro-Boer print from 1902, showing a woman and child amid burning farm buildings. The text at the bottom reads: "It is uncertain where fate will take us, may hope remain."*

ABOVE: *The young Transvaal lawyer-turned-outlaw, General Jan Smuts. Treated like a son by President Paul Kruger, Smuts was as respected for his legal brain as he was his tactical prowess.*

The Peace of Vereeniging

On May 15, 1902, the Boers met for the first time and shared horror stories of conditions at the front, the loss of men to the sweeps and blockhouses, rumours of Bantu risings, starvation, sickness, and defeat. Few had good news to share, but the Transvaalers in particular made for a miserable sight: their emaciated skin pulled tight and their clothing ragged.

Divisions quickly made themselves felt. The Free State delegates were all generals and they had agreed amongst themselves that no peace would be accepted at the cost of independence. The 30 Transvaalers were men of various ranks, from generals down to field cornets, and two were landdrosts, local magistrates. Only an intervention from the two most respected

"The Boers met for the first time and shared horror stories..."

A military band strikes up at Gundagai, New South Wales to celebrate the end of the Great Boer War.

ABOVE: *The Queen's South Africa Medal issued to anyone in the theatre from 1899. Those who served from 1901 were issued with the King's South Africa Medal which bore the profile of King Edward VII instead. This one was issued to Sergeant Major John Close who served with 1st Kitchener's Fighting Scouts.*
© Museums Victoria / CC BY

triumphed. Eventually, even Rey was forced to ask: "There has been talk of fighting to the bitter end. But has the bitter end already come?"

By May 17, the majority favoured some sort of settlement and a five-man negotiating team of Botha, Wet, Rey, Smuts and Hertzog met Kitchener and Milner at Melrose House in Pretoria. The first proposal - that the republics become British protectorates, allowing them to retain the fig leaf of independence whilst leaving them beholden to Britain - was rejected outright by Milner who never lost sight of his dreams of a single South Africa. For the second half of May, the Boers pleaded for any settlement that would allow them the dignity of their liberty, if in name only.

That they brooked the unthinkable is largely attributed to an understanding reached between Kitchener and Smuts. Growing frustrated with Milner's inflexible approach, Kitchener touched Smuts gently on the arm and led him outside for a stroll in the gardens. There he confided in Smuts that in his opinion Milner's patrons in government would be gone within two years and the Liberals would sweep to power with a far more favourable attitude towards the Afrikaners. The negotiators swallowed their pride and returned to Vereeniging on May 28 with Britain's terms: they would accept British sovereignty and the reality of the Transvaal and Orange River Colonies, lay down their arms and swear oaths of allegiance to King Edward VII. In return, there would be no prosecutions of those who surrendered and no executions of Cape rebels, prisoners would be released and returned to their farms, firearms would be retained but subject to license, and that there would be a return to civilian government as soon as possible. The British government ➡➡

legal minds present - the former state attorney Gen Jan Smuts and the hoary justice of the peace, 'Judge' Hertzog - promised a glimmer of progress. They argued that as a point of principle, a delegate was duty-bound to vote as they thought best and in accordance with the arguments presented, not as they had been instructed or had decided beforehand.

In the long hours of discussion that followed, the opinions of the great generals carried the most weight. Botha was for peace, Wet was for resistance, and Rey was on the fence. Botha argued that this was the last opportunity to avoid humiliation: "Terms might now be secured which would save the language, our ancient customs and national ideals. The fatal thing would be to secure no terms at all and yet be forced to surrender."

President Steyn, who was suffering from the neuromuscular disease myasthenia gravis and had travelled to Vereeniging in defiance of his doctor's orders, was too unwell to contribute and his son maintained years later that if his father had been present, the war party would have

ABOVE: *Schalk Burger, acting president of Transvaal following President Paul Kruger's flight to Europe. As a commandant general, he fought at Spion Kop and Modder River.* Zuid-Afrika Haus

What Happened Next?

Paul Kruger
Oum Paul found Europe unreceptive to his pleas for aid. Kaiser Wilhelm II could not risk antagonising Britain (or his grandmother, Queen Victoria) by meeting with him, and although Queen Wilhelmina of the Netherlands was more cordial, she also found hosting the old Boer politically awkward. After a brief stay in Utrecht, he moved to Switzerland where he died on July 14, 1904, after contracting pneumonia. His remains were repatriated with British consent and received a state funeral in Pretoria.

A cartoon from Puck *shows Paul Kruger as the mythical 'Wandering Jew' cast out of Europe.*

Jacobus 'Koos' de la Rey
Like his comrades, Rey remained politically active but unlike them he bitterly opposed South Africa's participation in World War One. Many Afrikaners were of German descent, and most remembered the support shown by Imperial Germany to the Boer cause. Rey held his tongue out of loyalty for Botha and Smuts but was still seen by many as a figurehead and he was sought out by General C.F. Beyers, who had resigned his post in protest at the war. The two were driving to meet another anti-war general when they encountered a series of police roadblocks, perhaps believing they were being targeted they carried on driving and were shot and killed. The roadblocks had been set up to catch a notorious gang of robbers and it was a tragic accident.

Christiaan de Wet
A defiant Free Stater and arch-bitter-ender, Wet remained active in politics and in 1914 became too active for his own good. As one of the leaders of the Maritz Rebellion to establish an independent Transvaal, he was defeated at Mushroom Valley by his old comrade in arms, General Botha. He was arrested, sentenced to four years, but served only one with a promise to take no further part in South African politics. Wet died peacefully at his farm on February 3, 1922.

ABOVE: *Crowds flood into Yonga Street, Toronto with news that the war has come to an end.*

Lord Kitchener handed over command to Lieutenant General Sir Neville Gerald Lyttelton and three days later he sailed for Britain. He left in his wake a final toll of over 100,000 British and colonial casualties, approximately 22,000 of them fatal.

As interim governor of Transvaal and the Orange River Colony, Milner was energetic and diligent. Soon the highveldt was garnished with railways, roads, telegraph lines and irrigation channels. His dreams had not quite come to pass, his efforts to persuade large scale British immigration failed and Afrikaner culture was able to thrive and resist his aspirations to conjure up a new Canada wholesale. Afrikaners continued to outnumber Brits and they continued to dominate the countryside, whilst the British settlers stuck to the cities. Milner's executive rule improved much, but it satisfied no-one. Taxes on the Rand were higher than ever to pay off the costs of war and Uitlanders continued to be denied a voice in the running of Transvaal, for there was no Volskraad in which it could be heard.

would make available £3 million (£245 million in modern money) for reconstruction and two principle fears of the Afrikaners were addressed, extending the vote to blacks would not be considered until self-government had been granted and Afrikaans would remain an official language.

It was a sombre reunion. The Peace of Vereeniging (as the treaty is called) was not the settlement any of them had hoped for, but it was the best they were going to get. By 54 to six, the delegates voted in favour and on May 31, 1902, the Boers returned to Melrose House to put their signatures to the document. Milner and Kitchener signed on behalf of Britain, the latter grandly as 'Kitchener of Khartoum'. The cost weighed heavily on the Boers and Schalk Burger reflected the mood: "We are standing here at the grave of the two republics. Much yet remains to be done, although we shall not be able to do it in the official capacities which we have formerly occupied. Let us not draw our hands

back from the work which it is our duty to accomplish. Let us ask God to guide us, and to show us how we shall be enabled to keep our nation together. We must be ready to forgive and forget, whenever we meet our brethren. That part of our nation which has proved unfaithful we must not reject."

Later that night at Vereeniging a small group of Burghers gathered around a small grave and buried the Vierkleur of the South African Republic. The next day the delegates returned to their commandos and their communities to explain what they had lost and what they had gained. Some were outraged - a handful of POWs refused to take the oath and went into exile - others despaired, but many were relieved. They fired their rifles into the air, smashed the butts into the ground, and then headed home to see what remained of their farms

Carrying the Cost

As keen to see the back of South Africa as his predecessor had been, on June 20, 1902,

ABOVE: *The cover of the satirical magazine* Puck *shows Britain's John Bull offering aid to the Boers after knocking the stuffing out of each other.*

Field Marshal Herbert Kitchener, 1st Earl Kitchener inspects Australian veterans of the Second Boer War during a visit to Adelaide, 1910.

ABOVE: *A group photograph of the veterans who had come to Adelaide's Government House to meet Lord Kitchener, 1910.*

ABOVE: *A small contingent of surviving veterans of the Great Boer War lead the Anzac Day parade through Adelaide, 1923.*

Milner invited the Boer leaders to participate in his administration, but they refused to hold any office which they had not been voted into by their own people. Jan Smuts especially remained persistent in holding him to account.

Milner had hoped to withhold self-government until the British population outnumbered the Boers by three to two, but he was dismissed following a scandal in April 1905 and replaced as high commissioner, by the less antagonistic William Palmer, 2nd Earl of Selborne. When responsible government arrived in June 1907, Afrikaners dominated the elected chambers of Pretoria and Bloemfontein as surely as they had the Volksraad, and when Milner's dreams of a single unified South Africa arrived in 1910, Afrikaners dominated that too and the signatories of the Peace of Vereeniging led South Africa through its first three decades of existence.

The British won the war, but the Boers won the peace. The conflict's real losers were those who had looked to the British Empire to improve their lot. Many Bantu who had fought alongside the British or toiled on the roads and railways, discovered that the rights they had promised had been sacrificed in the rapprochement between Briton and Boer. Acts were passed to limit their access to the workforce, to restrict land ownership, and to segregate towns and cities. In the years following Vereeniging, the Indian population organised to face discrimination and Mahatma Gandhi implemented the non-violent form of protest he dubbed satyagraha, and in response to the Natives Land Act of 1911, the South African Native National Congress was founded, later becoming the African National Congress (ANC) - the party of Nelson Mandela.

The 'White Man's War' had been a fiction, but this was a white man's peace. For South Africa's non-white population, the struggle for freedom and representation would take them through the ugly years of apartheid and well into the final decades of the 20th century.

The Boer War memorial in Hobart, Tasmania circa 1910.

Frederick Roberts, 1st Earl Roberts

Lord Roberts was adorned with glittering accolades on his return to Britain in 1901 and was appointed commander-in-chief of the British Army before the post was abolished in 1904. Over the next decade, Roberts became convinced that a great European war was coming, and he campaigned for conscription with the National Service League and for the training of civilians in firearms. In 1912 he warned that Germany was preparing for war. He was correct. Roberts died from pneumonia on November 14, 1914, whilst visiting troops of the British Indian Army in France. An 'Indian' until the end.

Lord Roberts's coffin, draped with the Union flag, and flanked by a French honour guard prepares to return to Britain.

Jan Smuts

Once one of Britain's most implacable enemies, Smuts eventually became one of its staunchest allies. Immediately after the war, he acted as deputy to Botha in Het Volk and held several cabinet posts in Botha's South African government. During World War One, Smuts led the Union Defence Force and occupied German Southwest Africa and then commanded the British Empire forces in the East African Campaign. He then served as prime minister of South Africa from 1919 until 1924 and from 1939 until 1948, becoming close to his British counterpart, Winston Churchill. His views on racial segregation eased in later life and his government extended welfare and pensions to non-whites. For every action, however, is an equal and opposite reaction and the hardline Nationalist Party were carried to victory in the 1948 election on a platform of apartheid. Smuts died at his farm two years later.

Jan Smuts in the uniform of a British general during World War One.

Martinus Steyn

Unwilling to consent to the peace and increasingly frail, Steyn left for Europe. In 1904 he relented, took the oath of allegiance, and returned to South Africa where he championed the rights of Afrikaners. He played a key role in the establishment of the Union of South Africa and founded the National Party, which hot-housed the poisonous philosophy of apartheid. He died of a heart attack in November 1916.

Valour
on the Veldt

Victoria Cross Heroes of the Great Boer War

The highest military decoration awarded to a British soldier, the nature of the fighting in the Great Boer War placed servicemen under incredible pressure and 78 rose to the challenge, receiving the Victoria Cross in recognition of their valour in the face of the enemy.

The conflict was also the source of a number of firsts, including the first VCs awarded by ballot for collective action, the first VCs awarded posthumously, and the first VCs awarded to men serving in the armed forces of Canada and Australia.

It was also the last time the medals were presented by their namesake, Queen Victoria - with the honour of being Her Majesty's final Victoria Cross hero falling to Private Charles Ward, the last man in a batch of five awarded in December 1900. Queen Victoria died on January 22, 1901, and the conflict's remaining VCs were instead awarded by her son and successor, King Edward VII.

Cap Charles FitzClarence

The Royal Fusiliers (City of London Regiment)
Mafeking, October 14 – December 26, 1899

RIGHT: *Captain Charles FitzClarence, in the dress uniform of The Royal Fusiliers (City of London Regiment)*

Dubbed the 'The Demon of Mafeking,' Cap Charles FitzClarence's Victoria Cross citation details three instances in which he distinguished himself as the leader of the irregular Protectorate Regiment. Firstly, on October 15, 1899, the month-old Protectorate Regiment rescued an armoured train and FitzClarence held his unsteady troopers firm despite being encircled. On October 27, he led them across open ground to make a night attack on the Boer trenches. He was the first

man in and killed four of the enemy with his sabre, beheading one in a single stroke. Finally, on December 26, 1899 FitzClarence again led from the front and was wounded severely by a bullet which passed through both legs during the unsuccessful raid on the Boers' formidable Game Tree Fort. During World War One, FitzClarence was brigadier general in command of the 1st Guards Brigade. His initiative during the First Battle of Ypres (October 19 - November 30, 1914) arguably saved the British lines from collapse, but he was later killed leading a night attack on November 12, 1914.

Cap Robert Johnston
Cap Charles Mullins

Imperial Light Horse
Elandslaagte, October 21, 1899

RIGHT: *Major Charles Mullins following his medical discharge from the Imperial Light Horse.*

Mullins and Johnston - an Irish rugby international who enlisted whilst touring South Africa with the touring side which ultimately became what we know as the British and Irish Lions - dashed forward under heavy fire at the Battle of Elandslaagte and rallied the battalion.

Cap Matthew Meiklejohn
Sgt Maj William Robertson

The Gordon Highlanders
Elandslaagte, October 21, 1899

Having lost their commanding officer in the vicious crossfire at Elandslaagte, Meiklejohn and Robertson both rushed on and called

RIGHT: *Major Matthew Meiklejohn's Victoria Cross and service medals on display at the Gordon Highlanders Museum. Before South Africa, he served on the North West Frontier with the 1st Gordons.*
MMP-1982 CC BY-SA 4.0

on the battalion to follow. Meiklejohn was wounded in four places and his right arm was amputated.

2nd Lt John Norwood

5th (or Princess Charlotte of Wales's) Dragoon Guards
Ladysmith, October 30, 1899

RIGHT: *Second Lieutenant John Norwood pictured in his civilian clothes prior to departing for South Africa.*

When one of his men fell, Norwood galloped back through heavy fire, dismounted, and carried the casualty on his back, leading his horse by the reins until they were out of range. Norwood later fought with the 2nd County of London Yeomanry and fell on September 8, 1914, during the First Battle of the Marne.

Lt Henry Douglas

Royal Army Medical Corps
Magersfontein, December 11, 1899

At the Battle of Magersfontein, the young medical officer advanced under enemy fire to treat a number of officers and other ranks who had been pinned down. Douglas himself was wounded in the action, when a shell burst nearby, tearing the flesh from his cheek. After the war, Douglas served in East Africa and

Major Henry Douglas (fifth from the right) with the Red Cross Society staff in Serbia, 1913. Though Captain Herbert St Maur Carter also wears RAMC collar pins and arm rank, Douglas is conspicuous as the only man wearing a medal ribbon. **Wellcome Collection CC BY 4.0**

India, joined Robert Stirling Clark's expedition to Northern China, and led a Red Cross hospital in Serbia during the Balkan Wars. Promoted to lieutenant colonel in World War One, Douglas served as Assistant Director of Medical Services for the 29th Division on the Western Front.

Cpl John Shaul
The Highland Light Infantry
Magersfontein, December 11, 1899

The 26-year old regimental bandsman led a stretcher party during the bloody Battle of Magersfontein, dressing wounds under continuous fire.

Cap Beachcroft Towse
The Gordon Highlanders
Magersfontein, December 11, 1899

Already a distinguished young officer, Towse's citation points to two occasions which merited the Victoria Cross. During the retreat in the disastrous Battle of Magersfontein, Towse attempted to hoist his mortally wounded commanding officer onto his back. When that proved impossible, he stayed with him until help arrived. Then on April 30, 1900 Towse and a company of 12 Gordons dug in on

RIGHT: *Captain Sir Beachcroft Towse on the cover of the National Institute for the Blind annual report. He is also pictured chatting to some blinded veterans of World War Two.*

Mount Thaba and held off an attack by 150 Boers. During the battle, Towse was blinded in both eyes by a bullet.

Retiring from the army in 1902, Towse spent the rest of his life working with the blind. He volunteered at a hospital in France in World War One and took up the role of chairman of the British and Foreign Blind Association (later the National Institute for the Blind), donating his house as their first rehabilitation centre. Knighted in 1916 (and further ennobled with a CBE in 1920 and a KCVO in 1928), he founded the British Wireless for the Blind Fund in 1928, was a trustee of the Association for Promoting General Welfare of the Blind (which still exists as an employment charity called Clarity) and served as vice patron of St Dunstan's Hostel (now Blind Veterans UK) from 1946 until his death in 1948.

Maj William Babtie
Royal Army Medical Corps
Colenso, December 15, 1899

At the Battle of Colenso, Babtie rode into heavy fire to tend to the wounded remnants of 14th and 66th Royal Field Artillery, going from man to man without thought to his own safety. Later he returned to the firing line to recover the body of Lt the Honourable Frederick Roberts. In World War One, Babtie was appointed Director of Medical Services in the Mediterranean, tasked with ongoing operations in the Dardanelles, Egypt, and Salonika. He was heavily criticised for the miserable casualty evacuations at Gallipoli, but despite the damage to his reputation Babtie was knighted in 1919.

Cap Walter Congreve
The Rifle Brigade (Prince Consort's Own)
Colenso, December 15, 1899

RIGHT: *A portrait of Lieutenant General Sir Walter Congreve by Francis Dodd, circa 1918.*

During the Battle of Colenso, Congreve braved the Boer fire to successfully retrieve two of the stricken guns of the 14th and 66th RFA. Seeing Lt Roberts fall, despite his own wounds he joined Maj Babtie and limped back to recover his body. During the action, Congreve was shot through the leg, through the toe of his boot, his elbow and shoulder had both been grazed by rifle fire, and his horse had also been shot in three places.

Congreve commanded the 18th Brigade of the British Expeditionary Force at the First Battle of the Aisne (September 12-28, 1914), and recorded the events of the 1914 'Christmas Truce'. Promoted to command XIII Corps, Congreve led his men into one of the bloodiest exchanges of the Somme, the Battle of Delville Wood (July 15 - September 15, 1916). Congreve's 25-year old son, Maj William 'Billy' Congreve, was also present at the battle when he was shot in the throat by a German sniper and posthumously awarded the VC, making them one of the few father and son duos with the distinction. In 1917, Congreve's left hand was peppered with shrapnel and he was forced to have it amputated - later taking to wearing an iron hook. Promoted to general and knighted in 1918, Congreve finished his career as governor of Malta.

Cpl George Nurse
Royal Field Artillery
Colenso, December 15, 1899

With his comrades lying dead and wounded, Cpl Nurse joined Congreve and Roberts in rescuing two of the abandoned guns - an operation that would have been considerably more difficult without the aid of an experienced artillery driver.

Pte George Ravenhill
The Royal Scots Fusiliers
Colenso, December 15, 1899

Ravenhill volunteered to join Congreve's party and was shot through the forearm. In 1908 he was imprisoned for stealing a quantity of iron, forfeiting his Victoria Cross and pension.

Cap Hamilton Reed
Royal Field Artillery
Colenso, December 15, 1899

Reed led three teams of 7th Battery to help recover the guns at Colenso and was wounded in the act. During World War One, Reed served as chief-of-staff to Lt Gen Sir Frederick Stopford - blamed for the failure of the Dardanelles campaign - and his successor. Reed escaped disgrace and went on to command the 15th (Scottish) Division in Belgium, successfully holding off the German Army's desperate Operation Michael offensive on March 28, 1918.

Lt the Honourable Frederick Roberts
The King's Royal Rifle Corps
Colenso, December 15, 1899

Handsome, gallant and the beloved only son of Field Marshal Frederick Roberts, 1st Earl Roberts, Freddy - as he was known - had all the makings of greatness before that was cut short retrieving the guns at Colenso. Fatally wounded in his abdomen and groin, Roberts became the first man awarded the VC posthumously.

RIGHT: *Roberts's grave at Chieveley War Cemetery, South Africa.* **Queensland University of Technology**

Cap Harry Schofield
Royal Field Artillery
Colenso, December 15, 1899

The last of the VCs awarded for the retrieval of the guns at Colenso, Schofield was ordered to make the first attempt by General Sir Redvers Buller. Initially recommended for the Distinguished Service Order on the basis that he was simply following orders, the snub seemed especially acute when Roberts was awarded the VC for the same undertaking courtesy of his influential father. The perceived injustice led to a press campaign and Schofield's DSO was upgraded to the VC in August 1901.

Sgt Horace Martineau
Protectorate Regiment
Mafeking, December 26, 1899

During the ill-fated raid on Game Tree Fort with FitzClarence, Martineau - despite being wounded in the side - rescued a fellow trooper laying only ten yards from the Boer lines and pulled him into cover. There, he bound his comrades' wounds and dragged him to safety, being shot a second time. His wounds were so severe that his arm had to be amputated at the shoulder. Martineau was in New Zealand when World War One broke out and enlisted on the spot, serving with the 14th (South Otago) Regiment as Battalion Transport Officer in Gallipoli. Whilst recuperating in Egypt from sickness, Martineau got into a slanging match with an officer of the RAMC but his VC shielded him from court martial and he was instead sent back to New Zealand. Now profoundly ill with gastroenteritis, Martineau died on April 7, 1916.

Tpr Horace Ramsden
Protectorate Regiment
Mafeking, December 26, 1899

During the attack on Game Tree Fort, Ramsden carried his brother - who had been shot through both legs - to safety.

Lt Sir John Milbanke, 10th Baronet
10th (Prince of Wales's Own) Royal Hussars
Colesberg, January 5, 1900

Milbanke's patrol came under fire on the outskirts of Colesberg and as they withdrew, he was shot in the thigh. Spotting one of his troopers had been unhorsed, Milbanke galloped back and pulled the stricken soldier onto his own mount. In World War One,

Milbanke was appointed lieutenant colonel of the 1/1st Sherwood Rangers Yeomanry and was killed in action at Gallipoli during the Battle of Scimitar Hill (August 21, 1915).

Tpr Herman Albrecht
Imperial Light Horse
Ladysmith, January 6, 1900

Facing a concentrated Boer assault on the unfinished Wagon Hill gun emplacement, Albrecht shot and killed Commandant de Villiers before being shot in turn.

Lt Robert Digby-Jones
Royal Engineers
Ladysmith, January 6, 1900

The second of the five Wagon Hill VCs, Digby-Jones was leading a working party on the gun emplacement when the Boers struck at various points along the line. Downing tools, Digby-Jones led a bayonet charge to keep the Boers from taking his position and he was shot in the throat.

Lt James Masterson
The Devonshire Regiment
Ladysmith, January 6, 1900

Masterson led three companies of the 1st Devonshire Regiment to drive the Boers from their position on Bester's Ridge, the closing action of the battle for Wagon Hill. Once they had taken the ridge, the Devons found themselves exposed to fire on two sides and Masterson crossed 100 yards of open ground to ask the nearby Imperial Light Horse for covering fire. Shot through both thighs, Masterson crawled the remainder of the way to deliver his message.

Pte James Pitts
Pte Robert Scott
Manchester Regiment
Ladysmith, January 6, 1900

With 14 of their comrades killed in the surprise attack, Scott and Pitts held the sanger on the left of Caesar's Camp - the larger hill adjacent to Wagon Hill - for 15 hours without food or water. In total, 33 Manchesters were killed and 40 wounded at Caesar's Camp, with Pitts the only man completely unscathed.

Sgt Alfred Atkinson
The Princess of Wales's Own (Yorkshire Regiment)
Paardeberg, February 18, 1900

During the murderous first day of the Battle of Paardeberg, Atkinson exposed himself to enemy fire seven times to bring water to his wounded comrades. On the seventh attempt he was fatally wounded.

Lt Francis Parsons
The Essex Regiment
Paardeberg, February 18, 1900

Having been ordered to attack the Boer laager from south of the river, one private found himself wounded and pinned down on the riverbank by Boer fire. Parsons crossed the open to dress his wounds and returned twice more, first to bring him water and then to carry him to safety. Sadly, Parsons was killed at the Battle of Driefontein (March 10, 1901).

Pte Albert Curtis
The East Surrey Regiment
Onderbank Spruit, February 23, 1900

Curtis made several attempts to rescue his wounded CO, eventually binding his wounds, and then, with the help of another man, bringing him back to safety.

Sgt James Firth
The Duke of Wellington's (West Riding Regiment)
Arundel, February 24, 1900

On two occasions during the action at Plewman's Farm, Firth carried wounded comrades to cover. On the second occasion, he was shot through the nose and eye but survived.

Lt Edgar Inkson
Royal Army Medical Corps
Colenso, February 24, 1900

During the fighting at Hart's Hill, Inkson carried a wounded officer to safety.

Photographed shortly after the Boer War, Captain Edgar Inkson of the RAMC wears his VC proudly.
Wellcome Collection CC BY 4.0

Cap Conwyn Mansel-Jones
The Prince of Wales's Own (West Yorkshire Regiment)
Tugela, February 27, 1900

During the relief of Ladysmith, Mansel-Jones rallied the stricken West Yorkshires in the face of a thundering Boer Maxim. Despite his wounds, he urged them onwards where they took the enemy positions. Although his health forced him into retirement, Mansel-Jones rejoined in 1914 and served as a staff officer, earning a DSO, a CMG and six mentions in despatches.

Sgt Henry Engleheart
10th (Prince of Wales's Own) Royal Hussars
March 13, 1900, Bloemfontein

Whilst undertaking a daring cavalry operation around Bloemfontein, the party were forced to break through the enemy lines across several spruits, the first of which was filled with Boers and could only be taken in a single-file. Engleheart led the way and surprise carried them through. At a later crossing, a comrade's horse faltered and refused to climb the bank. Trapped in the spruit and with Boers closing in, Engleheart helped to pull both man and mount free.

Dvr Horace Glasock
Gnr Isaac Lodge
Sgt Charles Parker
Maj Edmund Phipps-Hornby
Royal Horse Artillery
Korn Spruit, March 31, 1900

Driver Horace Glasock

Major Edmund Phipps-Hornby

The four were awarded the Victoria Cross on behalf of all the men of Q Battery who maintained steady fire in the chaos at the Battle of Sanna's Post.

Lt Francis Maxwell
Roberts's Light Horse
Korn Spruit, March 31, 1900

An officer of the Indian Staff Corps attached to an irregular unit, Maxwell joined Q Battery

Lieutenant Francis Maxwell photographed prior to his service in South Africa.

in trying to save the guns. His citation also mentioned an incident in the Chitral expedition of 1895 where Maxwell retrieved the body of his fallen commanding officer under fire. Whilst commanding the 12th Middlesex Regiment in 1916, Lt Col Maxwell captured the German positions around the village of Thiepval and was promoted to brigadier general leading the 27th Brigade. He was later killed by a German sniper whilst touring the lines during the Battle of Menin Road Ridge (September 21, 1917).

Lt William Nickerson
Royal Army Medical Corps
Wakkerstroom, April 20, 1900

Whilst attached to the Mounted Infantry, Nickerson advanced under heavy fire to treat a wounded man and he stayed with him until they were safe. In World War One, Nickerson first served as CO of the 6th Cavalry Field Ambulance in Belgium and then as assistant director of medical services in Salonika.

Cpl Harry Beet
The Sherwood Foresters (Derbyshire) Regiment
Wakkerstroom, April 22, 1900

Ordered to withdraw from a farm in the same operation, Beet stayed behind with a wounded NCO and dressed his wounds. He then kept the Boers away from the farm until night fell and they were evacuated.

Cp John MacKay
The Gordon Highlanders
Johannesburg, May 20, 1900

During a skirmish at Crow's Nest Hill outside Johannesburg, McKay repeatedly risked his life to tend to the wounded and bring one man into cover. ➤➤

Cpl Frank Kirby
Royal Engineers
Delagoa Bay Railway, June 2, 1900

After cutting the Boer railway line, Kirby rode back to rescue a comrade whose horse had been shot out from under him. In 1911, Kirby was posted to the newly formed Air Battalion of the Royal Engineers, which was later absorbed by the Royal Flying Corps. He served with the RFC during World War One and swapped his cap badge a third time when it became the Royal Air Force.

Pte Charles Ward
The King's Own (Yorkshire Light Infantry)
Lindley, June 26, 1900

With his picket surrounded by 500 Boers and their officers slain, Ward volunteered to run the gauntlet of fire to the signalling post 150 yards to the rear. Ward made it without a scratch but was wounded on the return journey. Ward's VC was the last one awarded by Queen Victoria before her death.

Cpl Arthur Richardson
Strathcona's Horse
Wolwespruit, July 5, 1900

Canada's first VC doubled back to rescue a fallen colleague when their patrol was ambushed. After the war, Richardson's career stalled as his wife became seriously ill and he fell into debt and alcoholism. They returned to Britain and following his wife's death he worked quietly and anonymously as a labourer on Liverpool's tramway. During World War One, an imposter posing as Richardson enlisted in the Gordon Highlanders, drumming up much publicity and even attending a garden party at Buckingham Palace. Only when the bootleg Richardson died and was buried with much fanfare in 1924 did the real Richardson make himself known.

Cap William Gordon
Cap Reginald Younger
The Gordon Highlanders
Krugersdorp, July 11, 1900

Ambushed on the road at the Battle of Dwarsvlei, Younger volunteered to bring an artillery wagon into cover. With the fire from the Boers in the ridges above them growing in intensity the attempt failed and so Gordon gathered some more volunteers and joined in. Together they managed to haul a gun to safety, although Younger was fatally wounded.

Lt Neville Howse
New South Wales Army Medical Corps
Vredefort, July 24, 1900

Howse dashed through crossfire to reach a fallen soldier - continuing on foot when his horse was shot out from under him - and brought the casualty back to safety in what he later dismissed as "a fit of insanity." He went on to serve at Gallipoli and became director of ANZAC medical services. After retiring from the army to enter politics, Howse became Australia's Minister for Defence and Minister of Health.

Pte William House
Princess Charlotte of Wales's (Royal Berkshire Regiment)
Mosilkatse Nek, August 2, 1900

Warned not to attempt it, House advanced under heavy fire to recover his sergeant and was wounded in the process. He died in 1912 from an accidental discharge of his own rifle.

Sgt Brian Lawrence
17th (Duke of Cambridge's Own) Lancers
Essenbosch Farm, August 7, 1900

Ambushed by a group of more than a dozen Boers whilst on patrol, Lawrence's partner was thrown from his horse, dislocating his shoulder. Lawrence placed the wounded man on his own horse, and wielding both men's carbines he held the Boers off until his comrade made it to safety. The Lancer then retreated two miles on foot with the Boers in pursuit, firing as he went.

Sgt Harry Hampton
Cpl Henry Knight
The King's (Liverpool Regiment)
Van Wyk's Viel, August 21, 1900

Hampton held the post until his small party of Mounted Infantry were forced to retreat. Despite taking a head wound, Hampton helped support a wounded corporal until the

A studio portrait of Major General Sir Neville Reginald Howse taken whilst stationed in Cairo during World War One.

man was hit a second time and killed, and then Hampton himself was injured again. In the same fierce encounter, Knight - at the head of a small rear guard - came under attack by 50 Boers and held them at bay for nearly an hour whilst his comrades withdrew. Unfortunately, two men were killed but Knight carried a third man who was wounded for two miles under heavy fire.

Pte William Heaton
The King's (Liverpool Regiment)
Geluk, August 23, 1900

Fighting around Geluk's Farm a few days later, Heaton volunteered to break out of a Boer encirclement to summon aid.

Pte Alfred Durrant
The Rifle Brigade (Prince Consort's Own)
Bergendal, August 27, 1900

During the final large-scale battle of the war, Durrant restrained a disorientated comrade who was attempting to charge the enemy and carried him back to cover.

Lieutenant Colonel William Gordon's medals on display at the Gordon Highlanders Museum. MMP-1982 CC BY-SA 4.0

Tpr John Bisdee
Lt Guy Wylly
Tasmanian Imperial Bushmen
Warm Bad, September 1, 1900

The first Australian-born VCs, Wylly and Bisdee were passing through a narrow gorge when they came under close fire, hitting six of the eight men and shooting several of their horses from under them. Bisdee pulled a fallen officer onto his horse and retreated, whilst Wylly gave his horse to a wounded man and hung back to cover their flight. Wylly was mentioned in dispatches twice and awarded the DSO for his service during World War One.

Trooper John Bisdee (pictured on horse-back) of the Tasmanian Imperial Bushmen, one of the first two Australian-born VCs. Lieutenant Guy Wylley (inset) was later decorated for his staff work in India and served as an aide-de-camp to King George V from 1929 to 1933.

The Duke of Cornwall and York - later King George V - presents one of nine Victoria Crosses at Maritzburg, August 14, 1901.

Maj Edward Brown
14th (King's) Hussars
Geluk, October 13, 1900

On three occasions during operations around Geluk, Brown assisted comrades who had become unhorsed.

Lt Alexis Doxat
Imperial Yeomanry
Zeerust, October 20, 1900

Coming under fire whilst scouting a Boer position, Doxat dashed back to recover a man who had been thrown from his horse.

Lt Hampden Cockburn
Lt Richard Turner
Sgt Edward Holland
Royal Canadian Dragoons
Komati River, November 7, 1900

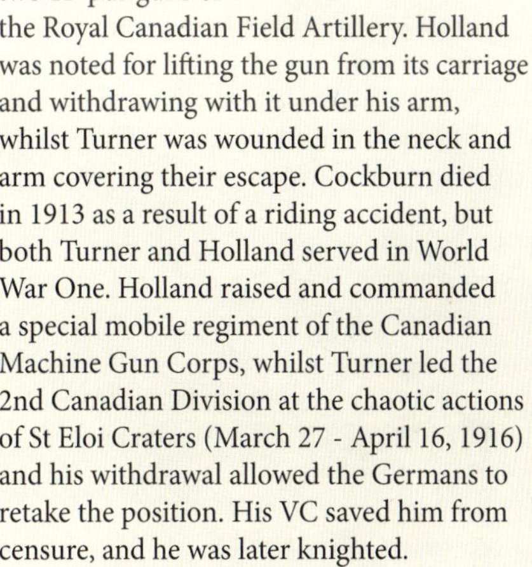

Sergeant Edward Holland, Royal Canadian Dragoons. During World War One, Holland held the rank of major commanding Borden's Motor Machine Gun Battery.
Inset: *Lieutenant Hampden Cockburn's Victoria Cross, shown front and back.*

Cockburn, Turner and Holland fought bitterly to keep 200 attacking Boers from seizing two 12-pdr guns of the Royal Canadian Field Artillery. Holland was noted for lifting the gun from its carriage and withdrawing with it under his arm, whilst Turner was wounded in the neck and arm covering their escape. Cockburn died in 1913 as a result of a riding accident, but both Turner and Holland served in World War One. Holland raised and commanded a special mobile regiment of the Canadian Machine Gun Corps, whilst Turner led the 2nd Canadian Division at the chaotic actions of St Eloi Craters (March 27 - April 16, 1916) and his withdrawal allowed the Germans to retake the position. His VC saved him from censure, and he was later knighted.

Pte Charles Kennedy
The Highland Light Infantry
Dewetsdorp, November 22, 1900

Kennedy carried a wounded comrade three-quarters of a mile under heavy fire. The next day, Kennedy volunteered to carry a message across open ground – he made it only 20 yards before he was shot, and was invalided home.

Pte John Barry
The Royal Irish Regiment
Monument Hill, January 7-8, 1901

Surrounded by the Boers, the wounded Barry smashed the breech of his company's Maxim gun to prevent it being used by the enemy. He later died of his wounds and it was only through the campaigning of Sgt Alfred Atkinson's grieving mother that a batch of posthumous awards were made, including one for Barry.

Sgt Donald Farmer
The Queen's Own Cameron Highlanders
Nooitgedacht, December 13, 1900

A Sudan veteran, Farmer carried his commanding officer to safety under heavy fire after their party of reinforcements was caught in the open. His great deeds were done but the battle was not and Farmer returned to the fray and was eventually captured.

Farrier Sgt Maj William Hardham
4th New Zealand Contingent
Naeuwpoort, January 28, 1901

Seeing one of his fellows had been wounded and unhorsed, Hardham galloped up to him under heavy fire, hoisted him onto his horse and then ran alongside until they were out of range. During World War One, Cap Hardham fought with the Wellington Mounted Rifles and was wounded at the Battle for No. 3 Post (May 28 - May 30, 1915) during the Gallipoli campaign.

Farrier Sergeant Major William Hardham, 4th New Zealand Contingent, photographed a year after the award of his VC.

Sgt William Traynor
**The Prince of Wales's Own
(West Yorkshire Regiment)**
Bothwell Camp, February 6, 1901

During a night attack, Traynor dashed from his trench to bring in a wounded comrade but was wounded in the process. Despite his injuries, Traynor remained at his post and in command of his detachment until the Boers had been driven successfully off.

Cpl John Clements
Rimington's Guides
Strijdenburg, February 24, 1901

Despite having been shot in the lung, when called upon to surrender by five Boers, Clements opened fire - wounding three - and took them prisoner instead.

Lt Frederic Dugdale
5th (Royal Irish) Lancers
Derby, March 3, 1901

Coming under heavy fire, Dugdale placed a wounded man on his horse and then recovered a riderless horse with which he rescued another casualty.

Lt Frederick Bell
West Australian Mounted Infantry
Brakpan, May 16, 1901

Bell gave his horse to a dismounted trooper and then covered the man's escape.

Lt Gustavus Coulson
The King's Own Scottish Borderers
Lambrechtfontein, May 18, 1901

During a rear guard action, Coulson took a fallen man on his horse but when the horse was wounded, he forced the man to ride the stricken horse to safety without him. He was shot and killed.

Sgt James Rogers
South African Constabulary
Thaba 'Nchu, June 15, 1901

Rogers rescued a wounded officer and brought him to safety, he then rode back to recover two more men who had lost their mounts. During World War One, Lt Rogers joined the Australian Army Service Corps and was wounded at Gallipoli.

Lt William English
Scottish Horse
Vlakfontein, July 3, 1901

English crossed open ground under heavy fire at extremely close range to get fresh ammunition for his comrades. He served in both world wars and died of a cerebral haemorrhage in 1941 whilst commanding the Royal Ulster Rifles.

Pte Harry Crandon
18th Hussars
Springbok Laagte, July 4, 1901

Crandon passed his horse to a wounded man and then running alongside he led it to safety. He was wounded during World War One.

Sgt Major Alexander Young
Cape Mounted Police
Ruiter's Kraal, August 13, 1901

Young led a small party in a charge against a Boer-held kopje and when they retreated, he carried on the charge, taking their commandant captive. Lt Young fought with the South African Scottish Regiment during World War One and was killed on October 19, 1916 during the Battle of the Somme.

Lt Llewellyn Price-Davies
The King's Royal Rifle Corps
Blood River Poort, September 17, 1901

Seeing the British guns in danger of being overrun, Price-Davies charged out alone with his revolver blazing. He was shot from his horse but survived and went on to serve as liaison officer to the 38th (Welsh) Division through some of their bloodiest battles of World War One.

Dvr Frederick Bradley
Royal Field Artillery
Itala, September 26, 1901

Seeing a fellow artillery driver shot down as he carried ammunition up a hill, Bradley brought him to cover and then carried the ammunition the rest of the way.

Pte William Bees
**The Sherwood Foresters (Derbyshire)
Regiment**
Moedwil, September 30, 1901

Tormented by the howls of a wounded Maxim gun team, Bees broke from cover to fill his camp kettle from a nearby spruit and hauled the water back across open ground to quench their thirst. The kettle was struck by numerous bullets, but Bees himself was unharmed.

Lt Leslie Maygar
Victorian Mounted Rifles
Geelhoutboom, November 23, 1901

Maygar gave his horse to a wounded comrade and then made his own escape on foot. During World War One, the aging Maygar lied about his age to rejoin and served with the 4th Light Horse Regiment at Gallipoli, and then commanded the 8th Light Horse in the Sinai and Palestine. He was fatally wounded by a German aircraft during the Battle of Beersheba (October 31, 1917).

Surgeon Cap Thomas Crean
Imperial Light Horse
Tygerkloof Spruit, December 18, 1901

A member of the British and Irish touring rugby squad with Robert Johnson, Crean tended to the wounded under heavy fire. Only when he was injured so severely that he was not expected to survive, did he finally rest. Crean served with the RAMC in World War One and was twice mentioned in dispatches and awarded the DSO.

Shoeing Smith Alfred Ind
Royal Horse Artillery
Tafelkop, December 20, 1901

Although the rest of his team had fallen, Ind continued to fire his Maxim gun into the approaching enemy until the very last minute

Surgeon Cap Arthur Martin-Leake
South African Constabulary
Vlakfontein, February 8, 1902

Martin-Leake repeatedly placed himself in harm's way to tend to the wounded, first by crossing open ground to treat a fallen man. Later, he was injured whilst tending to an offer's wounds and only gave up when completely exhausted. Even then he refused water until all the other casualties had been seen to. Martin-Leake volunteered with the Red Cross in the Balkan Wars and during World War One was awarded a second Victoria Cross - making him one of only three men to have been awarded the VC twice - for tending to the wounded within view of the enemy trenches.